Sri Aurobindo

Saga of a Great Indian Sage

Sri Aurobindo

Saga of a Great Indian Sage

Wilfried Huchzermeyer

DK PRINTWORLD

Publishers of Indian Traditions

Cataloging in Publication Data — DK
[Courtesy: D.K. Agencies (P) Ltd. <docinfo@dkagencies.com>]

Huchzermeyer, Wilfried.

Sri Aurobindo : saga of a great Indian sage / Wilfried Huchzermeyer.

p. cm.

Includes bibliographical references and index.

ISBN 9788124607022

1. Ghose, Aurobindo, 1872-1950. 2. Philosophers – India – Biography. 3. Nationalists – India – Biography. 4. Hindus – India – Biography. I. Title.

DDC 181.4 23

ISBN 13: 978-81-246-0702-2 (HB)
ISBN 13: 978-81-246-0706-0 (PB)
First published in India in 2013

Printed and published by:
D.K. Printworld (P) Ltd.
Regd. Office : *'Vedaśrī'*, F-395, Sudarshan Park
(Metro Station: Ramesh Nagar)
New Delhi – 110 015.
Phones : (011) 2545 3975, 2546 6019; *Fax* : 2546 5926
e-mail : indology@dkprintworld.com
Web : www.dkprintworld.com

Preface

A LONG time ago while staying in the Sri Aurobindo Ashram, I happened to overhear a sādhak[1] introducing a visitor on the basics of Integral Yoga. After a while I caught the sentence, "Sri Aurobindo's standpoint is Indian, but his viewpoint is Western".

This aphorism, enriched by a little play on words, outlines in an original way Sri Aurobindo's spiritual philosophy. We envisage him standing firmly on the soil of Indian tradition, but enlarging his perspective with his dynamic and evolutionary approach and his full acceptance of life and matter. We would have to add that he has also rediscovered and revitalized some aspects of the Indian tradition, especially the ancient Vedic culture.

In this present biography, I intend to present Sri Aurobindo's life and works comprehensively and in detail, but none the less a selection had to be made in view of the voluminous material that is available. In this context, an important criterion was the assumed relevance of the respective subjects for readers of our time. As for the interpretation, Sri Aurobindo has stated several times, ". . . it would be only myself who could speak of things in my past, giving them their true form and significance".[2] All the same, he has supported researchers through a large number of clarifications regarding his life so that it does appear possible to write about him on a solid foundation.

All the references to Sri Aurobindo's works are — if not otherwise mentioned in the footnotes — from the *Complete Works of Sri Aurobindo*[3] whose pagination is only in some cases identical with the earlier standard editions of the Sri Aurobindo Ashram. Most titles of the *Complete Works* can be viewed on the Ashram website.[4]

The Sri Aurobindo Ashram Trust has been kind enough to give permission to print the photo on the cover, and all the photos of Sri Aurobindo and the Mother. The same is the case with the photos of the Ashram, etc., unless specified otherwise in the captions.

In conclusion, I wish to thank all those who have helped in preparing this book through editing, proof-reading, photos and other contributions, and the Sri Aurobindo Ashram Trust for permission to quote from the Ashram literature and for the use of a large number of photos made available with the kind support of the Ashram Archives.

Wilfried Huchzermeyer

References

1 See Glossary.

2 *Letters on Himself and the Ashram*, 5.

3 See Literature.

4 See Internet addresses.

Contents

1

Childhood in India
(1872-79)

KRISHNA Dhan Ghose, Sri Aurobindo's father, was a gifted and ambitious man. Though grown up in poor circumstances he managed to complete medical studies in Calcutta. Thereafter, he worked as a doctor in a hospital and in the State medical service. But without additional training in England, he would not be eligible to further his career. Therefore he went to London in 1870, and a year later received his doctorate at King's College in Aberdeen, Scotland.

A few years before travelling to the West, Ghose had married Swarnalata Devi (twelve years of age at the time). She was the daughter of a famous Bengali named Rajnarain Bose who, at a later date, was given the honorary title "Grandfather of the Indian nation". He was a man of universal education and had a reputation as a leading representative of the Brahmo Samaj, the "society of the Brahmos". This was a reform movement in Hinduism, founded in 1828 by Raja Rammohun Roy in Calcutta, with the aim of a fundamental renewal of the religion of the Hindus. Old rituals, such as the worship of statues of gods, were rejected and replaced by the adoration of the One, an infinite God, who may be inwardly worshipped and who perhaps listens to prayers, but cannot incarnate as a human being. Deeply-rooted social evils (such as *satī*, the burning of widows) should be eliminated during a process of inner purification and renewal.

Ghose was proud to marry the daughter of such an eminent personality and the ceremony was performed according to the rites of the Brahmo Samaj. But his stay in England changed his mind and his values. Strongly impressed by the efficiency and glamour of the British civilization, he broke away from the tradition of Hinduism and began to think and feel like an Englishman. He had also studied the writings of Charles Darwin whose first epoch-making books were just published at that time in England; he became an atheist, though endowed with a positive faith in a progressive human evolution. For him the universe with all its creatures was the real God, "and when I worship that by action I worship Him".[1]

When Ghose returned to India as a deeply Anglicized man, his grandfather was quite disturbed. But after his education in England the doctor got a well-paid job in Rangpur, Bengal and moved there with his wife and two sons, Benoy Bhushan and Manmohan. By August 1872 the birth of another child was expected and Ghose sent his wife to Calcutta as there was danger of an outbreak of an epidemic in Rangpur. Swarnalata stayed at the home of his friend, lawyer Mano Mohan Ghose who owned a house in the best part of town.

Sri Aurobindo was born on 15 August 1872 around 5 a.m. shortly before sunrise and was given the name Aravinda Ackroyd Ghose. Aravinda means "lotus" in Sanskrit and Ackroyd was the name of an English lady with whom Ghose had formed a friendship in England. She took part in the ceremony. Sri Aurobindo later dropped this middle name, and when he moved from Baroda to Calcutta in 1906 he changed "Aravinda" to the Bengali form "Aurobindo".

Aurobindo grew up in his parents' home without speaking Bengali, since his father wanted his children to learn the English

---

[1] K.D. Ghose to J. Bose on 2 December 1890. Quoted in *The Lives of Sri Aurobindo,* 6.

language and culture from scratch, which he considered superior. But Aurobindo picked up some Hindustani (a popular version of Hindi) while talking with the servants in the house.

In 1877 Aurobindo, Benoy Bhushan and Manmohan were sent to Darjeeling, a picturesque hill station in the Himalayas of which the English had taken possession, using it for their recreation. While farmers had started growing tea on their plantations, missionaries had opened the Loreto Convent School, a boarding school conducted by the Loreto sisters, a group of Irish nuns. Here the three brothers received their first formal education — on Indian soil, though in a totally Anglicized environment, and English finally became their mother tongue. In later life, Sri Aurobindo said little about this period in such idyllic surroundings, but he had had a depressing experience which he described in 1926 in *Evening Talks*:

> I was lying down one day when I saw suddenly a great darkness rushing into me and enveloping me and the whole universe.[2]

Even before moving to Darjeeling, Aurobindo and his brothers had only little contact with their father who, as a highly placed public health officer, was almost constantly touring the region. But none the less they adored him very much. Their mother Swarnalata had started showing symptoms of mental illness soon after the birth of her first child, which gradually worsened during the 1870s. Manmohan was later to remark in a letter that he was seeking love and "crying for bread", but only got "a stone" in response. We do not know how far this also applied to Aurobindo, but we may assume that at least during the final years in Rangpur a normal motherly relationship and love no longer existed. Possibly this may have influenced the decision of Ghose to send his three sons to remote Darjeeling.

---

[2] Purani, *Evening Talks with Sri Aurobindo*, 393.

2

Education in England
(1879-92)

DUE to his education in England and his perfect mastery of the English language, Ghose was able to form a close relationship with Edward Glazier, the top-ranking civil servant of the region. Glazier helped him to realize his highest ambition regarding his three sons: to educate them in England, with the objective of admission into the renowned Indian Civil Service (ICS). Some special demands were made, such as completing a high level of education in England itself, which was a rather difficult condition for Indians who rarely succeeded in entering this lucrative and much sought-after career. During a homestay, Glazier contacted his relative William H. Drewett, a clergyman in Manchester, asking him to take care of the three boys.

In 1879 Ghose travelled to England with his wife, his three sons and daughter Sarojini (born some time after Aurobindo). Swarnalata was again pregnant at this time and her husband did not want her to remain alone in India. He rather wished to take her to London to be examined by a specialist, in view of her disquieting symptoms. He took his sons to Drewett and left his wife with a doctor in London, returning to India alone. In January 1880 Swarnalata gave birth to a son who was at first given an English name, but was subsequently renamed Barindra Kumar.

Private Lessons in Manchester

Drewett and Mrs Drewett, living in the industrial town of Manchester, had received strict instructions to give the boys in their care a European education and keep them at a distance from Indian compatriots. They followed this guideline. Thus the three brothers grew up without learning anything about the history, language and culture of their mother country. Before they were sent out to school, they initially received private lessons from their hosts: Drewett teaching them Latin and history, while his wife introduced them to French, geography and mathematics. Two years later Benoy Bhushan and Manmohan were sent to the Manchester Grammar School, whereas nine-year old Aurobindo continued his studies at home.

Drewett respected Ghose's wish not to impart any religious instructions to the boys, but it was inevitable that in the home of a clergyman they acquired some basic knowledge of the Bible and the Christian religion. Sri Aurobindo was later to refer to Jesus and his role as Son of God in a long passage in his epic poem *Savitri,* mentioning his work in the world in several aphorisms.[1] But Aurobindo was not really interested in the subject of Christianity, it rather bored him.

Once he reported an incident which took place when Drewett's mother took him to a religious meeting in Cumberland. After prayers some people stayed on for a while. A preacher approached Aurobindo and asked him some questions:

> I did not give any reply. Then they all shouted, "He is saved, he is saved" and began to pray for me while offering thanks to God. I did not know what it was all about.[2]

---

1 *Savitri,* 445; *Essays Divine and Human,* Thoughts and Aphorisms, 427, 444 (Aphorisms 39, 41, 169, 171).

2 Purani, *The Life of Sri Aurobindo,* 6.

The preacher then asked Aurobindo to pray and he did, in the manner of small children before going to sleep in order to keep up an appearance.

What Aurobindo was really interested in was reading poetry, especially the lyrical style of P.B. Shelley, which he devoured. He was fascinated by his work *The Revolt of Islam* and read it several times. Shelley described in this work a mythic freedom struggle in the Orient; this inspired Aurobindo with the idea that in the future he would make a similar contribution to the changing of the world. In the meantime his father had become disillusioned regarding the English. In his rare letters to his sons he sent copies of a Bengali newspaper in which he had marked certain passages which revealed how Indians were being mistreated by the English colonialists, whom he criticized as "heartless". A few decades later, Sri Aurobindo noted:

> At the age of eleven Aurobindo had already received strongly the impression that a period of general upheaval and great revolutionary changes was coming in the world and he himself was destined to play a part in it. His attention was now drawn to India and this feeling was soon canalised into the idea of the liberation of his own country.[3]

St. Paul's School in London

In 1881 Drewett gave up his work as a clergyman and emigrated to Australia a few years later. Shortly before leaving England in 1884, he gave the three Indian boys into the care of his mother, who moved to London with them. Aurobindo and Manmohan were sent to the renowned St. Paul's School which had a long tradition as an outstanding institution, attended by many important personalities in the English culture. St. Paul's imparted the classical education of that era,

---

[3] *Autobiographical Notes,* 15.

with Greek and Latin as the main subjects. Walker, head of the school, was quite impressed by Aurobindo's knowledge of Latin and gave him intensive private lessons in Greek; under his tutelage the boy quickly advanced to the school's top-level classes. Soon Aurobindo was able to read, in the original texts, the great authors Virgil, Cicero, Euripides, while also studying the New Testament in Greek as well as French literature. He attended classes in mathematics, but did not study the sciences.

Aurobindo was among the best in his class, but for some time he lost interest in his curriculum, preferring to read books of his own choice: English and French poetry, European history plus other subjects. He learned Italian on his own as well as some German and Spanish. As for sports, he had little inclination at school. St. Paul's School awarded many scholarships and prizes and in 1884 Aurobindo was able to secure a scholarship which freed him from the obligation of paying fees. Furthermore, at the end of this period at school, he resumed more intensive studies in his subjects, gaining a second prize in literature and an honorary prize in history.

The external living conditions in London were at times rather difficult. Mrs Drewett was a very pious woman, making the three Indian brothers share regular short Bible readings, which increasingly irritated them. Once Manmohan made a disrespectful remark (about Moses) which enraged the old lady so much that she moved to another place, because she did not want to live under the same roof with an "atheist". The young Indians were now freed from the religious indoctrination, but henceforth they had to get along on their own and so moved on, into new lodgings. At the beginning of their stay Ghose had sent regular remittances, but due to his own difficulties money came more and more rarely, so that Aurobindo lived in great poverty for a period of time. For a whole year "a slice or two of sandwich, bread and butter and a cup of tea in the morning and in the evening a penny saveloy formed the only food".[4] Moreover, they had no firewood during a very cold winter, thus Aurobindo experienced extreme privation.

Aurobindo's plan after completing school was to study for two years at a university, since this was the main condition for admittance into the ICS. At the end of 1889 he went to Cambridge to take the difficult examinations for a scholarship, upon which would depend the continuation of his academic career. The tests were mainly in his favourite subjects of Greek and Latin and so he was very successful and came out on top. The scholar and poet Oscar Browning who examined his papers was to state later that Aurobindo's papers were the best he had ever seen.

A few months later Aurobindo had to take the entry examination for the ICS which was far more difficult. This time there were tests in ten subjects, and once more his thorough knowledge of the classic languages helped him secure an excellent ranking among the large number of applicants. In 1890 Aurobindo, who was now 18 years of age, could move to Cambridge with good prospects. His brother Benoy Bhushan did not pass the required exams, while Manmohan aspired for a career as a poet.

Studies in Cambridge

Aurobindo's financial situation was now more comfortable due to the scholarships from Cambridge University and the ICS, but by no means rosy since with this money he also had to support his two brothers. This was necessary because Ghose had stopped sending remittances for his sons almost entirely when he came to know about the scholarships. Only after having received some urgent letters from the historian G.W. Prothero who knew Aurobindo very well, Ghose reacted by

---

4 *Autobiographical Notes,* 116.

sending some money which helped Aurobindo make several overdue payments.

But apart from these problems, this was a relatively happy period for him. He was quite absorbed in his diverse studies at one of the two leading universities of England, with time-honoured buildings and traditions and mostly highly qualified teachers. His ICS curriculum included subjects such as administrative and criminal law, history, geography and foreign languages, even Bengali. However, the latter was taught by a somewhat incompetent Englishman who could hardly speak the language himself, using antiquated texts. Sanskrit, too, was part of the curriculum, but Aurobindo learned it on his own by studying again and again the story of Nala and Damayantī in the *Mahābhārata*. Meanwhile, he had to appear regularly for intermediate examinations which were required in order to obtain extensions for the scholarships.

Aurobindo had chosen the classical languages as the main subject for his university studies, which enabled him to deepen further his knowledge of Greek and Latin. Aurobindo made a number of friendships, mostly with Indian fellow-students or with Irishmen and continental Europeans, less often with Englishmen. He really admired France as a cultural nation, whereas England, in his perception, was a country of trade and commerce which he did not hold in great esteem. One of the reasons was, of course, that the British had made his home country a colony; he revolted more and more against this status and consequently patriotic feelings were born. Thus he became a member of the Indian Majlis, a club of students where he expressed his feelings in several speeches.

During his studies, Aurobindo devoured a great deal of literature even beyond the prescribed readings, probing deeply the European history of thought. He read well-known authors such as Virgil, Dante, Racine, Shakespeare and Milton in the original; he especially liked poets of the Romantic period such as Byron, Shelley and Keats. Some poems which he published in 1898 under the title *Songs to Myrtilla* probably date back to this period.

He was interested in inspired poetry or life-relevant concepts and ideas rather than those of abstract logic and philosophy. That is why the writings even of Kant or Hegel had no attraction for him. When in 1935 he tried to explain the working of yogic force to a disciple, he pointed out:

> How was it that I who was unable to understand and follow a metaphysical argument and whom a page of Kant or Hegel or Hume or even Berkeley left either dazed and uncomprehending and fatigued or totally uninterested because I could not fathom or follow, suddenly began writing pages of the stuff as soon as I started the *Arya* and am now reputed to be a great philosopher?[5]

But Aurobindo studied Plato's dialogues and he very much appreciated the *Republic* and the *Symposium* as great literary works.[6] At this stage he wrote *The Harmony of Virtue*, a title inspired by the Platonic dialogues in which basic questions of virtue and beauty are discussed. He concludes in this early writing that "a life of perfect beauty" leads to "the peace of God that passeth all understanding".[7]

Aurobindo took a few of his intermediate examinations for the ICS without great interest, but he was able to secure two first prizes for the best verses in Greek and Latin. In the end he passed with distinction the Tripos (the final examination for the BA), thus fulfilling the essential conditions for the ICS career. However, he did not receive an academic degree, since according to the rules he would have to pass yet another year

---

5 *Autobiographical Notes*, 223-24.

6 *The Life Divine*, 313.

7 *Early Cultural Writings*, 77.

at the university. This was impossible for him as there was increasing pressure from his father in India, who was eager to see at least one of his sons starting a glorious career (as he considered it) in his home country, and he was already making preparations by using his contacts with Englishmen in the administration.

Meanwhile Aurobindo had passed the final written examination for the ICS without great interest and only the obligatory riding test was left now as the last hurdle. But he had no experience in riding and lacked money to pay for the required lessons. That is why he failed in two tests and did not appear for the third. The examining board allowed him to take a few more tests, but he did not appear at the appointed dates. Finally, he was declared to be excluded from the ICS After this decision, some prominent friends of the Ghose family in England tried to put in a word for him, but their efforts failed. Actually, some later statements of Sri Aurobindo show that he did not really want to pass the test, since the ICS had no attraction for him and he preferred to evade the career of a subordinate officer of the British administration. "By certain manoeuvres he managed to get himself disqualified for riding without himself rejecting the Service, which his family would not have allowed him to do," he later commented in one of his letters.[8]

Aurobindo had no more examinations to pass; now he freely chose his own readings. During his studies he had acquired only some superficial knowledge of Indian philosophy, but now he started going deeper into it, studying the Upaniṣads and their teaching of the *ātman* (the immortal Self) in human beings which is one with the *brahman* (the Absolute) beyond and behind everything. At this stage his knowledge of Sanskrit was not yet sufficient for reading the

---

8 *Autobiographical Notes,* 31.

original texts, therefore he used translations of the well-known Indologist Max Müller. He felt strongly attracted to some of the teachings of the Upaniṣads, but many interpretations in the Sacred Books of the East irritated him, since they were inspired by the conviction of a European cultural superiority, showing little sensitivity for several aspects of the Indian tradition or insight into them. Aurobindo revolted more and more against this kind of arrogant approach and around the end of his stay in England he joined, along with his brothers, a secret society named "Lotus and Dagger" founded by some Indian students in London. Every member of the group took an oath to work henceforth for the liberation of India and to take up some special activity for this purpose. But ". . . the society was still-born" and there was only a single meeting.[9]

In the meantime James Cotton, a friend of the Ghose family, made efforts to open an alternative career for Aurobindo. When in November 1892 Sayaji Rao Gaekwad[10] of Baroda came to London, Cotton arranged a meeting with him in which Aurobindo and Benoy Bhushan took part. They reached an agreement that Aurobindo would be employed with a monthly salary of Rs. 200 (a rather small amount in view of Aurobindo's high qualifications).

Meanwhile Ghose, in India, had no knowledge of all these recent developments and the failed ICS career. He had been transferred from Raṅgpur to Khulna since a new British officer-in-charge of his district felt that Ghose had become too influential. This transfer very much embittered the doctor, but none the less in Khulnā, too, he became engaged in many social activities, gaining popularity and respect from the local people. But problems intensified with his wife Swarnalata who had moved to her parents' place after returning to India; she

[9] *Autobiographical Notes*, 33.

[10] Mahārājā. Also spelt Gaekwar.

stayed at some distance from them in separate lodgings with Sarojini and Barin. Her children had a rather difficult time with their mentally ill mother, who suffered from strong mood swings. Finally Ghose managed to take the children away from her and arranged for their stay with an acquaintance in Calcutta.

In September 1892 Ghose had travelled to Bombay (Mumbai), expecting Aurobindo's arrival and wishing to receive him with pride, back in his home country. But his son's announced arrival was an error, therefore Ghose returned home in a dejected mood. Some time later in December he received a telegram from Bombay informing him that the steamer on which Aurobindo was travelling had sunk, and that his son was among those who had drowned.[11] This fatal misinformation was too much for a father so full of expectation, whose health was already affected by his problems with Swarnalata. Therefore, after reading the telegram Ghose fell quite ill and died a few days later.

Meanwhile, on 11 January 1893 Aurobindo booked his passage on the postal steamer *Carthage* and arrived in Bombay at the beginning of February. There he had a deep spiritual experience, feeling "a vast calm which descended upon him at the moment when he stepped first on Indian soil after his long absence, in fact with his first step on the Apollo Bunder in Bombay". That experience continued for a few months; it was one of those inner experiences ". . . coming of themselves and with a sudden unexpectedness, not part of a *sadhana*".[12]

---

11 Actually, there is evidence that in October 1892 a ship to Bombay had sunk near the coast of Portugal and that only nine passengers had survived.

12 *Autobiographical Notes,* 110.

3

Baroda
(1893–1906)

BARODA was one of hundreds of small states in colonial India governed by *mahārājās*, more or less like autonomous princely states. The respective rulers enjoyed a great deal of independence and could pursue their own interests undisturbed by the British as long as they accepted their supremacy and recognized them as their protecting power. After India's Independence, Baroda became at first part of Bombay Presidency, but since 1960 it belongs to the state of Gujarat and has today a little less than two million inhabitants.

When Sri Aurobindo started his work in the princely state in February 1893, he saw for the first time busy Indian life in the streets and marketplaces, he moved amidst a crowd of people whose language he did not understand, but which he soon began to learn. The Mahārājā gave him work in the Survey Settlement Department, later he was posted to the Stamp and Revenue Department and also worked for some time in the State Secretariat. Although he never became officially the private secretary to the Mahārājā, the latter entrusted him with all kinds of tasks such as drafting letters, speeches or documents.

Once the Mahārājā took Sri Aurobindo with him on a private tour to Kashmir as his secretary, but tension developed between them and there was no second joint journey. Certainly one of the main reasons was that Sri Aurobindo had a very self-confident personality and did not act as a servile subordinate, as was customary in India in this kind of relationship. Moreover, he had a superior intellect as well as literary competence. When the Mahārājā once found that a speech written for him by Sri Aurobindo was too excellent and therefore feared that people might suspect it was not his own creation, he wanted to have it revised. But Sri Aurobindo declined and said,

> Do you think, Maharaja, that if it is toned down a little, people will believe it to be yours? Good or bad, whatever it be, people will always say that the Maharaja always gets his lectures written by others.[1]

Over time Sri Aurobindo became more and more interested in teaching at Baroda College, where first he became a part-time lecturer in French, later a full professor of English and finally vice-principal.

Although the teaching job was greatly more satisfying than office work, he now had to put up with the particular habits of Indian students, who were very eager to literally copy the lectures and to learn everything by heart for passing examinations. There was no independent individual reflection on the subjects, as Sri Aurobindo had experienced during his college studies in England. Sometimes it even happened that students pointed out to him with great concern that his own comments were not in agreement with those of their textbooks.

But Sri Aurobindo always maintained cordial relations with his students and regularly invited some of them to his home. In their later reports they described how he used to give his lectures with natural ease and harmonic speech while standing in front of them almost motionless, the audience captivated by his words. That is why he was also a popular speaker at

---

[1] Purani, *The Life of Sri Aurobindo*, 39.

special occasions at the College. As for his academic work, he was not by nature the meticulous scholar patiently exploring endless details; his real gift was rather the inspired and brilliant interpretation of a text, revealing its special genius.

Sri Aurobindo used his free time in Baroda for intensive linguistic and literary studies. He deepened his knowledge of Bengali and Sanskrit and began an English translation of verses from the epic *Mahābhārata*, completing more than two chapters and attaining a remarkable quality of language and translation. He also acquired a good knowledge of Marathi and Gujarati, two modern Indian languages spoken in the state of Baroda, and after a while he knew sufficient Hindi for reading books and newspapers in this most important language of northern India. Thus he was now familiar with twelve European and Indian languages, being able to speak and read English, French and Bengali, having mastered Latin, Greek and Sanskrit and commanding a good knowledge of Gujarati, Marathi and Hindi. Moreover, he was able to read classical literature in German, Spanish and particularly Italian. But his main language always remained English, since his Bengali studies had started too late for attaining a similar mastery.

First Political Writings

At the time Sri Aurobindo began taking part in the political debate in India at the end of the nineteenth century, the country had assumed an attitude of resignation, of passive acceptance of the fact of British colonialism. The elite had been trained at British institutions and had a rather idealized perception of London politics and the parliamentary system. Nevertheless, there were also critical voices and some discontent, and therefore the Indian National Congress was founded in 1885 (with British collaboration) in order to create an outlet for those who protested. It became an institution where Indians of the higher classes came together, giving endless speeches and passing numberless resolutions with naïve hopes, all of which were ignored by the British administration to which they were directed.

Due to his long stay in England, Sri Aurobindo had a thorough understanding of English politics and now he got an opportunity to share this knowledge with his countrymen. K.G. Deshpande, his best friend at Cambridge University and editor of the weekly journal *Indu Prakash* invited him to publish articles in it. Sri Aurobindo wrote a series of articles from 1893 to 1894 under the title *New Lamps for Old* in which he tried to awaken his countrymen, pointing out the wrong, illusory and futile approach of the Congress members:

> I say, of the Congress, then, this — that its aims are mistaken, that the spirit in which it proceeds towards their accomplishment is not a spirit of sincerity and whole-heartedness, and that the methods it has chosen are not the right methods, and the leaders in whom it trusts, not the right sort of men to be leaders; — in brief, that we are at present the blind led, if not by the blind, at any rate by the one-eyed.[2]

Sri Aurobindo called for the participation of the lower classes in the political process because only in this way could the latter acquire sufficient dynamism for a deep change; he made it clear that he would prefer an upheaval similar to the French Revolution rather than an orderly parliamentary procedure, which was likely to last endlessly under the given circumstances. But this kind of articulation was very risky in a British colony and therefore Deshpande was soon warned by Mahadev Govind Ranade, a former editor of the *Indu Prakash*, that he was in danger of being arrested. Deshpande then talked to Sri Aurobindo, asking him to tone down his articles, to avoid provoking the British rulers. Sri Aurobindo

---

[2] *Bande Mataram*, 21.

followed this request, but quickly lost the inspiration for writing these cautious articles, formulated in a more innocuous academic style, and therefore the series was discontinued in March 1894.

Visiting Relatives

In the same year Sri Aurobindo undertook for the first time a major journey, visiting relatives in different places. To begin with he met his brother Benoy Bhushan and then he went to see his grandfather Rajnarain who received him warmly with his family. Sri Aurobindo was also taken to his mother who stayed in a village nearby. She found it difficult to recognize him as her son, but then she remembered a cut on one of his fingers he had suffered as a child, and on seeing the scar, she was at last convinced. Over time, Sri Aurobindo developed cordial relations with his many family members, but especially with his younger brother Barin and his sister Sarojini with whom he occasionally exchanged letters. Sarojini later reported that it was not quite easy to reach his mind and to establish communication with him.

Once while on vacation visiting the home of his aunt in Calcutta, his cousin Basanti observed him unpacking his suitcases. She assumed they would contain clothes and other practical things; with great surprise she realized they were full of books, which Sri Aurobindo read with great intensity. However, she happily noted that this did not prevent him from sharing the merry talks of the other family members who were all in a holiday mood and who could hardly understand Sri Aurobindo's "hobby" of continuous reading. Actually, his thirst for books was tremendous; there are reports that every month — sometimes even every week — he would order masses of books from Bombay and Calcutta. Dinendrakumar Roy, a Bengali author who occasionally assisted Sri Aurobindo with his language studies and was in close touch with him, remembers:

> Sitting in a chair before a table, undisturbed by the terrible biting of the mosquitoes, Aurobindo read at night until one o'clock by the light of a "jewel lamp". I saw him sitting there for hours at a stretch, his eyes glued to the page, his attitude unchanging, like an ascetic rapt in contemplation, oblivious of the world. I don't think he would have noticed if the house caught fire.[3]

Marriage to Mrinalini Bose

In large parts of the Indian society it has been customary that pressure is put on single people to find a partner for marriage, with the ceremony becoming a major event often connected with heavy financial strain. Aged twenty-eight, Sri Aurobindo had already been rather long in the single status; all his elder brothers were married. In those days Indian women were often married while still children, with the partnerships being arranged by the parents. Young Hindu girls were prepared early on for their role as a loyal and obedient wife, seeking through her devotion to make her partner happy.

In 1900 Sri Aurobindo placed a marriage advertisement.[4] According to Bengali custom at that time, he went to the prospective brides' homes for a brief meeting, and after many such visits, without hesitation upon seeing Mrinalini Bose, he made his decision. Aged fourteen, she was a beautiful, kind-hearted girl though without any special gifts and in no way a match for her husband's high intellect. Before the marriage there was, however, a problem to be solved, since from the orthodox Hindu viewpoint Sri Aurobindo had become impure

---

3 Dinendrakumar Ray, *Aurobindo Prasanga* (Calcutta: Sri Aurobindo Pathmandir), 43.

4 Purani talks manuscripts, 5:97; *The Lives of Sri Aurobindo*, 53. See also Iyengar, *Sri Aurobindo*, 64.

through his journey to England. It was necessary for him to purify himself through certain religious rites which included, for instance, a complete tonsure of his head. But Sri Aurobindo was unwilling to undergo such rites, which made it very difficult to find a priest for the marriage ceremony. Eventually a brāhmin agreed to perform the rites of marriage after having been persuaded by extra payment.

After the marriage the newly-wedded couple travelled to Deoghar[5] to spend a month there with Sri Aurobindo's relatives. Accompanied by Sarojini, they proceeded to Nainital, a beautiful hill-station in the western Himalayas where the Gaekwaḍ owned a bungalow. After a while, all three of them proceeded to Baroda.

The relationship with her husband was a great challenge for Mrinalini because he was a genius, not only married to her, but also to his books and later on to his political activities and his Yoga. Sarojini's presence may have helped the young girl, grown up in a well-to-do middle-class family to get used to the new situation. But during their marriage there were again and again long phases of privation when Sri Aurobindo was absent, or imprisoned as a freedom fighter, and finally beyond reach in distant Pondicherry.

Often Sri Aurobindo tried to give her inner support through long, loving letters, but their content makes us assume that he may have expected too much of her, with his reports about his activities and statements on his personal philosophy. Mrinalini had to undergo many crises. Sri Aurobindo was glad and relieved upon hearing one day that she had received spiritual initiation from Sarada Devi, the wife of Sri Ramakrishna.

Their marriage remained childless and we hardly have

---

[5] Situated in today's State of Jharkhand, north-east India.

any documents in the Indian biographical literature to inform us how they lived together. However, we know that Sri Aurobindo kept his usual working routine and that among his relatives there was the impression that he did not feel naturally drawn towards family life. His inner concentration and detachment was too deep and intensive for that. In a letter to his father-in-law he once noted:

> I am afraid I shall never be good for much in the way of domestic virtues. I have tried, very ineffectively, to do some part of my duty as a son, a brother and a husband, but there is something too strong in me which forces me to subordinate everything else to it.[6]

When Sri Aurobindo was later asked why great spiritual personalities should marry at all, being hardly able to live a normal marital life, he answered:

> Perfectly natural — they marry before the change — then the change comes and the marriage belongs to the past self, not to the new one. . . . Do you think that Buddha or Confucius or myself were born with a prevision that they or I would take to the spiritual life? So long as one is in the ordinary consciousness, one lives the ordinary life — when the awakening and the new consciousness come, one leaves it — nothing puzzling in that.[7]

Some letters from 1905 confiscated before the Alipore court

6 *Autobiographical Notes*, 147. A new document has been published by Manoj Das in his series *Sri Aurobindo: Life and Times of the Mahayogi* (Mother India, November 2012, p. 802). He refers to Manomohan Gangopadhyay's title *Shruti-Smriti* (Bengali) in which the author reports about a meeting with Sri Aurobindo after the Alipore Conspiracy Case. When they discussed about the possibility of celibacy in married life, Sri Aurobindo is said to have made a very clear statement that he had been practising celibacy all the time.

7 *Nirodbaran's Correspondence with Sri Aurobindo*, 576.

case and used during the process have been preserved as valuable documents of the correspondence between Sri Aurobindo and Mrinalini. They were originally written in Bengali and later translated into English. A letter dated 30 August 1905 is especially important, as it throws light on Sri Aurobindo's relationship with his wife and his general thoughts on the relationship. He addresses the question of his unconventional way of life, which would appear hard to bear even for a self-sacrificing devoted Hindu wife. Sri Aurobindo points out that from the viewpoint of ordinary humans he would indeed be "mad", as his goals were extraordinary, his activities uncommon.

> They label all these as madness, but if the mad man succeeds in the field of action, then instead of calling him a lunatic, they call him a great man, a man of genius.[8]

For a woman, Sri Aurobindo continues, marriage with such a husband necessarily means suffering because her life is focused on the well-being and happiness of the family, and this natural desire to have a normal family life is inconsistent with the high-flying aspirations of the genius. It is, therefore, her choice either to trust him blindly and to follow his hardly comprehensible ways, or else to consider him a mad man, and to leave him. Sri Aurobindo then proceeds to declare that he has three "madnesses".

First, his belief that all the gifts and possessions he has do not belong to him, but are only entrusted to him by God. He is only allowed to keep for himself, Sri Aurobindo says, what he absolutely requires; all the rest must be used for the work given to him. This means concretely that he can give only a limited support to his wife, since the whole of India is now his family, in need of his help.

---

[8] The source of this and the following quotations is *Sri Aurobindo Mandir Annual*, 1967, 117-20. See also Iyengar, *Sri Aurobindo*, 198-200.

Second, Sri Aurobindo declares that he has the deep desire to see God and experience him face-to-face. However, what he has in mind is not the religious experience, but the living realization. For this purpose the sacred writings of India have laid down certain disciplines: "I have begun to observe them and within a month I have been able to ascertain that the words of the Hindu Dharma are not untrue." Sri Aurobindo invites his wife to follow him on this path, but it would be her own free decision, to do so, or not.

The third "madness" is his special relationship with his own home country, Mother India. "Whereas others regard the country as an inert piece of matter and know it as the plains, the fields, the forest, the mountains and the rivers, I know my country as the Mother, I worship her and adore her accordingly." Now, he continues, he sees a demon (the British colonial power) sucking his mother's blood and that is why he has to rush for her support and cannot spend his time sharing petty enjoyments with wife and children. He has to face the battle, but "I am not going to fight with a sword or a gun, but with the power of knowledge". This, he says, is his mission on earth, "at the age of fourteen the seed of it had begun to sprout and at eighteen it had been firmly rooted and become unshakable".

Once more Sri Aurobindo invites Mrinalini to follow him on the path, to support him as his *śakti* sharing his noble goals instead of listening to the doubting voices from some of the relatives. But the demand Sri Aurobindo makes on her by speaking more as a *guru* than as a husband, is very high — too high for Mrinalini. And as we shall see later, it was the destiny of another woman to become Sri Aurobindo's *śakti*. Mrinalini always made efforts to play her role to the best of her capacity, but she was suffering because Sri Aurobindo's financial support for her was insufficient to live decently. Therefore she received financial help from her relatives during those long periods when she lived separately from her husband. Even when he was employed in Baroda, she often stayed for one reason or another with family members in Bengal and had to be content with her correspondence with Sri Aurobindo, who dedicated much time to the reading and answering of her letters.

The Political Work

With his articles in the *Indu Prakash* Sri Aurobindo had tried for the first time to participate in the political debate of the country or rather to initiate it. The limits imposed upon him by the editor stood in the way of his making much effect. But in the following years he never lost sight of his goal: to win for the Indian population the ideal of attaining independence. He followed political events with great attention. Even while the Indian National Congress kept passing its numberless vain resolutions, there was a glimmer of hope with the appearance of Bal Gangadhar Tilak who, along with his group of followers from Maharashtra, was ready for a more radical approach.

Tilak was a journalist and activist from Poona who had studied at the University of Bombay. He was able to move skilfully on the stage of high-level politics and to reach the masses as an inspired orator. His newspaper *Kesari* in the Marathi language circulated tens of thousands of copies, which was much more than English papers could ever hope to sell. In 1897 he was condemned to eighteen-months imprisonment on the charge of sedition. According to the prosecution, articles in his newspaper had inspired two Indians in Poona to kill a high British government official in the town. But when Tilak was released from prison, the populace celebrated him as a national hero.

In 1898 Sri Aurobindo had met a Bengali named Jatindranath Banerji, who had wanted to become a soldier but failed to get into the Indian Army. However in Baroda he was smuggled into the State Army with the help of a young army officer Madhavrao Jadhav, a close friend of Sri Aurobindo. For about two years Banerji received training there and spoke with Sri Aurobindo and like-minded people of the possibility of a political upheaval in the country.

After this training Banerji was sent to Bengal in order to establish a centre of physical education. It was planned that in this way young men should be found who could, at a later stage, be prepared for some revolutionary activity. However, Bengalis were better known as intellectuals rather than fighters who would be ready to challenge the British foreign power. Therefore, Sri Aurobindo believed that a period of up to thirty years might be required to see any result.

The aim of this undertaking was

> to establish secretly or, as far as visible action could be taken, under various pretexts and covers, revolutionary propaganda and recruiting throughout Bengal. This was to be done among the youth of the country while sympathy and support and financial and other assistance were to be obtained from the older men who had advanced views or could be won over to them.[9]

It was planned for this purpose to establish centres in every town and in every village. Societies for the practice of *lāṭhī* (an Indian martial art performed with bamboo sticks) often served as the outer cover. Sarala Devi Ghosal, a grand-daughter of Devendranath Tagore (the father of Rabindranath) became active in helping to spread *lāṭhī* practice while Sister Nivedita, a prominent Irish disciple of Swami Vivekananda, made efforts to strengthen the Bengali youth. She helped to found a society for physical education whose director was Pramathanath Mitra, a highly-placed lawyer and *lāṭhī* expert in Calcutta.

---

9 *Autobiographical Notes*, 49.

When Banerji came to Bengal, he contacted this society named Anushilan Samiti[10] and joined it for common activities. He travelled too through other districts of Bengal, in order to meet like-minded people, to win them over for collaboration and thus lay a foundation for a revolutionary upheaval.

At the end of 1902 Sri Aurobindo's younger brother Barin suddenly turned up in Baroda. He had discontinued his studies at a college in Patna after six months and was now roaming about the country in search of his destiny. For some time he stayed with his brothers Manmohan and Benoy Bhushan, trying without success to set up some small trading business. Subsequently he stayed with Sri Aurobindo, who supplied him with a large number of books and took him out for political discussions within a circle of friends. Soon Barin came to know that a secret society had been founded which included some politicians from Maharashtra among its members.

In December 1902 the Gaekwad of Baroda gave a brilliant speech in Ahmedabad (with some remarkable passages written by Sri Aurobindo). The Gaekwad pointed out that if India would want to take her proper place in the world, it would require "a great national movement in which each man will work for the nation and not for himself or for his caste". For this purpose action would be required,

> but until you realise that the ultimate remedy lies in your own hands, and that you have to carry it out by yourselves, no external reform can help you.[11]

Finally, he even pleaded for the institution of a "national government". His courageous speech, given on the occasion of an industrial fair, was much applauded by the audience.

---

[10] Literally, cultural society.

[11] *Early Cultural Writings*, 718, 720.

A few days later there was a session of the Indian National Congress at the same location. Sri Aurobindo was present; he met Tilak who explained to him the reasons for his rejection of the toothless Congress politics, and described the kind of action he had initiated in Maharashtra. After this talk Sri Aurobindo had the impression that Tilak might be capable of leading a future revolutionary party.

At the beginning of 1903 Sri Aurobindo introduced Barin to the secret society where he swore an oath in a solemn ceremony to fight unto death for the freedom of India. Then he went to Calcutta to help Banerji with his activities there. But Barin was an intellectual type of man and with limited physical strength, so he did not get along well with the robust, giant Banerji. Again and again there arose discord between them, with Sri Aurobindo trying indefatigably to mediate. Barin was ready to listen to his elder brother regarding the political work and would have preferred receiving instructions directly from him exclusively, but he found it very hard to submit to Banerji. In the end their conflict could not be solved and the two separated. Thereafter revolutionary activities in Bengal which had progressed well in some places, lost power, and became more or less extinguished.

After this set-back the work of the independence fighters gained an unexpected new impetus when Lord Curzon, Viceroy of India, decreed the partition of Bengal in 1905 which was officially declared as part of major administrative reforms. But there was the clear political intention behind this move to weaken the community of Bengali-speaking Hindus according to the well-tried principle of *divide et impera* (divide and rule). This group was the most politically active community in India, threatening to disturb the otherwise unchallenged British domination. The reforms provided for the creation of two new provinces, East Bengal and Assam, and as a result the Hindus would be minorities in the respective districts, dominated by Muslims. This was of great importance for the overall power structure in that Lord Curzon had succeeded in winning over to his side the Muslims.

A storm of indignation was created among the Hindus due to this administrative act of the British. Large meetings took place attended by thousands; protest was voiced against the reforms as the people swore they would stop buying products imported from England (such as salt, sugar and cloth) and instead of them purchase only native (*swadeshi*) products. Within a short period of time a Swadeshi movement developed out of the protests, gaining great momentum. But boycott also meant sacrifice, as the native products were often much more expensive, and therefore some parts of the population did not support it; the daily struggle for survival had a greater priority than striving for noble goals that were somewhat irrelevant from their viewpoint.

On 7 August 1905 a huge gathering was held in Calcutta and a unanimous resolution was passed to support the boycott. After the meeting, students went through the streets chanting slogans and calling out *bande mātaram*[12] which quickly became a *mantra*. The two words were taken from a song by the eminent Bengali poet Bankim Chandra Chatterjee (which still remains popular). Thus regionally a national movement was born along with a wave of enthusiasm in large parts of the population, especially the Hindu middle class. The British administration reacted to these protests by strictly prohibiting the new *mantra* and by banning all large gatherings.

Sri Aurobindo knew the chances connected with the revolt and the national enthusiasm of the people, but he was also aware of the dangers of an uncontrolled process. In a note unpublished at that time he wrote the following lines which

---

12 The Bengali version of Sanskrit *vande mātaram*, "I bow before the Mother [India]".

possibly, for the first time in this context, contained the term "passive resistance" which was to make Gandhi famous many years later:

> Let the authorities remember this, that when a Government breaks the Law, by their very act the people are absolved from the obligation of obeying the Law. But let the people on their side so long as they are permitted to do so abstain from aggressive violence, let them study carefully to put their oppressors always in the wrong; but from no legitimate kind of passive resistance should they shrink.[13]

Spiritual and Occult Experiences

Sri Aurobindo's main interests in life were initially poetry and literature, and additionally political activities. An important aspect of his literary exploits was the study of Sanskrit works. Having translated some sections of the *Mahābhārata* as mentioned previously, he next took up Kālidāsa, writing some elaborate treatises on the great Indian poet's work and translating some parts of it.[14] Thereafter he read the Upaniṣads with commentaries by Indian and Western authors such as Śaṅkarācārya and Paul Deussen. His impression was that they did not convey the true sense of the Upaniṣads, and that he might require some training in *yoga* in order to be able to understand their real essence. His friend Keshavrao Deshpande had had some experience in *yoga* and was ready to share it with him, but at this stage Sri Aurobindo declined to go into it, since it appeared to him that *yoga* had something to do with withdrawing from life, which was out of the question for him.

All the same he had some important spiritual experiences.

---

13 *Bande Mataram*, 103.

14 Published in the volume *Kalidasa: Essays and Translations*. Sri Aurobindo Ashram, 2004.

Previously mentioned was his perception of a wide silence after his return from England, as he stepped onto Indian soil at the Apollo Bunder in Bombay. Moreover, there was

> the realisation of the vacant Infinite while walking on the ridge of the Takht-i-[Sulaiman] in Kashmir, the living presence of Kali in a shrine on the banks of the Narmada, the vision of the Godhead surging up from within when in danger of a carriage accident in Baroda in the first year of his stay.[15]

In Poona again he had a significant experience when visiting a shrine dedicated to Bhavānī, the Mother-Godhead, and expressed it four decades later with the two lines,

> The Soul of all that lives, calm, pure, alone
> Revealed its boundless self mystic and bare.[16]

These were inner experiences which occurred spontaneously and unexpectedly, not as part of a *sādhanā* (spiritual discipline). Sri Aurobindo had a friend, A.B. Devadhar, who finally taught him some yogic practices. Devadhar was a disciple of Swami Brahmananda of Gange Math in Chandod, some 30 miles from Baroda. Brahmananda was a renowned *yogī* and Sri Aurobindo, deeply impressed with him, met him personally several times, receiving his blessings. There are reports that Brahmananda looked at Sri Aurobindo with open eyes during his last visit, whereas usually he kept them closed or half-closed. Sri Aurobindo was amazed at the beauty of the *yogī*'s eyes; he had never before seen anything comparable.

Brahmananda is said to have reached a very great age with the help of *haṭha-yoga* practices as well as *rāja-yoga* meditation: some reports speak of 200 or 300 years.[17] But he

---

15 *Autobiographical Notes,* 110.

16 *Collected Poems,* 622.

17 See also: *Letters on Himself and the Ashram,* 15-16, and Purani, *Evening Talks,* 514.

was not the *guru* of Sri Aurobindo and therefore the latter followed a spiritual path on his own. In 1904 he started practising *prāṇāyāma* for three hours in the morning and two hours in the evening and felt a remarkable, energizing effect. There was a kind of mental freshness and illumination; he was able to effortlessly write 200 lines of poetry within an hour, whereas formerly he would only write 10 lines a day. Moreover, his health and memory improved, his skin became more smooth and he felt a sort of aura around his head. He noted a pleasant sweet taste in his saliva and he experienced some supernatural visions.[18]

While being in search of a *guru*, Sri Aurobindo met a Nāgā *saṁnyāsī*.[19] Although he could not accept him as his teacher, the ascetic confirmed his belief in the effectiveness of yogic force, for when Barin fell ill with a dangerous mountain fever, Sri Aurobindo saw the *saṁnyāsī* curing his brother, "by merely cutting through a glassful of water crosswise with a knife while he repeated a silent *mantra*".[20]

In Europe at the beginning of the twentieth century occult experiences such as séances and table moving were very much in vogue and the wave reached India. The basic idea was to contact invisible worlds with their hidden forces and beings, and receive messages from them (which is today called "channelling"), always combined with the expectation of attaining knowledge which transcends that of the earth sphere. Sri Aurobindo and his circle tried the so-called automatic writing, in which a being of the invisible worlds is supposed to guide the medium's hand and to transmit texts. Regarding the background of these practices Sri Aurobindo later clarified:

---

[18] Purani, *Evening Talks*, 613.

[19] A Hindu ascetic of a certain sect.

[20] *Autobiographical Notes*, 110.

> The writing was done as an experiment as well as an amusement and nothing else.[21]

Barin particularly received some remarkable texts

> in a very brilliant and beautiful English style and remarkable for certain predictions which came true. . . .[22]

Among the predictions there were also statements on the future progress of the national movement and the actions of Tilak. Sri Aurobindo, impressed by the experiments when they proved to be correct, decided to probe more deeply into the matter. But in the end the results did not quite satisfy him. He gave up these experiments entirely after further sessions later in Pondicherry. He came to realize that certain phenomena of interaction with beings of another plane of existence do occur, but that the majority of these writings came

> . . . from a dramatising element in the subconscious mind; sometimes a brilliant vein in the subliminal is struck and then predictions of the future and statements of things [unknown] in the present and past come up, but otherwise these writings have not a great value.[23]

Of messages with some higher value he counted that of the great Yogi Ramakrishna Paramahamsa, contacted by himself and three companions with the question of what they could do for their country. They received the instruction *mandir gaḍo* (Bengali words for "build a temple"). At first this was taken literally, but later Sri Aurobindo was more inclined to give it a symbolical interpretation.

Thereupon his companion Deshpande founded a school near Chandod, a place of pilgrimage, which aimed at a modern education with a national outlook, connected with Sanskrit

---

21 *Autobiographical Notes*, 95.

22 Ibid.

23 Ibid., 96.

studies. Some time earlier Barin had developed the idea that a *saṁnyāsī* order be founded dedicated to the political work. For this purpose he searched for a place in a remote region, far from big cities. When he asked Sri Aurobindo to support his idea by writing a pamphlet, he acquiesced with a booklet titled *Bhawani Mandir* by the middle of 1905.

In this booklet he suggested that a temple for the Mother (the Śakti or infinite Energy) should be erected somewhere in a hilly region and that all children of the Mother would be called upon to help with the work. The monks of the temple would be *karma-yogīs*[24] going out into the world carrying "the flame of Bhavānī" into all parts of the country. Their work was to be based on the spiritual knowledge of Vedānta, the teachings of the Upaniṣads and the *Bhagavad-Gītā*.

Barin's search was unsuccessful and he returned from the hills with mountain fever. Actually Sri Aurobindo had only half-heartedly taken up this idea of a Bhavānī Mandir.[25]

The Last Days in Baroda

Many students took part in the Swadeshi movement such as picketing in front of those shops which continued selling imported products. Therefore the British colonial government decided to take action against the students by prohibiting their joining any political gatherings. Furthermore, the school and college principals were informed in a circular letter that they would lose government grants if their students took part in

---

24 Practising *karma-yoga*, the *yoga* of works.

25 It is interesting to note the parallel to Matrimandir, the "Temple of the Mother" which Sri Aurobindo's spiritual collaborator Mirra Alfassa dreamed of and had built many decades later in Auroville. However, Matrimandir represents the universal Śakti beyond all national and religious objectives. Moreover no adoration takes place in it; it is a place for meditation and for receiving spiritual force.

the boycott activities. This blackmailing on the part of the authorities caused great irritation; there were Bengali intellectuals who began to think how they might overcome dependence on British support.

Finally they took up an idea which had already been discussed earlier: founding their own national institutions for the education of the youth. Subodh Chandra Mullik, a wealthy patron, offered a very large amount of money for realizing these plans. He and Sri Aurobindo had met in 1904, finding that they shared many ideas. Mullik's understanding was that in connection with his donation he would claim the privilege of personally nominating the director of the national college that was to be founded.

At the end of November 1905 Sri Aurobindo went to Calcutta to have a look at the current political scene there. He stayed at Mullik's house where he met Bipin Chandra Pal, the leader of a group which called itself "the new party" as it promoted the boycott movement. Sri Aurobindo encountered some young people associated with Pal. Now the subject of "national education" became more and more important and therefore a board of experienced educators was formed with the aim of developing plans for a committee on the national level.

At the end of December 1905 the annual Congress session took place in Bengal and there was a clash between the more radical and the moderate forces. Tilak and some of his followers succeeded, in spite of great difficulties, in seeing that a resolution passed in favour of the boycott. For this purpose they were compelled to accept a compromise with the moderate forces which they celebrated as a first victory over their opponents.

Meanwhile, Sri Aurobindo continued his work in Baroda. In 1905 he had been appointed acting principal of Baroda

College since A.B. Clarke, the official British principal, preferred spending most of his time at home in England. This resulted in a good deal of administrative work as well as teaching while inwardly he felt more and more drawn to Bengal at this stage; his desire was to join the political movement there. When Clarke came to Baroda in 1906, Sri Aurobindo took a four-month leave, thinking of finishing his employment in Baroda thereafter.

A friend noticed that Sri Aurobindo, as he packed his suitcase, seemed quite inspired. On being enquired the reason for this, Sri Aurobindo explained that the time had finally arrived to dedicate himself entirely to the service of his country, and that he would soon leave Baroda.[26] On 28 February he answered an invitation from a photo studio which was run by some former students of Baroda College. A photo, probably taken on this occasion, shows him sitting amidst eight students of his class wearing a three-piece Western style suit, a tie and a walking stick as well as a turban as worn in north India.

Shortly before his departure to Calcutta at the beginning of March, he quickly wrote a letter to Mrinalini (who stayed with her relatives) indicating that he might soon call her to his place, although this would not be certain since much work was awaiting him in Bengal.

---

26 R. Parkar, *Reminiscences*, 190. *The Lives of Sri Aurobindo*, 97.

4

The Freedom Fighter
Calcutta (1906-08)

When Sri Aurobindo moved to Calcutta he was known largely to his local colleagues, but not yet as a reputed personality in the eyes of all. Many considered him as an outsider who had so far spent his life in distant England followed by a sojourn in remote Baroda serving for a long time as secretary of a *mahārājā* and finally, as vice-principal of a college. His articles in the *Indu Prakash* had been published more than ten years earlier. People were hardly aware of them any more and his past activities in Bengal had failed to show concrete results due to Barin's weaknesses.

What was helpful for his introduction was a fact known to all insiders that he would become the director of a future national college. At the outset a National Council of Education was founded, with Sri Aurobindo as one of ninety-two founding members, many of whom were respected members of the society: scholars, big landowners, etc. It was a high-calibre board that speedily worked out plans for the college.

In that same year of 1906 Sri Aurobindo and Barin launched a Bengali newspaper named *Jugantar*[1] (The New Age). Its purpose was to reveal Sri Aurobindo's political ideas to a larger public. For the first time he published an article (in Bengali) demanding that India throw off the chain that tied it to British colonial power. The Congress, he explained through

[1] Also spelt *Yugantar*.

an image, merely wanted to replace the iron chain by a golden one — a policy of timidity which he had repeatedly rejected.

Sri Aurobindo, unaccustomed to writing in Bengali, contributed only a few leading articles in the first issues; all the others were written by Barin and two colleagues. *Jugantar* became an influential publication, reaching within a year an unexpectedly high circulation of 10,000 copies. However from an economic point of view the paper was a fiasco, since all those involved lived entirely in a world of their own political ideals. They did not care to occupy themselves with finances.

In April 1906 the Barisal Conference would be held, a regional meeting of the Congress; to be discussed in particular would be the consequences of the partition of Bengal. Problems with the British police arose even before the gathering. The delegates were chanting the forbidden *mantra "bande mātaram"* on the way to the convention site, refusing to refrain chanting it in the future as well as refusing the banning of processions, as ordered by the police chief. On the contrary, the delegates escorted the president of the conference in a demonstrative procession to the meeting while chanting *bande mātaram*. Sri Aurobindo marched in the first rank with other veterans of the movement and the large police detachment let them pass without intervention. But the police asked the younger volunteers in the back ranks to dissolve the procession, violently beating them with their *lāṭhīs* (sticks) when they refused the order. Many young activists suffered serious injuries, whereupon the leaders of the procession rushed to the police chief to stop the brutal action. The veteran Surendranath Banerjea declared himself responsible for everything, which resulted in his arrest plus a heavy fine.

This was a decisive moment in the resistance movement because for the first time, Indians of repute were in open revolt against the British executive power. Banerjea as leader attained a kind of martyr status in the eyes of the population. Actually, some volunteers had wanted to join him in this role, but police chief F.E. Kemp had turned them away. Retrospectively, the Sri Aurobindo biographer K.R.S. Iyengar notes:

> Thus did defiance of the law acquire respectability and sanctity at Barisal, and the abortive conference made history more than it would have, had it been allowed to be held in peace.[2]

Bande Mataram

Today the terms "radical" and "extremist" carry a very negative connotation. As a rule in world politics our sympathies are with the moderate forces that are willing to compromise. But in the political setting of India at that time the situation was different: large parts of the population and the elite had so much resigned themselves to the British colonial government that the mere thought of shaking off foreign rule appeared to them radical and extreme. But in reality the "extremists" inspired by Sri Aurobindo were freedom fighters, claiming the legitimate rights of their country for self-determination, some of them ready to accomplish this goal by the use of force if necessary.

The Moderates, however, did not intend to question the foreign rule in such a manner. They preferred to confine their actions to influencing the acceptance of reforms, to working for the right of the Indian population to gain a say in political life. From the viewpoint of Sri Aurobindo and his comrades this was a policy of shameful begging *vis-à-vis* the British, who were at most ready to make some trivial concessions to the Indians to pacify them, while basically unwilling to change the *status quo*. When the group of Hardliners — we shall refer to the extremists as such in the following — kept gaining power there was an increasing confrontation with the established Moderate forces. The growing differences became evident

[2] Iyengar, *Sri Aurobindo*, 203.

during the annual sessions of the Congress. Even before the meetings took place conflicts arose regarding the nomination of the president, who was, to some extent, in a position to determine the course of the sessions in which the Hardliner's aim was to pass their resolutions demanding independence.

At the end of 1906 there was a major clash of the two parties in connection with a nomination and the heated debate finally found its way into the columns of several newspapers. Although the Hardliners controlled a few papers such as *Jugantar*, they had no English language paper to represent their position throughout the country. This was felt to be a handicap: in August 1907 Bipin Chandra Pal, though short of funds, launched a daily newspaper with the provocative name *Bande Mataram*. Pal approached Sri Aurobindo, who had not been informed of this plan, requesting him to write articles for the newspaper. Sri Aurobindo at once agreed and wrote a text on John Morley as the first of hundreds of contributions. The latter had just been appointed as the new Secretary of State for India in London; he was more friendly towards India than his predecessor, a fact that raised exaggerated and unrealistic expectations for many Indians. Meanwhile, Pal undertook a journey to East Bengal to find readers for his newspaper there. After his return, Hemendra Prasad Ghose and Shyamsundar Chakravarty joined the paper as managing editors.

By this time Sri Aurobindo was teaching at the National College of Education, founded on his birthday, 15 August 1906. He gave lectures in English and history, performed a good deal of administrative work and helped prepare examinations. His salary was much less than it had been in Baroda so that he had to reduce his expenses, especially for books. He stayed at Mullik's house where he met some members of the cultural elite of Calcutta.

Regarding *Bande Mataram,* he suggested that the Hardliners in Bengal should form an alliance with Tilak and his people in Poona, establishing themselves as a national party of India and use the newspaper as its organ of communication. A volunteer who was ready, if necessary, to go to prison gave his name in the imprint as responsible editor. However, the texts were very carefully worded so as to avoid offering the colonial government an opportunity of charging the paper with sedition. The revolutionary contents were evident to the readers, but they were expressed through subtle suggestions and allusions which in themselves did not violate any laws. Sri Aurobindo developed a great mastery writing in this special style and soon the London press became aware of those brilliant articles, frequently quoting from them.

It was not his strategy to attack the British personally but to demand persistently the right of the people to freedom and self-determination. However, many attacks were directed against the Moderates and their policy of endless vain petitions. Again and again Sri Aurobindo and Pal stressed that it could not be the right path to follow for India: begging, combined with the expectation that the British government after many reforms would one day become a nice, acceptable administration. Rather the country would have to rediscover its true self, shake off all foreign control and take charge of its own destiny in full autonomy.

In the *Bande Mataram* articles Sri Aurobindo's style of writing had not yet attained that of a global sage. We see him here very much as an Indian with fiery emotions, often using flowery language very rich in imagery, appealing to the mind of many Hindus. In the following example he addresses the question of passive resistance and its effectiveness. Unlike Gandhi, Sri Aurobindo believed that non-violent resistance should not be made an absolute rule. If the opponent himself makes use of violence and unfair means it is legitimate, he says, to face him too with violence, if there is really no other way:

> The work of national emancipation is a great and holy *yajna*[3] of which boycott, Swadeshi, national education and every other activity, great and small, are only major or minor parts. Liberty is the fruit we seek from the sacrifice and the Motherland the goddess to whom we offer it; into the seven leaping tongues of the fire[4] of the *yajna* we must offer all that we are and all that we have. . . . But every great *yajna* has its Rakshasas[5] who strive to baffle the sacrifice, to bespatter it with their own dirt or by guile or violence put out the flame. Passive resistance is an attempt to meet such disturbers by peaceful and self-contained *brahmatej*;[6] but even the greatest Rishis of old could not, when the Rakshasas were fierce and determined, keep up the sacrifice without calling in the bow of the Kshatriya.[7]
>
> Vedantism[8] accepts no distinction of true or false religions, but considers only what will lead more or less surely, more or less quickly to *moksha*, spiritual emancipation and the realization of the Divinity within. Our attitude is a political Vedantism. India, free, one and indivisible, is the divine realization to which we move — emancipation our aim. . . . Passive resistance may be the final method of salvation in our case or it may be only the preparation for the final *sadhan*.[9] In either case, the sooner we put it into full and perfect practice, the nearer we shall be to national liberty.[10]

Thus long before Gandhi, Sri Aurobindo sounded the possibilities and limits of passive resistance, deeply reflecting on this subject. Since the British were a relatively civilized

---

3 Sacrifice.

4 An image from the *Ṛgveda*.

5 Demons.

6 Spiritual force.

7 Warrior.

8 See Glossary.

9 Means, way, accomplishment.

10 *Bande Mataram*, 302-3.

political force (as compared to other political powers such as Russia) he assumed that passive resistance could achieve a good deal if supported by large parts of the population which would, however, require sacrifice and renunciation. Most of the boycott measures could be carried out within the framework of the existing laws but their breaking he considered legitimate, or even a duty if the laws or decrees themselves jeopardized basic rights of the people.

Regarding the role of the newspaper, Sri Aurobindo later explained:

> The *Bande Mataram* was almost unique in journalistic history in the influence it exercised in converting the mind of a people and preparing it for revolution.[11]

Some prominent personalities in different parts of the country were inspired by Sri Aurobindo's leading articles, and outside India Gandhi and Nehru, among others, became aware of the paper. The *Times* in London published long extracts from it regularly.

Meanwhile, the conflict with the British colonial government increased. In the Punjab the local president of the Congress was arrested after riots; farmers had revolted against raised water rates and revenue assessments. Lala Lajpat Rai was deported to Burma (Myanmar) without trial and Sri Aurobindo protested vehemently against this measure in an article in *Bande Mataram.*

At this point Bipin Chandra Pal started campaigning in south India for the national cause whereupon the governor of Madras urged the viceroy, Lord Minto, to deport Pal as well, but Morley in London intervened with his veto. In June *Bande Mataram* and *Jugantar* were advised by British authorities to use a more moderate language in their articles, or, face legal action. In fact, some editors in Bombay and in the Punjab had

[11] *Autobiographical Notes,* 56.

already been given prison sentences due to sedition. However the authors of *Jugantar,* who sometimes criticized the government openly and whose texts had always been more radical than those of *Bande Mataram* were not impressed by this threat. They described the British empire as a huge sham which would collapse if you pushed it just a little.

In July the government reacted by ordering a police raid of the *Jugantar* office. A co-worker named Bhupendranath Dutt declared himself to be in-charge of the paper and was consequently arrested on a charge of sedition. But a short time later he backed down from his statement and wanted to be free of the consequences. Sri Aurobindo grew angry upon being informed, although he knew that Dutt was not actually the editor. He urged him, for the sake of the cause, to take responsibility for *Jugantar* and the articles. Furthermore, Dutt was to refuse to defend himself, making a statement to this effect which Sri Aurobindo himself formulated. Thus Dutt was made to change his mind and he followed Sri Aurobindo's instructions, declaring before the prosecution,

> I have done what I considered my duty to my country. . . . I do not wish to make any further statement or *to take any part in the case.*[12]

Through his refusal to co-operate with a British law court Dutt broke new ground in India, establishing a precedent which was later taken up by Gandhi and his followers. Dutt was sentenced to one year's rigorous imprisonment, none the less he could draw comfort from the fact that the Indian population celebrated him as a hero.

The Trial Against Sri Aurobindo and Bande Mataram

Sri Aurobindo had always carefully avoided publishing his name or that of other authors in the imprint page of the journal.

---

12 *Bande Mataram,* 613.

When once it did happen due to the negligence of a co-worker, it brought about one of the few moments in Sri Aurobindo's life that his companions witnessed him enraged.[13] He was determined to act only behind the curtain, all the more so since at that point he had not yet officially finished teaching at Baroda College; he was only on extended leave. One of the two co-editors had learned to write in Sri Aurobindo's style which enabled him to publish leading articles on his behalf whenever Sri Aurobindo was travelling. But external observers (the British authorities) generally believed that Sri Aurobindo was the author of those brilliant texts about which they were increasingly concerned, since they did not fail to notice the influence those texts had on political thought all over India.

After the prosecution had taken action against *Jugantar*, the editors of *Bande Mataram* felt sure that the police would show up sooner or later in their office. Therefore precautions were taken that Sri Aurobindo's name should not appear anywhere in the files of the newspaper and wherever this was the case, they removed his name with a knife. At the end of July the police arrived at the office of *Bande Mataram* with a search warrant plus a warrant for Sri Aurobindo's arrest, but before serving it they wanted to examine whether there was any evidence against him to be found in the office. Although they could not discover any incriminating material they decided none the less to arrest Sri Aurobindo and informed the editor on duty about it a little later. When Sri Aurobindo came to know, he surrendered to the police on his own. He was subsequently released on payment of large sureties arranged by two friends.

This arrest instantly made Sri Aurobindo famous in the country. He was still little known outside Bengal, and some people assumed there might be other authors, too. But now that his identity had been officially confirmed by the British authorities a wave of sympathy was generated in the press and

[13] *The Lives of Sri Aurobindo*, 112.

in the population. Even newspapers Sri Aurobindo had criticized because of their moderate political positions now published articles praising him. In August 1907 Rabindranath Tagore wrote some lines of appreciation in Bengali which appeared in *Bande Mataram* in September and were later to become famous:

> Rabindranath, O Aurobindo, bows to thee! O friend, my country's friend, O Voice incarnate, free, of India's soul. . . . The fiery messenger that with the lamp of God hath come. . . . Rabindranath, O Aurobindo, bows to thee.[14]

There are reports that Sri Aurobindo faced the action of the prosecution with its prospects of a long prison term with great equanimity. But as one of the key figures in the political scene of the country, he was not ready to surrender to the British without fighting and therefore decided to stand up to them in court. Actually the prosecution had a serious problem: there was no evidence that Sri Aurobindo really was the editor of the newspaper. They could not even prove that he had received a regular salary, for although he was entitled to receive it he had rarely accepted it, merely a few small amounts as he knew the paper was short of funds.

The prosecution now accused Sri Aurobindo, the manager and the printer of the newspaper for having published offensive articles from *Jugantar* in an English translation. Furthermore, they were said to have printed a letter to the editor which was seditious in content. In the subsequent trial the prosecution attempted to prove at first that Sri Aurobindo was in fact the responsible man behind the paper, and they called Bipin Chandra Pal as a witness. Pal had been pushed out of the team by the other editors some time earlier, against Sri Aurobindo's will, at a moment when he had been ill with fever.

---

[14] Quoted from: sriaurobindosociety.org.in/sriauro/aurolife.htm. According to Iyengar, *Sri Aurobindo* (pp. 229-30) the poem was first published on 8 September, 1907, in Bengali in *Bande Mataram.*

Pal, refusing to make a statement, remained loyal to Sri Aurobindo and was given a six-month prison sentence for contempt of court. The manager, Shyamsunder Chakravarty, declared that the paper had no editor. Sri Aurobindo himself made a written statement that he had no connection with it. Justifying this obviously incorrect statement at a later time, he explained that a nationalistic editor

> . . . owes no moral obligation of quixotic candour to antagonists who themselves recognise no moral obligation in their struggle with him. Whatever he owes is to his people and the mission he has to discharge.[15]

In September 1907 Douglas H. Kingsford pronounced his judgement; the texts taken from *Jugantar* as well as the letter to the editor were indeed seditious therefore the printer had to take responsibility for them, according to the laws of the country. There was insufficient evidence to prove Sri Aurobindo's responsibility as editor and therefore he was acquitted; the welcome judgement was celebrated throughout the country.

Sri Aurobindo would have preferred now, in tune with his nature, to resume acting from backstage but due to Pal's imprisonment it was on him to further the Hardliners' cause in the important political places. Of special note was the next annual session of Congress which was to take place in Nagpur, Maharashtra, a stronghold of the Hardliners. An executive committee was elected in which the nationalists had a majority of the votes. The Moderates wanted to change this by irregular new elections, which resulted in vehement protests from the Hardliners. The Moderates understood that resistance in this locality was too strong and so they decided to move the gathering to Surat near Bombay where they had many followers. Rashbehari Ghose was nominated as the candidate for chairing the meeting.

---

15 *Bande Mataram*, 693.

Actually, even with the regional Congress gatherings there were disputes regarding the question of which of the two parties would be entitled to present the president, and thus enabled to pass its choice of resolutions. The Hardliners, who had been defeated in this struggle, considered a splitting. Eventually Tilak convinced them of his strategy: to remain active in the Congress for a while with an extra session to be arranged only for the Hardliners, separate from the regular sessions.

The gathering in Nagpur was preceded by a regional meeting of the Bengalis in Midnapore. Again the Moderates had a majority of the votes and named the chairman, K.B. Dutt. Before and during the session the Hardliners urged him to speak about *swaraj* and national self-determination, but he refused to do so. Then a small group equipped with *lāṭhī*s revolted against Dutt during his speech, forcing the discontinuation of the session by creating an uproar. The Moderates thereupon chose to withdraw into another hall where they passed their usual resolutions.

Just before travelling to Midnapore Sri Aurobindo had quickly written a letter to Mrinalini, trying to make it clear to her that he was very much under pressure with various duties and that in view of the current political developments, he would hardly be able to fulfil her wish that he devote more time to her:

> Would you listen to a request of mine? I am passing through very anxious times, the pressure from all sides is sufficient to drive one mad. And at such a time if you also get upset it will only add to my anxiety and worry; a letter of encouragement and comfort will give me special force, and I will overcome all obstacles and dangers with a cheerful heart.

In fact, Mrinalini felt somewhat lonely and forsaken, but she had married a man who followed entirely his inner destiny and could only tell her:

> This suffering is your inevitable lot . . . because, unlike ordinary Bengalis, I am unable to make the happiness of the relatives and of the family the main aim of my life. In these circumstances what is my Dharma is also your Dharma; and unless you consider the success of my mission as your happiness, there is no way out.[16]

Hence Sri Aurobindo prepared for the session in Nagpur. On 20 December he had a meeting with Henry Nevinson, a foreign correspondent for the *Manchester Guardian*, who studied revolutionary movements with great interest. Sri Aurobindo explained his plans in detail, referring to the Irish struggle for freedom in his talk. Nevinson was deeply impressed by his meeting with

> the youngish man whose intent dark eyes looked out from his thin, clear-cut face with a gravity that seemed immovable, but the figure and bearing were those of an English graduate.[17]

The Congress Session in Surat

Due to the *Bande Mataram* trial Sri Aurobindo had become well known to large parts of the Indian population. Also there had been some public appearances with short speeches. About his journey by train to Surat, Barin noted later:

> Aurobindo the new idol of the nation was hardly known then by his face, and at every small and big station a frantic crowd rushed about in the station platform looking for him in the first and second class carriages, while all the time Aurobindo sat unobserved in a third class compartment. By the time this fact became known and he was found out, the train was about to start.[18]

---

16 sriaurobindoashram.com/E-Library/Other Editions/ writings in Bengali Translation/Letters to Mrinalini, 356.

17 Nevinson, *The New Spirit in India*. Quoted in *The Lives of Sri Aurobindo*, 136-37.

18 B. Ghose, "Sri Aurobindo as I Understand Him". Quoted in sriaurobindoashram.org/- research/Sri Aurobindo's speeches and his meeting with Lele/2

At some stations however, where the train had longer stops, Sri Aurobindo disembarked to address the people. In Bombay he and his comrades were escorted to a meeting at the seaside, received by an enthusiastic crowd. On 24 December they reached Surat where the Moderates and Hardliners stayed in separate camps. All of them sensed that there might be a clash of the two parties; preparations were made for the imminent struggle for supremacy in the Congress. The leaders among the Moderates were well known and respected personalities such as Pherozshah Mehta and Gopal Krishna Gokhale from Poona, who had chaired the Congress session in Benares in 1905, as well as Surendranath Banerjea, an influential veteran of the independence movement.

Among the Hardliners Sri Aurobindo and Tilak were the eminent leaders — Sri Aurobindo with his reputation as an author and with his inspired ideas, while Tilak, by profession a teacher of mathematics as well as a journalist, was a brilliant orator with the capacity of mobilizing and controlling a large number of delegates from Maharashtra. This was indispensable for neutralizing the Moderates in the Congress who were superior in number. Tilak had a very strong and unshakable personality; he was willing to withstand sacrifice and suffering having already endured two prison terms because of activities against the British. Sri Aurobindo appreciated his capacities and tried to co-ordinate his own tactics with Tilak as much as possible. Thus a strong alliance between the Nationalists from Bengal and from Maharashtra could be formed.

In the afternoon Sri Aurobindo took the chair at a first meeting of the Hardliners as Tilak explained the proposed action of the Nationalists. It was their intention to ask Rashbehari Ghose to give up his candidacy for the chair in favour of Lajpat Rai, a renowned activist who had just been released from prison outside the country. Furthermore, it was planned to promote resolutions supporting national self-determination.

Sri Aurobindo declared at the end of the meeting that he would prefer seceding from the Congress, although he would avoid taking this step if it meant breaking with Tilak. The next morning Lajpat Rai was received at the railway station but the Nationalists were disappointed upon learning that he did not wish to accept a nomination for the chair; he preferred to mediate between the two parties.

In the evening there were hectic consultations and debates in the two camps: a clash at the Congress session seemed now unavoidable. The Hardliners approached Surendranath Banerjea offering a compromise which he considered acceptable, but the chairman of the reception committee controlled by the Moderates refused to receive anyone.

In the afternoon of 26 December the first sessions of the Congress began with 10,000 people present. There were only 1,100 Nationalist delegates as opposed to 1,300 Moderates and, they were treated condescendingly by the Moderates because of their inferior number.[19] It was only at the beginning of the session that Tilak received the texts of the resolutions to be passed, shocked to see that the Nationalists were expected to give up some important ground they had conquered at the last session. When Rashbehari Ghose was proposed to the chair the Hardliners protested vehemently and the session was then disrupted amid tumultuous scenes. Surendranath Banerjea, who had supported Ghose's nomination and had climbed on a table to make himself heard was also shouted down. In the evening he invited the Bengali delegates to his tent in an attempt to persuade them to sign an agreement involving a compromise. But the Hardliners, led by Sri Aurobindo, refused to accept it.

The session was continued at noon the next day. After a

---

19 According to Nevinson's estimate, there were 1,600 delegates, with about 500 Hardliners. The other figures are given by Sri Aurobindo (*Autobiographical Notes*, 82).

speech from Banerjea, R. Ghose was elected president. When Ghose was about to start his opening speech, Tilak rose to his feet to make an amendment. But Ghose did not allow him to speak and Tilak was shouted down by the activists of the Moderates bringing yet another great tumult. In Sri Aurobindo's words:

> There was a tremendous uproar, the young Gujerati volunteers lifted up chairs over the head of Tilak to beat him. At that the Mahrattas became furious, a Mahratta shoe came hurtling across the pavilion aimed at the President, Rash Behari Ghose, and hit Surendra Nath Banerji on the shoulder. The young Mahrattas in a body charged up to the platform, the Moderate leaders fled and after a short fight on the platform with chairs the session broke up not to be resumed.[20]

In the evening the Moderates proceeded to have their own separate session under police protection and did not admit any Hardliners inside. They resolved to dissolve the Congress and establish instead a national conference whose constitution would be framed in such a way that the Moderates alone could control it for a long period of time. The Hardliners too had a separate gathering to discuss the new situation. There still exists a photo of it which shows Sri Aurobindo as the chairman sitting at the table with a motionless face while the stout Tilak, standing on his left, gives a speech. The delegates decided to found a national committee with Sri Aurobindo as president, to keep track of further developments.

A few days later Tilak issued a press report signed by Sri Aurobindo as a reaction to a statement of the Moderates. In the text it was said that the Moderates had provoked the splitting of the Congress by not informing the Hardliners in advance of the resolutions that were to be passed, and by

---

20 *Autobiographical Notes*, 82-83.

reversing agreements arrived at in Calcutta a year earlier. Furthermore, Tilak was not given the opportunity of moving his amendment.

Many observers believed that Tilak may have wanted the split, but this was not the case. Sri Aurobindo later explained the real background:

> History very seldom records the things that were decisive but took place behind the veil; it records the show in front of the curtain. Very few people knew that it was I (without consulting Tilak) who gave the order that led to the breaking of the Congress. . . .[21]

This happened when some younger Nationalists from Maharashtra approached him for consultation after it had leaked out that the Moderates wanted to change the constitution in their own favour. Thereupon it was decided — without informing Tilak or other veteran leaders — to blow up the Congress if it would not be possible to control it.[22]

However, it is quite conceivable that the break might have taken place even without this secret consultation, since there was no real option to de-escalate the confrontation of the two parties effectively and lastingly. The key issue was the question of the possibility to gradually obtain additional rights conceded to the Indians within the framework of British colonial rule or, whether the rule should be shaken off entirely to secure *all* rights, without restrictions. There was no compromise imaginable, and now the way ahead had been pointed. Actually, further developments showed that the new organization of the Moderates was not very popular. It failed to become an important political force.

It was also at the end of December 1907 that Barin tried to

---

21 *Letters on Himself and the Ashram*, 26.

22 *Autobiographical Notes*, 83.

organize a conference of the revolutionaries from all over India. He had gathered a small group of militant young men in the Maniktala Gardens: an old, overgrown family plot with a small, dilapidated house where they learned the handling of weapons and manufacture of bombs. They tried twice to kill Lieutenant Governor of Bengal Sir Andrew Frazer, but both attempts failed and he escaped without injury.

Now Barin invited his brother and his friends and many others to the conference but nobody attended, so the responsibility for those dangerous revolutionary activities remained with Barin alone. When Sri Aurobindo was later asked about his connection with Barin's group, he commented:

> I had nothing to do with them. It was all Barin's work. I never knew who these boys were and never saw them. Only once Barin brought a troop of them in my house but they were all waiting below. It is true that Barin used to consult me or Mullick for advice. But the whole movement was in his hands. I had no time for it. I was more busy with Congress politics and *Bande Mataram*.[23]

Although Sri Aurobindo never ruled out entirely the possibility of an armed revolution as the last means, it had never been his idea "that by throwing a few bombs we could overthrow the British government".[24]

---

23 Nirodbaran, *Talks with Sri Aurobindo*, vol. I, 502 (28 February 1940).

24 Ibid., 237.

5

Meeting with Lele
(1908)

SRI Aurobindo has stated himself that he began *yoga* around 1904.[1] He had a great inner poise by nature and his intensive *prāṇāyāma* exercises of up to six hours a day had brought about a powerful flow of energy, better health and poetic inspiration. A special effect, very useful in India, was the following:

> Whenever I used to sit for Pranayama, not a single mosquito would bite me, though plenty of mosquitoes were humming around.[2]

But his steadily growing political activities and responsibilities forced him to give up this practice. In November 1906 he was bedridden, seriously ill with fever for some time. Probably the cause of illness was that his body, used to an intensive flow of energy now disrupted through less frequent practice, lost its balance.[3] But his interest in *yoga* remained active in the background and from it he specifically expected fresh energies for his work.

Meanwhile, Barin had an idea that he should find a spiritual guide for his political *saṁnyāsīs* and so he spent some time searching for the right person. Retrospectively he spoke with regret on this plan (which was never fulfilled in the intended

1 *Autobiographical Notes*, 107.

2 *Talks with Sri Aurobindo*, vol. I, 107 (5 January 1939).

3 Ibid., 128 (5 January 1939).

way) saying that his group had turned to the cult of violence under the influence of the Irish freedom movement and the Russian secret societies and that they had wished to put divine power to the service of their "dark mission".

> "It was no wonder then that we wished to take to spiritual means for a holy war against the British, this idea of God helping the righteous even in murder and bloodshed being ingrained in man from his savage days.[4]

Then one day in a friend's home Barin happened to meet Vishnu Bhaskar Lele, a *yogī* from Maharashtra whom he had already seen once before in the Ashram of a renowned *yogī*.

> He made me sit in a dark room with him for a few minutes and as a result three days afterwards I had my first glimpse of spiritual awakening, my first psychic experience.[5]

Barin was quite impressed by this experience and told his brother about it, in whom an interest developed for meeting Lele. After the Congress session in Surat, Barin sent Lele a telegram requesting him to meet Sri Aurobindo in Baroda. When the latter arrived there, he was enthusiastically received by the students of Baroda College, who unyoked the horses from his carriage to pull it with their own hands.

Sri Aurobindo gave some lectures on the political situation in the country and was idolized by numberless persons who sought his advice or approached him for various reasons which made it difficult for him to find time and privacy for the meeting with Lele. Barin describes the further events as follows:

> Lele suddenly spirited Aurobindo away from the midst of

---

4 *Sri Aurobindo (As I Understand Him)*. Quoted in sriaurobindoashram.org/research/Sri Aurobindo's speeches and his meeting with Lele/4.

5 Ibid.

> all this commotion to a lonely old place tucked away in the heart of the city. There, day in and day out, the two of them sat wrapped in deep meditation facing each other. Their simple needs were looked after by Vishnu Bhaskar's wife. . . . I was also there and used to sit in meditation with them morning and evening in my restless and perfunctory way. My mind was divided between my ambitious national work and this inner life of Yoga.
>
> Seven days passed almost in continuous and silent meditation while batches of young men traversed the town in search of their newly-found leader who had so suddenly and mysteriously disappeared from among them. . . . When Aurobindo was at last permitted to come out and attend a meeting in the famous gymnasium there among his ardent admirers, a great and abiding peace had descended on him which from thence onward formed the basis of all his future Sadhana. . . .[6]

Lele was a simple man employed as a government clerk without higher education or any special talents. But Sri Aurobindo saw in his eyes sincere devotion and some force, so he decided to entrust himself to Lele for spiritual instruction. He told Lele that he had given up his *prāṇāyāma* practice under the pressure of work, though basically he was ready to resume it; he expected to acquire more force for his activities from *yoga*. Lele told him that there was no need to give up his activities, but first a few calm days were necessary. They moved into the first floor of a house of a friend of Lele's, where undisturbed their sessions of meditation could take place, which led Sri Aurobindo very quickly to an overwhelming experience:

> "Sit down," I was told, "look and you will see that your

---

6 *Sri Aurobindo (As I Understand Him)*. Quoted in sriaurobindoashram.org/research/Sri Aurobindo's speeches and his meeting with Lele/4.

> thoughts come into you from outside. Before they enter, fling them back." I sat down and looked and saw to my astonishment that it was so; I saw and felt concretely the thought approaching as if to enter through or above the head and was able to push it back concretely before it came inside. In three days — really in one — my mind became full of an eternal silence — it is still there.[7]
>
> From that moment, in principle, the mental being in me became a free Intelligence, a universal Mind, not limited to the narrow circle of personal thought as a labourer in a thought factory, but a receiver of knowledge from all the hundred realms of being and free to choose what it will in this vast sight-empire and thought-empire.[8]

Sri Aurobindo now had an experience of the classical traditional Indian spirituality, that is, the infinite silence of the *Brahman* on whose background the world with its appearances passes like a film. We may call it *nirvāṇa* in the sense of Vedānta, the extinction of the ego and union with the one supreme Reality. This experience is the foundation of the teaching of Māyāvāda (or illusionism) and can result in contempt for the world and of life in it — a position to which Sri Aurobindo was basically quite opposed. The first stanza of a poem *Nirvana* which he wrote later summarizes the experience as he perceived it during his subsequent stay in Bombay:

> *All is abolished but the mute Alone.*
> *The mind from thought released, the heart from grief*
> *Grow inexistent now beyond belief;*
> *There is no I, no Nature, known-unknown.*
> *The city, a shadow picture without tone,*
> *Floats, quivers unreal; forms without relief*

[7] *Letters on Himself and the Ashram*, 247.

[8] Ibid., 244.

Flow, a cinema's vacant shapes; like a reef
Foundering in shoreless gulfs the world is done.[9]

How could a human being perform his activities in such an inner state? K.R.S. Iyengar aptly describes the new situation as follows:

> This immaculate crown of Advaitic or Nirvanic realisation, while inducing the supernal inner calm, rendered even normal surface activities an unreal continuum of unconsciousness. Things were happening, he was apparently engaged in activity, but he himself didn't know how or why.[10]

Actually language reaches its limits here because it is not that "someone has an experience" in the same way as when we say "I had a good meditation". Sri Aurobindo explains it in paradoxical language, "When I had the experience of *Nirvana*, I forgot myself completely. I was a sort of nobody."[11] However, we can at least state that the "extinction" is not absolute, there remains an individual entity of whatever kind, because otherwise it would be impossible to continue life. But the normal procedure would be that a *yogī*, after such a radical entering into an absolutely new space of consciousness would withdraw for a long period of time in order to assimilate the experience and to find a new inner poise.

However Sri Aurobindo could not withdraw under the given circumstances. Along with Tilak he was one of the two leading personalities of the freedom movement and there were urgent tasks to be looked after, such as consolidating the Hardliners' party after the splitting from the Congress. Lele's original intention had been to support Sri Aurobindo in his

---

9 *Collected Poems*, 561.

10 Iyengar, *Sri Aurobindo*, 261.

11 Nirodbaran, *Talks with Sri Aurobindo*, vol. I, 19 (13 December 1938).

work, he did not want him to have this experience of the *impersonal Brahman* but rather an opening to the divine voice within which then guides one's life even in practical matters. But Sri Aurobindo had to reappear in public in spite of this particular inner state and Lele accompanied him for a while to watch his further progress. They accepted invitations to Bombay and Poona where Sri Aurobindo gave speeches on the political development. His mind was vacant and he doubted whether he would find words at all, but Lele assured him that the language would rise from within, and this is how it actually occurred, in the right moment.

Sri Aurobindo gave his most outstanding speech on 19 June in Bombay in the presence of about 3,000 persons. Once more he felt helpless in view of his vacant mind, but Lele instructed him to make *namaskāra*[12] to the audience and then wait for the inspiration to come from within. As in a trance, he stood on the podium and the words started coming, not fluently as with an experienced orator, but articulated in short sentences with mantric force, deeply moving the soul of most listeners. The subject of the speech was "nationalism" in a very specific sense, not referring to anything narrow-minded; the term meant primarily the freedom and self-determination of the country and the courage to be committed to these goals. For Sri Aurobindo nationalism was something religious and God-given in the sense that India should be true to her real, spiritual destiny. At the same time he critically remarked in his speech, which was noted down,

> Have you got a real faith? Or is it merely a political aspiration? Is it merely a larger kind of selfishness? Or is it merely that you wish to be free to oppress others, as you are being oppressed?[13]

---

12 The Indian manner of greeting with folded hands.

13 *Bande Mataram*, 819.

Today it is difficult to properly understand his texts whose true meaning, as perceived in those days, may not be fully accessible to our mentality. But it should be mentioned that even in his time some people found it hard to follow his approach and did not like his linking of God, religion and nation. The following passage shows how much Sri Aurobindo's whole political work was based on a high, idealistic vision:

> Another thing which is only another name for faith is selflessness. . . . This is the second aspect of our religion, and is the absolute denial of the idea of one's separate self, and the finding of one's higher eternal Self in the three hundred millions of people in whom God himself lives.[14]

Sri Aurobindo remained in Bombay for a few days and then consulted with Lele about his future spiritual path. Lele first gave him some instructions regarding regular meditation, etc., but then realized that his role had come to an end. Therefore, he advised Sri Aurobindo to entrust himself entirely to the inner guidance and to follow its voice. Sri Aurobindo did so henceforth, and thus the *guru–śiṣya*, relationship between them came to completion.

---

[14] *Bande Mataram*, 827-28.

6

Calcutta and Alipore
(1908-10)

BEFORE returning to Bengal, Sri Aurobindo, at the request of some followers, visited several towns in Maharashtra and gave many speeches. Everywhere he was received like a dignitary and thousands came to listen to his addresses, although most of them did not understand his English. But he was not deluded by his fame, for due to his knowledge of world history he was aware that it might be transitory. So at the beginning of February he noted in *Bande Mataram* that in times of revolution popularity might be short-lived and

> the man whose carriage is today dragged through great cities by shouting thousands amid cries of "Bande Mataram" and showers of garlands, will tomorrow be disregarded, perhaps hissed and forbidden to speak. . .[1]

Sri Aurobindo's style as a speaker was described as very reserved by many contemporaries. Calm like a Buddha he stood on the podium, keeping the audience spellbound with his slow, rhythmic voice, whereas some of his colleagues articulated their arguments in a dramatic style.

After returning to Calcutta, he informed Mrinalini in a letter of his inner change:

> But henceforth I have no freedom of my own, you will have

---

1 *Bande Mataram*, 868.

> to understand that all that I do depends not on my own will but is done according to the command of the Divine. When you come here, you will realise the significance of my words. I hope the Lord will show you the light of His infinite Grace which He has shown me. . . .[2]

He resumed his work at the newspaper *Bande Mataram* and participated in a session of the executive committee of the National Council of Education where plans were discussed for his future lectures at the National College.

At a regional conference of the Bengal Congress once again there were differences between the Moderates and the Hardliners regarding the chair. Finally they agreed that Rabindranath Tagore, who was highly respected by all of them, should take the chair, and Tagore consented. Some resolutions were passed at this session, notwithstanding heated discussions on formulations regarding *swarāj*, self-determination. However they did arrive at an agreement on this point because the Hardliners did not want to break with the Moderates (who were inferior in number) as they feared this might weaken the common cause.

On 18 February Sri Aurobindo, full of confidence, noted in *Bande Mataram* that nationalism had been given a new spirit at this conference and that the resolutions passed had a practical use.

> We have hitherto been engaged in dispute about ideals and methods. We are confident that the country, at least Bengal, has now reached a stage when this dispute is no longer necessary. Whatever we may say out of policy or fear, the whole nation is now at one. Swaraj is the only goal which the heart of Bengal recognises, Swaraj without any limitation or reservation.[3]

---

2 Aurobindo to Mrinalini Ghose, 17 February 1907, in Sri Aurobindo, *Bangla Rachana*, 355-56.

3 *Bande Mataram*, 873.

Even president Tagore, he wrote, had given up all caution in his final address due to the inspired atmosphere, speaking in a very lively style on the ideal of *swarāj*, a subject close to his heart.

In Calcutta Sri Aurobindo moved into a new house at Scott's Lane No. 24, spending much time in meditating and looking after his manifold duties. There is a report that one day a co-worker of *Bande Mataram* came to fetch the text of a leading article by Sri Aurobindo. But it was not yet written. So Sri Aurobindo took a piece of paper and wrote the text in one piece, without pause or thinking or correcting. After his experience with Lele he had found a new basis for his work:

> In the condition of absolute inner silence I was making speeches and conducting a newspaper, but all that got itself done without any thought entering my mind or the silence being in the least disturbed or diminished.[4]

Meanwhile Barin continued his dangerous revolutionary activities. After the Surat Congress he invited Lele to visit the Maniktala Gardens, hoping to receive some new inspiration for himself and his companions. But Lele saw that they were involved in violent terrorist activities including the construction of bombs. He tried to change their minds, to keep them away from it, explaining to them that these things had no place in spiritual life. He even warned them that their approach would not only fail to bring about success, but rather end in disaster. In their heated emotional state the young men did not, unfortunately, listen to him but continued their activities. A little later they went to Deoghar to test a bomb in the hills. It exploded, but one of the boys died during the test and another was seriously injured.

Their sticking to the path of violence can be explained by

---

4 *Letters on Himself and the Ashram*, 260.

the background of the political situation in India. The British government persecuted the insurgents with increasing severity, often imposing merciless punishments such as very long prison terms under unbearable conditions as well as whippings. The freedom fighters reacted with anger and outrage to these humiliations, seeking compensation through their activities against the representatives of the British empire.

Even John Morley, the Secretary of State for India in London, was increasingly worried and noted in a letter to the viceroy:

> I must confess to you that I am watching with the deepest concern and dismay the thundering sentences that are being passed for sedition, etc. We must keep order, but excess of severity is not the path to order. On the contrary, it is the path to the bomb.[5]

In an article dated 14 April 1908 Sri Aurobindo addressed the subject of violence, disassociating himself from the "extreme of bombthrowing anarchism" in Europe: "Is India to be infected with the disease?"[6] Actually, he had tried at the beginning of April in a conversation with Barin to dissuade him from his terrorist attempts but was unable to convince him; so he let him follow his own path. We do not know whether Barin would have listened to his brother if the latter would have strictly insisted on his position. But generally Sri Aurobindo was not inclined to play the role of "the boss" imposing his will on others. So the fatal activities in the Maniktala Gardens continued, with Sri Aurobindo involuntarily in the same boat with the small group since Barin was his brother and since the plot was also registered in his own name.

---

[5] Quoted in Iyengar, *Sri Aurobindo*, 290.

[6] *Bande Mataram*, 1039.

It was high court judge D.H. Kingsford in Calcutta who in particular imposed severe punishments on the freedom fighters. One day he decreed the whipping of a fifteen-year old boy who swooned and collapsed under the beating. The outrage of the Indian population was so tremendous that Kingsford had to be transferred to the remote provincial town of Muzaffarpur for security reasons. The revolutionaries secretly followed and observed him; they had already tried in Calcutta to kill him with a parcel bomb but the judge, short of time, did not open the parcel and just laid it aside.[7] Next they planned to throw a bomb into his carriage during his drive home from a club where he and his wife played bridge with the wife and daughter of a lawyer named Pringle Kennedy.

When the four came out of the club, they entered two carriages. In the first carriage sat the wife and daughter of Kennedy, followed by the Kingsfords. The two revolutionaries Prafulla and Khudiram were waiting nearby hidden behind trees, and when they saw the first carriage approaching, they assumed it was that of the Kingsfords. Rushing towards it, they threw their bomb into the carriage through the open window. This time the attempt was successful, but it hit the wrong persons, and the two women suffered fatal injuries.

The two assassins were able to escape unrecognized amidst the turmoil and started their journey home separately. However, Khudiram was arrested the next day at a railway station not far away, whereas Prafulla managed to travel some distance by train before he was recognized. Just as he was about to be arrested, he fled firing at the police that pursued him, and then shot himself.

Even some time earlier the police had succeeded in smuggling an informer into the local revolutionary group in

---

7 As it is, he never opened it. When the police later defused it, they found that the bomb would have left him no chance.

Midnapore, who was able to access important insider information. The authorities who were intensively investigating on account of the bombing attempts now came to know about the activities in the Maniktala Gardens. They decided not to intervene yet as they wanted to observe the revolutionaries for some time. Not only Barin, but Sri Aurobindo was also named as one of the suspects.

A few weeks after his moving into Scott's Lane, Mrinalini joined him and they lived together for the first time after a long interval. Some time later Sri Aurobindo moved with Mrinalini and his sister Sarojini to Grey Street, the seat of the office of the Bengali newspaper *Nabashakti,* whose editor he was to become. During the day he heard about the bombing in Muzaffarpur. Therefore when he returned to Grey Street in the evening, he knew there was imminent danger and made sure that there was no evidence against him to be found in his rooms. Then he instructed Barin to remove all weapons, etc. from the Maniktala Gardens. But they had a lot of material and could not figure out any other solution than hiding the material in little holes they dug into the earth, also burning some incriminating documents. Then, greatly exhausted, they took rest. They intended to rise early in the morning and get away, for during the day some suspicious persons had shown up asking questions, which made them assume they were under observation.

The Empire Retaliates

The young revolutionaries slept longer than planned and were awakened by the police the next morning. Nolini Kanta Gupta later reported:

> . . . We were all arrested in a body. The police made us stand in a line under the strict watch of an armed guard. They kept us standing the whole day with hardly anything to eat. . . . In the evening, the order came, "Follow us". . . . We

were taken to the lock-up at the Lal Bazar police station."[8]

Herded into a single cell, they had to stay there for two days. Then they were taken to the prison in Alipore (a district of Calcutta) where they were permitted their first proper meal in three days.

On 2 May 1908 the police raided Sri Aurobindo's place. Around 5 a.m. he was awakened by his agitated sister, with the British inspectors and Indian policemen suddenly standing in front of him with pistols in hand. We are quite well-informed about his arrest and further events, because Sri Aurobindo has described them in detail in his writing *Kara Kahini*, which was first published in the original Bengali and later published in English under the title *Tales of Prison Life*.[9] Sri Aurobindo has written it as a living report and runs down his British tormentors with inspired irony. Thus the text is not marked by lamentation, but it rather shows his triumph over extreme adversity amidst which he discovers an inner joy and eventually achieves powerful spiritual experiences. Apart from these autobiographical documents, there are also a few other sources of contemporary witnesses.

As Mrinalini hurried terrified out of the bedroom, Sri Aurobindo, sitting on his bed, began taking note of the situation. Superintendent Cregan ascertained his name and then arrested him. Due to his ICS training in England Sri Aurobindo had a thorough knowledge of legal matters and first requested to see the search warrant; while studying its text, he learned the serious charges against him. He signed the warrant although it was not an arrest warrant, which would have been legally required. But he realized that any protest would be in vain in the given situation and therefore kept

---

8 Nolini Kanta Gupta, *Reminiscences*, 22-23.

9 English translation by Sisirkumar Ghose.

silent. They handcuffed him and tied a cord round his waist, only to be removed half an hour later. The police also arrested two other residents of the house.

The rooms were searched until late morning, but no incriminating objects or documents could be found. Meanwhile Sri Aurobindo's lawyer Hirendranath Datta tried to see Sri Aurobindo but was denied access to his house. Simultaneously there were searches at several other places. The police found important incriminating material not only in the Maniktala Gardens, but also in two houses that belonged to friends of the revolutionaries.

When Barin realized that the situation was hopeless, he made up his mind to confess everything and to co-operate with the police. Thus he wanted to take maximum personal responsibility to save the others involved in the investigation, including his brother. He showed the inspectors the weapons and bomb material hidden on the plot, and in the building the police found also many documents which the revolutionaries had not managed to burn in time. Barin, and two of his companions who had joined him in his role as sole responsible culprit, could now be rather sure to face death by hanging.

When the searching at Grey Street was finished around 11:30 a.m. Sri Aurobindo, along with his two companions Abinash Bhattacharya and Sailen Bose were taken to the local police station, where they were given a small meal and allowed to take a shower. Then they were taken to the police headquarters at Lal Bazar and two hours later to a station at Royal Street where an inspector tried, in a crude manner, to elicit a confession from Sri Aurobindo.

The next morning the three prisoners were driven back to Lal Bazar and Inspector Halliday ordered Sri Aurobindo to be locked in a solitary cell. Sri Aurobindo reports:

> When others had left, Halliday asked me: "Aren't you

ashamed of being involved in this cowardly, dastardly activity?" "What right have you to assume that I was involved?" To this Halliday replied: "I am not assuming. I know everything." At this I said: "What you know or do not know is your concern. I wholly deny having any connection with these murderous acts."[10]

Later that Sunday there were more interrogations without any legal assistance. Sri Aurobindo became aware now that the officers were very intent on proving his connection with Barin and his activities. Twice they gave him a meagre meal of which he took just a little.

On 5 May Sri Aurobindo and the other prisoners were taken to the court of the examining magistrate. At last he was permitted to talk to a lawyer and to a relative. The lawyer told him that the police claimed to have found incriminating papers with him, which Sri Aurobindo had thought impossible. But actually they had found, amongst others, a letter from Barin to his brother written on 22 December 1907 in which he wrote, "We certainly need sweets — ready for use — all over India. . . ."[11] It was evident that "sweets" was a code word which probably meant "bombs". Sri Aurobindo also spoke with his relative asking that he calm his family members at home, assuring them that his innocence would be clearly proven:

From that period on I had a firm belief that it would be so. In the beginning, during solitary imprisonment, the mind was a little uneasy. But after three days of prayer and meditation an unshakable peace and faith again overwhelmed the being.[12]

In fact, during the first few days after his arrest, Sri Aurobindo

---

10 Sri Aurobindo, *Tales of Prison Life,* Sri Aurobindo Ashram 1997, 9.

11 Quoted in *Jours de Prison,* tr. Michèle Lupsa 1988, Glossary.

12 *Tales of Prison Life,* 11.

had experienced the agony of someone who has sincerely and entirely given himself to the Divine but suddenly realizes that he is in hell. In a speech at Uttarpara he afterwards stated that for a while he was indeed shaken in his faith when he was arrested and taken to Lal Bazar,

> for I could not look into the heart of His intention. Therefore I faltered for a moment and cried out in my heart to Him, "What is this that has happened to me? I believed that I had a mission to work for the people of my country and until that work was done, I should have Thy protection. Why then am I here and on such a charge?" A day passed and a second day and a third, when a voice came to me from within, "Wait and see." Then I grew calm and waited.[13]

Alipore Jail

On 5 May Sri Aurobindo found himself locked in a cell of Alipore Jail, about 9 ft long and 5 ft in width, without windows, with iron bars at the entry in front. The latter opened towards a small courtyard enclosed by a brick wall which had a wooden door in it, which mostly stood open. There was a small hole in the door through which the sentry could have a look into the cell.

The prison conditions were extremely hard. The prisoners only had a plate, a tin water container and a bowl. The latter served many purposes,

> in the prison cell it helped in the act of ablution; later with the same bowl I gargled, bathed; a little later when I had to take my food, the lentil soup or vegetable soup was poured into the same container; I drank water out of it and washed my mouth. Such an all-purpose priceless object can be had only in a British prison. Serving all my worldly needs the bowl became an aid in my spiritual discipline too. Where

---

13 *Tales of Prison Life*, 109.

> else could I find such an aid and preceptor to get rid of the sense of disgust?[14]

Two baskets with a tar coating were kept in the room for relieving oneself. They were as a rule cleaned only twice a day and a veritable scourge for the prisoners, "but to have, in a small cell, a bedroom, dining and w.c. rolled into one — this is what is called too much of a good thing", Sri Aurobindo later noted laconically in his report.[15] But at the beginning he had at least sufficient water for his bath in the courtyard, arranged for him by a prisoner who was in-charge of the neighbouring cowshed. For the night there were two prison blankets one of which served as a pillow.

During the summer life in the cell turned into a real torture; it was heated like an oven and the burning thirst could only be quenched by drinking lukewarm water which caused sweating and even greater thirst. Once more Sri Aurobindo takes hardship as a challenge and learns to overcome the sensation of thirst. After some time he is given an earthen jug that keeps the water at a pleasant cool temperature.

The food was the same everyday, "coarse rice, even that spiced with husk, pebbles, insects, hair, dirt and such other stuff".[16] A heavily watered lentil soup with vegetables and greens mixed with grass and leaves was additionally given. However, Sri Aurobindo had an unshakeable faith in the divine Grace and it was only the first few days which he felt really hard to bear. Then ". . . the mind had risen above these sufferings and grown incapable of feeling any hardship."[17] Certainly it was helpful that he had an ascetic strain in his nature; his preference for travelling by third class train has

---

14 *Tales of Prison Life*, 16.

15 Ibid., 17.

16 Ibid., 24.

17 Ibid., 20.

already been mentioned. Thus in his imprisonment report Sri Aurobindo even writes words of praise for the humanitarianism of the British prison director, and notes that he had never before come across such a magnanimous person as the prison's physician, Vaidyanath Chatterji.

> It was as if he had been born to help and do good to others. Whenever he heard of a case of suffering, to try to lessen it had become for him almost a natural and inevitable act.[18]

His superior, Daly, a physician of Irish descent, also treated the prisoners with great fairness and care. When once Sri Aurobindo fell ill with fever during the monsoon season, he intended to counteract the illness through his spiritual force. But Daly urged him to take treatment in the hospital, he arranged for good food and even proposed to keep the patient there for a longer period. But Sri Aurobindo declined to accept this privileged treatment.

All the while he regards the loneliness of solitary confinement as a great challenge. He feels the mental strain it causes, and realizes that it can break even the strongest character. He tries to remain in a state of meditation for as long as possible, but is only able to concentrate for one or two hours. Then the mind tires and revolts, thinking grows more and more paralysed, there are no objects for reflection:

> There was for a time a condition when it seemed a thousand indistinct ideas were hovering round the doors of the mind but with the gates closed; one or two that were able to get through were frightened by the silence of these mental states and quietly ran away.[19]

In this void uneventful state even the mere observation of two columns of red and black ants offers a welcome change.

---

18 *Tales of Prison Life*, 37.

19 Ibid., 39.

But after a while Sri Aurobindo discovers an absolute inner freedom and has a feeling that even twenty years of loneliness would not have the power to shake him. Increasingly he sees God's hand in all outer circumstances and the darkness begins to recede; all that happens in the world appears to express the infinite Grace. Right in the midst of hell he refuses to negate God's omnipotence and recognizes hidden intentions of the Supreme which are beyond human understanding.

Then one day a relapse occurs: a current of confused thoughts sweeps his mind so powerfully that he fears he may lose control of it. In deep agony he invokes God and instantly receives a response by way of a great inner freshness, a lightness, bliss and peace as never before:

> Just as a child sleeps, secure and without fear, on the lap of his mother, so I remained on the lap of the World-Mother.[20]

All this does not mean to imply that there is no more pain and suffering. Dry periods continue to come, but due to the inner force they leave no more traces. The torments are pearling ". . . as water drops on a lotus leaf". When after a few days he is permitted at last to have some books sent — in particular the Upaniṣads and the *Bhagavad-Gītā* — he is convinced that even without the books he would have endured the hardship. In the end he concludes, with reference to the extremely difficult period of the first days, that ultimately this experience had given him additional strength and that his compassion for the victims of human cruelty had become greater yet. Then he adds, "I also realised the extraordinary power and efficacy of prayer".[21]

Some time later due to the intercession of Daly and the vice-director of the prison, he is given permission for regular long walks outside and gladly accepts. For up to two hours he keeps walking every morning between the workshops and

20 *Tales of Prison Life*, 43.

21 Ibid., 44.

the cowsheds, reciting verses from the Upaniṣads and discovering in them a source of light and power. He meditates on the *mantra sarvam khalvidam brahma* (all this is the *Brahman*) and tries to perceive in all he sees the divine presence: in all human beings, animals, trees and buildings. Gradually he has a new vision of his surroundings. Even the prison wall seems to be vibrating with a universal consciousness and he has a feeling that love is flowing towards him from all beings and objects.

> Once in a while it seemed as if God Himself was standing under the tree, to play upon his Flute of Delight, and with its sheer charm to draw my very soul out.[22]

Soul-inspired feelings such as love, goodness, compassion and non-violence open in him as an unshakeable peace settles in his being. He is full of confidence that God himself has taken him to this prison for his own best, and that he will eventually be released from it.

The Trial

There were doubts in parts of the British administration whether bringing a charge against a prominent personality such as Sri Aurobindo would be advisable in view of the scarce evidence. In a report to Home Secretary E.A. Gait, the chief secretary of Bengal stated that the accused had acted skilfully indeed, but there could be no doubt of his connection with the extremists.

> The conviction of the other persons concerned would be of no avail if Arabinda were set free; for, in that case he would lose no time in starting a fresh conspiracy, and the work now done would be altogether in vain. . . . In the interest of peace and good government, it is absolutely necessary that this man should be removed from the political arena.[23]

---

22 *Tales of Prison Life*, 47.

23 Quoted in Iyengar, *Sri Aurobindo*, 296.

The British administration employed Eardley Norton, its most capable man for the prosecution, offering him very generous pay. This was a threatening move which had to be countered, and therefore Sri Aurobindo's sister appealed in deeply moving words to her countrymen to donate money for an adequate defence for her brother. Some leading newspapers supported her case and individuals and institutions all over the country responded to the call. Money was even sent from Europe, Australia and America.

According to British law there was at first a preliminary trial, which started on 19 May before the Officiating District Magistrate L. Birley. The accused were charged with organizing a criminal gang for waging war against the government, and the trial lasted until 19 August. By the time the trial began, Sri Aurobindo had succeeded in transforming his prison cell and its surroundings into a kind of Himalayan cave for his spiritual path. Now he was abruptly thrown back into the world outside and the balance of his *yoga* was in question. For many hours he had to listen to boring debates before the court and was not able during the first few days to detach from the external proceedings.

> I found that while spending one's time in solitary imprisonment had grown easy and pleasant, it was not that easy in the midst of the crowd and in the life-and-death game of a serious political case.[24]

Now he met again companions who greeted each other happily, talking and laughing exuberantly while being driven to the court in a van with barred windows.

In his report on imprisonment Sri Aurobindo gives much space to a description of the Crown's prosecutor, E. Norton. This Englishman argues with great skill, displaying his brilliant

24 *Tales of Prison Life*, 48.

mastery of law and rhetoric while causing confusion and fear in the minds of witnesses. He even dominates Judge Birley, a weak character, making a great effort to justify his huge fee of Rs. 1,000 a day, so that his country should not suffer any loss. Norton describes Sri Aurobindo as a clever and highly intelligent rogue who was personally in-charge of all activities with the aim of undermining the foundations of the British empire.

In the Vaiṣṇavite tradition there is a "Yoga of Hatred"[25] which implies that one can attain God even while hating him intensely because one's thoughts are permanently focused on him and eventually you assume the qualities of the one upon whom you concentrate. With reference to this tradition Sri Aurobindo notes in an ironical style typical of large parts of his report:

> It is a pity I was not born as an Avatar; otherwise, thanks to his intense devotion and ceaseless contemplation of me for the nonce, he would surely have earned his release, *mukti,* then and there and both the period of our detention and the government's expenses would have been curtailed.[26]

In Sri Aurobindo's eyes the proceedings are just a farce. Two hundred twenty-two witnesses are called, some of them against their will, others eager to support the prosecution, with thousands of pieces of evidence presented. The trial becomes a play, directed by Norton and approved by Birley. Some obviously false statements of witnesses result in momentous conclusions, and thus Sri Aurobindo realizes that in the course of such a trial innocent persons may be found guilty, deported or even executed. He reflects on the helplessness of human beings before a British court, suffering the agony of possible life-long imprisonment, and he denounces the loss of human dignity.

---

25 *Samrambha yoga.*

26 *Tales of Prison Life,* 56.

While the co-accused in the courtroom were reading or merrily talking and laughing in spite of the serious penalties to be expected, Sri Aurobindo continued his secret *yoga*. Increasingly he succeeds in detaching from the external proceedings, focusing on his inner experiences. In his speech at Uttarpara he later described how Kṛṣṇa spoke to him after he had been permitted to walk up and down outside his cell:

> When you were cast into jail, did not your heart fail and did you not cry out to me, where is Thy protection? Look now at the Magistrate, look now at the Prosecuting Counsel.
>
> I looked and it was not the Magistrate whom I saw, it was Vasudeva, it was Narayana who was sitting there on the bench. I looked at the Prosecuting Counsel and it was not the Counsel for the prosecution that I saw; it was Sri Krishna who sat there, it was my Lover and Friend who sat there and smiled.[27]

At the beginning the prisoners were heavily guarded by the police during their transports. But gradually security measures were reduced and the authorities permitted visits and contacts with relatives more and more. On 13 June the accused were transferred from their single cells into a large common cell with a main hall and two wings, and this change resulted in much social activity. Sri Aurobindo alone did not welcome it, since now once more he had to readjust his *yoga* to the new circumstances. He withdrew into a corner where the more intellectual and contemplative prisoners had assembled, but he found it hard to maintain his previous concentration.

In this large cell Narendranath Goswami, one of the prisoners, sought contact with him. He was the son of a wealthy landowner and hoped to be released early with the help of expensive lawyers. Goswami told Sri Aurobindo that

---

27 *Tales of Prison Life*, 112.

he was in touch with some police officers who had offered him the chance to act as crown witness, which would imply immunity from prosecution. Sri Aurobindo observed Goswami with mistrust all the time and had the impression that his character was unstable. The other revolutionaries mistrusted him too, more and more, and finally stopped talking to him.

On 20 June the accused were transferred into yet another big cell but without wings, which made it even more difficult for Sri Aurobindo to separate himself from the noisy activities of his companions. Meanwhile, the prosecution succeeded in winning over Goswami, which Norton announced before the court on 22 June. This was the worst possible development for the accused, for Goswami talked freely about whatever he knew. He reported that he had become a member of the secret society in 1906 and came to know at that time that Sri Aurobindo was one of the two leaders. He identified Sri Aurobindo and gave the names of other as yet unknown persons who took part in the revolutionary activities, who were promptly arrested by the police. This second group had to wait for its trial in prison, while that of the first group continued.

As the behaviour of the prisoners had been very peaceful all the time, their supervision became more and more negligent. They discovered that they could smuggle messages outside with the help of visitors and it was possible as well to bring things inside like tobacco, or opium, hidden in the cloth of the visitor's *dhotī* or *sāṛī*. When this smuggling had repeatedly worked, the revolutionaries next asked for weapons and soon received them. Barin developed a complicated plan for a breakout but Sri Aurobindo rejected it for himself, since he wanted to face the trial in any case.

On 13 August the accused were brought before the judge. All of them refused to give evidence, and those who had already pleaded guilty withdrew their statements, now declaring them invalid. Much depended now on Goswami's charges. The counsels for the defence twice sought permission for a cross-examination, but Judge Birley rejected it arguing that the proceedings "should not last forever".

The preliminary trial was finished on 19 August. Birley ruled that thirty-one accused should be tried before the Alipore District Court for waging war against the British Crown. He considered Sri Aurobindo deeply involved in the case, as was made evident through Goswami's evidence and through Barin's letter (mentioned above). At this stage, Sri Aurobindo was facing a possible life-long stay in a penal colony on the Andaman Islands, far away from all civilization, where brutal wardens often gave extremely rough treatment to the prisoners.

While the revolutionaries were waiting for the main trial, Barin became active. He asked a visitor to bring a revolver which was then passed on to his cousin Satyen Bose who, consulting with some companions, concluded that getting rid of state witness Goswami would be more important than a breakout. Satyen made a pretence of his intention of also turning king's evidence and thus succeeded in getting in touch with the traitor. Early in the morning of 29 August he and his companion Kanailal Dutt shot Goswami dead and surrendered without any resistance to the wardens. They had to pay with their lives for the attack, but from the Indian viewpoint they became martyrs, having made a great sacrifice for the cause of freedom for India. The prison authorities reacted with strict measures. All cells were thoroughly searched and all the accused were punished with six weeks solitary confinement. A crack regiment was ordered to watch them day and night; they were not allowed to leave their cells even in the case of illness.

Meanwhile, Sri Aurobindo continued his *sādhanā* and had some extraordinary experiences about which he reported later in talks with his disciples. Once he wondered whether the *siddhi*s of the Indian tradition, that is supernatural powers and capacities such as levitation were actually possible. Then suddenly he found himself lifted to a position above the ground which he could not have reached through muscular effort:

> Only one part of the body was slightly in contact with the ground and the rest was raised up against the wall and I know I could not have held my body like that normally even if I had wanted to. I also found that the body remained suspended like that without any exertion on my part.[28]
>
> Then again, I was practising for a time to raise my hands and keep them suspended in the air without any muscular control. Once in that condition I fell asleep. The warder saw me in that posture and reported that I was dead. The authorities came and found me quite alive. I told them the warder was a fool.[29]

Sri Aurobindo had many such experiences and explained that they belonged to the vital plane, upon which his *yoga* at that time was practised. But soon they ceased and thereafter never returned.

Another experience was an inner encounter with Swami Vivekananda, the most well-known disciple of Ramakrishna.

> It is a fact that I was hearing constantly the voice of Vivekananda speaking to me for a fortnight in the jail in my solitary meditation and felt his presence. . . . The voice spoke only on a special and limited but very important field of spiritual experience and it ceased as soon as it had finished saying all that it had to say on that subject.[30]

In his *Talks* he referred in greater detail to these instructions, pointing out that the focus was on higher levels of

---

[28] Purani, *Evening Talks,* 393.

[29] Nirodbaran, *Talks with Sri Aurobindo,* vol. I, 13-14 (11 December 1938).

[30] *Autobiographical Notes,* 98-99.

consciousness which were later to play an important role in his integral *yoga* and which he named intuition, overmind, supermind, etc.

> It was Vivekananda who, when he used to come to me during meditation in Alipore jail, showed me the Intuitive Plane. For a month or so he gave instructions about Intuition. Then afterwards I began to see the still higher planes.[31]

One day the opening of his artistic vision was added:

> [I] knew something about sculpture, but [was] blind to painting. Suddenly one day in the Alipore jail while meditating I saw some "pictures" on the walls of the cell and lo and behold! the artistic eye in me opened and I knew all about painting except of course the more material side of the technique.[32]

Regarding his external appearance, it struck one of Sri Aurobindo's companions that his hair was shining as if he were using hair oil. But Sri Aurobindo explained to him that it was due to his *sādhanā*. At one stage he felt such a strong flow of energy that for ten days he kept fasting without suffering the slightest loss of energy, and he slept only one night. But he lost around one pound of weight each day and therefore decided to resume taking his normal food.

The Main Proceedings

In the morning of 19 October 1908 the trial against the accused began. The prisoners were brought into the courtroom under very strict security measures. The judge was Charles Porten Beachcroft, a fellow student of Sri Aurobindo at Cambridge. At the entrance examination for the ICS Sri Aurobindo stood first in Greek, while Beachcroft finished second. Later they

---

31 Nirodbaran, *Talks with Sri Aurobindo*, vol. I, 35 (18 December 1938). Also see the talk of 10 January 1939.

32 *Letters on Himself and the Ashram*, 264.

met occasionally when taking Bengali lessons where Beachcroft had better results than Sri Aurobindo. It must have been a strange feeling for both of them, to meet again in such unequal roles, before a court of law.

The charges against him were those of waging war against the British Crown as well as conspiracy and instigation of conspiracy. Fifteen lawyers with different kinds of qualifications had assembled to defend the rights of the accused all of whom pleaded "not guilty". Norton opened the proceedings declaring that he would present evidence that Sri Aurobindo was the leader of the conspiracy. He had 1,500 documents and objects to support his case, and those witnesses who had already made incriminating statements in the preliminary trial were invited once again. Norton also wanted to present Narendranath Goswami's testimony as evidence, but the counsels for the defence objected to it. Beachcroft considered the issue for two days and then declared that Birley had violated procedural law by preventing Goswami's cross-examination by the defence. Beachcroft's decision implied that the complete testimony of the state witness had suddenly lost all value for the prosecution, because it could not be used in the trial. This was a dramatic development in favour of Sri Aurobindo, who was affected by Goswami's statements more strongly than all the others accused.

Sri Aurobindo was defended by Byomkesh Chakravarty, a prominent barrister from Calcutta. His fees were very high and exceeded the financial means of the supporters, therefore after a little less than a month a young lawyer named Chittaranjan Das was asked to take over the defence. He was a friend of Sri Aurobindo's family, he had no great name as yet, but he was a great patriot who dedicated himself to his task with all his heart, taking only minimal fees. During the following six months until the end of the proceedings, he worked day and night for the defence, screening thousands of documents. He felt he served a great cause and in the end he sacrificed his health for it.

The defence mainly focused on proving that there was no conspiracy against the British Crown and that the bomb attempts had been planned and executed by individuals who wanted to take revenge on British officials. Das went so far as to suggest that some apparently incriminating documents may actually have been forged by the police. Apart from that, he said that there was no doubt that Sri Aurobindo had advocated the independence of India in his numberless articles and stuck by that. However, those texts were philosophical and political statements that did not violate British laws.

At the beginning of the trial Sri Aurobindo had been giving his counsellors Chakravarty and Das short notes with instructions, but his inner guide directed him to withdraw entirely from those external events. Das would free him from prison:

> Put aside those papers. It is not you who will instruct him. I will instruct him.[33]

The strict conditions imposed on the prisoners after the killing of the chief witness Goswami were gradually relaxed again. They were allowed to eat outside their cells, to take a bath, wash clothes and do physical exercises. Once a Scottish warden who liked to provoke Sri Aurobindo jostled him while he was doing his exercises, whereupon Sri Aurobindo gave the warden such a stern look that he was frightened and ran to the prison director to complain about the "insubordination". The other prisoners were also enraged because of the warden's behaviour, but the director himself came to calm the situation and said that "like good Christians they should all of them bear their respective crosses".

---

[33] *Karmayogin*, 8.

Moreover the accused had to face humiliating circumstances in the courtroom, where they were kept inside a locked cage enveloped with meshed wire. But the British authorities thought this necessary since they considered the situation highly dangerous, all the more so because several attempts took place during the trial: in the same building in February 1909 one of Beachcroft's colleagues was shot by a revolutionary.

The closing arguments of the prosecution and the defence began in March and lasted for several weeks. The brilliant address of Chittaranjan Das took eight days. He presented Sri Aurobindo as an idealist who was deeply committed to the cause of his country and its development — a development which in the true sense of the word could only be realized by a free nation in tune with her true self. He did not pursue his goals with methods which were opposed to the tradition of his country:

> The doctrines he preached are not doctrines of violence but doctrines of passive resistance. . . . He says, believe in yourself; no one attains salvation who does not believe in himself. Similarly, he says, in the case of a nation.[34]

Furthermore, Das pointed out by speaking in the first person on behalf of Sri Aurobindo:

> The whole of my case before you is this. If it is suggested that I preached the ideal of freedom to my country, which is against the law, I plead guilty to the charge. If that is the law here, I say that I have done that and I request you to convict me. . . . If that is my charge, you can chain me, imprison me, but you will never get out of me a denial of that charge.[35]

---

34 P.C. Roy, *Life & Times of C.R. Das*, 62, quoted in Iyengar, *Sri Aurobindo*, 313.

35 Closing Speech of C.R. Das, Alipore Bomb Trial Records, quoted in *The Lives of Sri Aurobindo*, 180.

Next Das proceeded to present his own vision of the case:

> My appeal to you is this, that long after the controversy will be hushed in silence, long after this turmoil, the agitation will have ceased, long after he is dead and gone, he will be looked upon as the poet of patriotism, as the prophet of nationalism and the lover of humanity. Long after he is dead and gone, his words will be echoed and re-echoed, not only in India, but across distant seas and lands. Therefore, I say that the man in his position is not only standing before the bar of this Court, but before the bar of the High Court of History.[36]

On 5 May 1909 Sri Aurobindo had remained exactly one year in Alipore Jail; one day later Beachcroft pronounced his judgement. Barin and Ullaskar were sentenced to be hanged, many other defendants were given a life sentence or very long imprisonment and deportation.

However, Sri Aurobindo left the courtroom a free man. Beachcroft had discussed his case in no less than fifty pages of his opinion — the other accused he referred to on only one or two pages — and pointed out that the evidence against Sri Aurobindo was too weak to find him guilty of such a massive charge as preferred against him.

We may enquire at this point whether Beachcroft was favouring his former fellow student or whether he was just keeping the flag of an independent judiciary flying. This question cannot be answered with certainty, but we can state as a fact that he was using the scope he possessed in such a way that it was to Sri Aurobindo's advantage. Beachcroft's decision at the beginning of the trial not to admit Goswami's testimony as evidence was a first step. The second was his reserved assessment of the "sweets letter" which Barin had addressed to his brother and in which he mentioned bombs

---

[36] P.C. Roy, 59-64, quoted in Iyengar, *Sri Aurobindo,* 313.

in code language. The judge ruled that this document (as well as another piece of writing) was not sufficiently conclusive, and thus the way was paved for Sri Aurobindo's freedom.

Das appealed against the two death sentences at the higher courts and achieved a change to lifelong deportation. Over time there were further mitigations, and after about ten years all prisoners were at large again.

Karmayogin

After his release, Sri Aurobindo went at first to his lawyer's house and a little later moved to the home of his maternal uncle. The latter was in prison and his family felt helpless and forlorn without its head. Therefore, Sri Aurobindo took over this role for the next ten months, staying there with his aunt and three cousins. Mrinalini did not join the household but stayed in Calcutta in the house of a friend of her father.

Sri Aurobindo had returned to a changed world. The newspaper *Bande Mataram* no longer existed. After his arrest Shyamsundar Chakravarty had disassociated himself from the bomb attempt at Muzaffarpur in a leading article declaring:

> Outrages of this kind have absolutely no sanction in our ancient tradition and culture.[37]

He wrote that they were an imitation of European anarchism and as foreign to the spirit of nationalism as the position of the Moderates. But the paper lost many readers after Sri Aurobindo's arrest and its financial situation worsened more and more. Finally, the editors decided to enact a heroic end of the paper by deliberately publishing a provoking article which caused the British authorities to close down the paper.

The manifold drastic measures of the government against the Hardliners did not fail to produce effects: the fire of the

---

37 10 May 1908, quoted in Iyengar, *Sri Aurobindo*, 291.

national movement was largely extinguished, the meetings and speeches of the freedom fighters were not attended any more by thousands, but only by a few hundred. The most prominent victim of the numberless deportations was Tilak who had been taken to a penal colony in Burma due to some imprudent statement. Thus the repressive measures of the British had created an atmosphere of fear, with every Indian knowing very well that a single wrong word could have disastrous consequences.

Sri Aurobindo also had to act with caution in this tense atmosphere, for his acquittal was not a guarantee of future immunity. In fact, Beachcroft's judgement had caused irritation in some circles and the authorities in Bengal had asked some external legal experts to find out whether an appeal might be fruitful. The experts believed there were good chances in the case of a new trial, but could not assure a great certainty of success. Therefore in the end the idea was rejected. Sri Aurobindo remained under observation by the authorities. In the meantime he had resumed his yogic practices and made himself acquainted with the current political situation through readings and talks with friends. The British government was making efforts to be in closer touch with the Moderates (who now controlled the Congress entirely) trying to win them over to their side by conceding some insignificant, unsubstantial reforms.

Sri Aurobindo found this new situation unsatisfactory; he developed plans to publish his own weekly journal, discussing subjects such as national religion, literature and philosophy. At the end of May he made a speech at Uttarpara which was later to become famous. In this address to the public he reported his arrest and his experiences in Alipore Jail. He pointed out that even a month before his imprisonment he had received an inner call to leave aside all activities, to withdraw and enter into communion with the Divine, but

> I was weak and could not accept the call. My work was very dear to me and in the pride of my heart I thought that unless I was there, it would suffer or even fail and cease; therefore I would not leave it. It seemed to me that He spoke to me again and said, "the bonds you had not the strength to break, I have broken for you".[38]

Sri Aurobindo also referred in this speech to Hinduism, Sanātana Dharma, the eternal teaching or religion, as it is called in Sanskrit, giving this term a very wide spiritual interpretation. This doctrine has been equated with Hinduism, because it was only on the Indian subcontinent, encircled by the ocean and the mountains, that it has survived from ancient times to the present and, because it has been a special mission of Indians to ensure its survival. Nevertheless he believed that basically the Hindu religion.

> . . . is not circumscribed by a single country, it does not belong peculiarly and for ever to a bounded part of the world.[39]

A narrow-minded sectarian religion, he continued, could only serve a limited purpose and exist for some time whereas the true, eternal religion lasts forever, for it is based on the knowledge that God dwells in all human beings and in all objects.

In fact, a closer look at his text shows that his philosophy of a national religion as presented in this speech would be different from that of a right-wing Hindu nationalism because, what he has in mind here are essential principles of spirituality, expressed not only in Hindu scriptures such as the *Bhagavad-Gītā* or the Upaniṣads but also in important scriptures of other religions. Thus, he says, all of them proclaim the basic unity and equality of all human beings although in different ways:

---

38 Sri Aurobindo, *Tales of Prison Life*, 110.

39 *Karmayogin*, 11.

> Christianity says we are all brothers, children of one God. Mahomedanism says we are the subjects and servants of one Allah, we are all equal in the sight of God. Hinduism says there is One without a second. In the high and the low, in the Brahmin and the Shudra, in the saint and the sinner, there is one Narayana, one God and he is the soul of all men.[40]

At this stage Sri Aurobindo frequently receives invitations to give speeches. He travels by train and steamer to Barisal in East Bengal and it is during this journey — on 17 June 1909 — that he begins a long series of diary notes on his inner experiences which were discovered very late, first published as a book in 2001 under the title *Record of Yoga*.[41] The subject of these notes is a certain phase of Sri Aurobindo's *sādhanā* as well as many supernatural experiences on the subtle physical plane, some of which are also referred to in ancient yogic texts such as the *Yoga-Sūtras*.

Sri Aurobindo begins the journey on a spiritually significant day dedicated to the Goddess Kālī, feeling that some great progress is imminent. He is doing *sūrya-trāṭaka* on the steamer, a yogic practice in which you glance at the radiant sun with open eyes.[42] He describes in detail the different after-images and their exact shades of colour. Then suddenly a note: "Realisation of Vasudeva". He has various *samādhi* experiences such as *savikalpa* and *savicāra*[43] and writes:

---

40 *Karmayogin*, 70. However, there are also later statements of Sri Aurobindo where he is critical of religions and their followers. See, for example, Purani, *Evening Talks*, 295 (29 June 1926).

41 First serial publication 1986-94. The content and meaning of these comprehensive notes will be discussed in detail in the eighth chapter.

42 A practice hardly possible anymore because of the thinner ozone layer.

43 *Savikalpa* means, in his terminology, a type of *samādhi* in which the mind is open to all kinds of inner experiences. In *savicāra*, →

> Exposure to sharp cold wind, no feeling of cold; to strong sun, only feeling of pleasant warmth.[44]

Thus manifold experiences take place, especially visions before his inner eye, and all of it happens while he is travelling, while he has contact with other people and is even talking with them.

On 19 June 1909 Sri Aurobindo founded the *Karmayogin* as "a weekly Review of National Religion, Literature, Science, Philosophy, etc." The cover illustration shows a motif from the *Bhagavad-Gītā* of Kṛṣṇa and Arjuna in the chariot. One of the mottos of the journal has also been taken from the *Gītā*: "Yoga is skill in works".[45] In fact, a *karmayogin* is someone who performs works in the spiritual sense with detachment and out of a higher inspiration. The concrete purpose of the journal was to help build India as a nation, to work for her freedom, unity and greatness so that she could fulfil her mission in the world.

> This is the faith in which the *Karmayogin* puts its hand to the work and will persist in it, refusing to be discouraged by difficulties however immense and apparently insuperable.[46]

The current political developments were also to be considered, but only in so far as they were relevant for the growth of the national life and the soul of the country. The essential aim of the *Karmayogin* was to help its readers to realize their true purpose in life:

> We have yet to know ourselves, what we were, are and may be; what we did in the past and what we are capable of doing in the future; our history and our mission. This is the

→ the mind does not reason logically, but it judges and perceives. (Explanations according to the *Glossary of Yoga*. In Classical *yoga*, these terms have a slightly different significance.).

44 *Record of Yoga*, 33.

45 *Bhagavad-Gītā* II.50.

46 *Karmayogin*, 23.

> first and most important work which the Karmayogin sets for himself, to popularize this knowledge.[47]

Sri Aurobindo then points out that his object is not religion in the Western sense, but rather spirituality,

> the force and energy of thought and action arising from communion with or self-surrender to that within us which rules the world.[48]

He wants to offer the Indian soul a key for its further growth; his intention is to help his country find its path into the future.

In the first issues Sri Aurobindo published his English translations of the *Īśa, Kena* and *Kaṭha Upaniṣad*. In the literary section there were translations from a work of Kālidāsa as well as some of his own poems, essays with titles such as "The National Value of Art" or "The Ideal of the Karmayogin". In an article entitled "A System of National Education" he expounded for the first time some basic ideas which were later to be tried at the Sri Aurobindo International Centre of Education. He expressed the essential thesis of this system as follows:

> Every one has in him something divine, something his own, a chance of perfection and strength in however small a sphere which God offers him to take or refuse. The task is to find it, develop it and use it. The chief aim of education should be to help the growing soul to draw out that in itself which is best and make it perfect for a noble use.[49]

At times Sri Aurobindo had to deal with rationalistic critics of other publications who were doubting, for instance, his reports of spiritual experiences in Alipore Jail, or who mocked his idealism.

---

47 *Karmayogin*, 20.

48 Ibid., 21.

49 SABCL, vol. 17, *The Hour of God*, 204.

The journal received a great response and was financially successful from the outset. There were subscribers not only in Bengal, but as far away as Madras, and after some time editions in Bengali, Hindi and Tamil were brought out. On 23 August 1909 Sri Aurobindo founded additionally the Bengali journal *Dharma,* in which he wrote articles in Bengali. His knowledge of the language had improved through his stay in the large common cell in Alipore Jail. His Bengali could be described as highly Sanskritized and the style of his writings as somewhat old-fashioned, though accomplished in its own way.

For the British administration this was a good period. They were glad to see that the revolutionary movement had collapsed more or less. Now there was only Aurobindo left who disturbed the pleasant peace, becoming active once more, giving speeches and writing articles to mobilize his countrymen. A lot of correspondence was exchanged between the central government and the top officials of the regional administration in Bengal to discuss his case and consider appropriate action. There was a proposal to bring a new charge against him and to deport him, but in the end it was rejected. Informers were taking notes of his speeches and presented some sentences which would have supported a charge, but Sri Aurobindo did not do the British the favour of publishing those dangerous passages. Furthermore, there was also an apprehension on the part of the administration that a new charge against Sri Aurobindo might cause again an uproar among the people who were quiet at the moment. But nevertheless, the possibility of deportation continued to be discussed as an option.

In July 1909 Sister Nivedita warned Sri Aurobindo that there were plans to remove him from the country, she had come to know this through informers in the government. She therefore recommended that he leave British India and continue his work outside the country. Sri Aurobindo was not ready to accept this proposal. He decided to publish an open letter to his countrymen in which he referred to the menace of being deported. This letter appeared in the *Karmayogin* on 31 July and Sri Aurobindo hoped in this way to foil the plan of the British government. Furthermore, he wanted to encourage his companions to keep fighting for their cause in case he was deported. If he were not there anymore, he wrote, someone else would come with the proper qualifications to complete successfully the struggle whose goal was not only the freedom of India, but the future of the entire world.

Actually the British did not take any action against him, but the respective decision had already been taken a week before the publication of the article.[50] The Viceroy of India, Lord Minto, still believed that something must be done, but the Secretary of State for India in London did not favour any such plans. On 25 December Sri Aurobindo published a second open letter. He was deeply reflecting now on the situation in the country, considering the question whether he should withdraw for some time from the political stage,

> . . . as the national movement seemed otherwise threatened with a complete pause. A Home Rule movement or a movement of the South African type suggested themselves to him[51] and he foresaw that they might be resorted to in the near future; but he decided that such movements were not for him to lead and that he must go on with the movement for independence as it was. In the second letter also he rejects the reforms as inadequate and advocates a continuance and reorganisation of the Nationalist movement.[52]

---

50 *The Lives of Sri Aurobindo*, 153.

51 Sri Aurobindo (writing about himself in the third person) meant a self-government as in Ireland which however fell quite short of the ideal of complete independence, or a movement of intensive passive resistance as organized by Gandhi in South Africa. (W.H.)

52 *Autobiographical Notes*, 86-87, see also p. 62.

Meanwhile by the beginning of September a regional conference of the Congress was due to be held at Hooghly, Bengal, which resulted in another confrontation between the Hardliners and the Moderates. The latter were superior now and even tried to exclude Sri Aurobindo from the meeting. But they failed in this effort: Sri Aurobindo did attend the conference and attempted to represent the interests of the Hardliners. When the Moderates prevailed regarding several procedural issues and the Hardliners could not pass their boycott resolution, Sri Aurobindo was ready to compromise and he refused to yield to the pressure of other members of his party who favoured another splitting to take place. Raising his arm during the session he calmed the revolting Hardliners, asking them to leave the hall silently without further protest, thus expressing their disapproval of a position of the Moderates they could not accept. The Hardliners followed this advice and it became evident to all those present how much authority Sri Aurobindo still exercised among his companions.

The Anniversary of the Partition of Bengal was commemorated on 16 October. Sri Aurobindo tried to arrange some meetings and speeches, but the response was small as compared to former times. Therefore he now concentrated especially on his literary works which were published in the *Karmayogin.* He also kept contact with some young revolutionaries (such as Nolini Kanta Gupta who was later to become the Ashram Secretary) and gave instructions on the *Gītā* as well as French lessons. As for language studies, it was his idea that "grown-ups" should not study from textbooks written for children, but should rather start off with high level literary texts. He succeeded with this method in his small circle.

Sri Aurobindo's cousin Basanti, the daugher of his uncle Krishna Kumar Mitra, has given a loving description of scenes from his private life during this period:

I never saw [him] getting angry. Auroda is sitting and

> writing. His sandals are lying at a little distance. My mother comes, puts on his sandals and goes up to the terrace to take her constitutional walk. After some time people come to see Auro. He gets up, searches all around for his sandals. In the meantime he sees his aunt, smiles and asks her: "Little aunty! have you put on my sandals? There are visitors who have come to see me." His aunt gives him his sandals. That she took them away — that he had to wait — nothing of this has made him angry.[53]

One day Sri Aurobindo received a prominent visitor from England — Ramsay MacDonald, the leader of the Labour Party and later Prime Minister. From a British perspective he was entering the lion's cave, meeting one of the most dangerous opponents of the Empire. But he saw a man sitting under a printed verse from the Bible:

> I will go on in the strength of the Lord God.[54]

Sri Aurobindo appeared to MacDonald

> . . . far more of a mystic than of a politician. He saw India seated on a temple throne. But how it was to arise, what the next step was to be, what the morrow of independence was to bring — to those he had given little thought. They were not of the nature of his genius.[55]

At the beginning of February the British government, through a new law, began taking a tougher line against publishers. Henceforth printing presses were required to make a deposit which was seized, along with the press, if objectionable texts were printed. Sri Aurobindo realized at once that he could no longer publish political articles in the *Karmayogin* and accordingly explained this to his readers. He pointed out that

53 Purani, *The Life of Sri Aurobindo*, 116.

54 *Psalms* 71:16.

55 *The Awakening of India*, 49, quoted in *The Lives of Sri Aurobindo*, 199.

as long as the present conditions continued he would write no further political commentaries, but readers should be confident that better times were to come and realization of the pursued goals were only postponed, not given up.[56]

Chandernagore

In February 1910 nine deported activists of the freedom movement were released, among them was Sri Aurobindo's uncle Krishna Kumar Mitra. Sri Aurobindo met him at the station and felt relieved that he was now free from the duty of playing the role of a family head of the latter's household. Meanwhile the Government of Bengal revised its position *vis-à-vis* Sri Aurobindo. After having rejected the proposal of his deportation seven months earlier, they now decided to take him plus fifty-two other members of the Hardliners out of the country. Although the Government of India did not consent, they continued their close observation awaiting the proper opportunity to take action.

On 24 January the situation became hugely critical when a young Bengali revolutionary named Birendranath Dutta Gupta shot detective Shamsul Alam on the premises of the Calcutta High Court, because Alam had made great efforts to persecute the revolutionaries. On 29 July the *Karmayogin* commented defensively on the attempt:

> All we can do is to sit with folded hands and listen to the senseless objurgations of the Anglo–Indian Press, waiting for a time when the peaceful expression and organisation of our national aspirations will no longer be penalised. It is then that Terrorism will vanish from the country and the nightmare be as if it never had been.[57]

One day in mid-February as Sri Aurobindo was sitting in the *Karmayogin* office with some companions, their friend

56 *Karmayogin*, 444.

57 Ibid., 426.

Ramchandra Majumdar burst into the room with great agitation announcing that Sri Aurobindo's arrest was imminent. He said that a relative working in the police department had informed him of it. Actually this message was somewhat imprecise, since an arrest warrant was only to be issued six weeks later (the background a charge of sedition in connection with Sri Aurobindo's second open letter) and the next day only a search of the office rooms was planned. Considering several options the small group took the news very seriously. Sri Aurobindo reported later:

> While I was listening to animated comments from those around on the approaching event, I suddenly received a command from above, in a Voice well known to me, in three words: "Go to Chandernagore".[58]

Sri Aurobindo did not hesitate and set off at once with Ramchandra Majumdar, Biren Ghose and Suresh Chakravarty (also called Moni). Chandernagore[59] was one of five French enclaves in India, situated some 20 miles north of Calcutta and to be reached via the Hooghly, a long branch river of the Ganges River. The enclaves under French jurisdiction were inaccessible to the British judiciary and therefore already served as a refuge for some freedom fighters. When the four men left the house they noted with surprise that there were no informers loitering in front of the house, as was usually the case. Ramchandra led the small group through narrow winding streets, through north Calcutta to the banks of the Hooghly where they hired a boat. Ramchandra was sent back, whereas Biren and Suresh started off on the journey with Sri Aurobindo.

The two boatmen had to row all night, reaching Chandernagore early the next morning. Sri Aurobindo knew only one person there, a former freedom fighter named

---

58 *Autobiographical Notes*, 89.

59 Today known as Chandannagar.

Charuchandra Roy, who had spent a few months with him in Alipore Jail. Since Roy was not as sturdy as the other young revolutionaries he had suffered extremely from imprisonment, crying frequently until he was released, due to the intervention of the French authorities.[60] When Sri Aurobindo sent Biren to him asking for lodging Charuchandra declined, as he was not ready to get involved again in dangerous activities. And perhaps he also felt that his high social status in the town was at risk. But Motilal Roy, another freedom fighter who very much adored Sri Aurobindo, came to know of his arrival through Charuchandra and rushed to the riverside. Highly pleased to personally meet his great idol he gladly offered to arrange for his lodging in Chandernagore.

Sri Aurobindo accepted the offer and sent Biren and Suresh back to Calcutta. He instructed them to inform Sister Nivedita of the new developments and to ask her to take over the editing of the *Karmayogin*. Following Motilal to his house in the small town he took lodging there. Occasionally he was taken to other places, since he did not wish anyone to learn of his identity or his place of lodging. Sri Aurobindo wanted to practise his *yoga* undisturbed, concentrating on his inner experiences. At this period he had many visions on the subtle-physical planes, meeting in his meditations three Vedic goddesses whom he later identified as Ilā, Māhī and Sarasvatī,[61] who represent symbolically the forces of revelation, the luminous vastness of truth and inspiration.

Sri Aurobindo remained in touch with his people in Calcutta asking them to send clothes and other things. He wrote a few articles for the *Karmayogin* which were never published. The journal was continued by Sister Nivedita who

---

60 Nirodbaran, *Talks with Sri Aurobindo*, vol. I, 184-85 (21 January 1939).

61 Purani, *The Life of Sri Aurobindo*, 132.

brought out a few texts of Sri Aurobindo which he had written before his departure, and made her own contributions to several pieces which he had started.

In the meantime his absence was noted by the public and all kinds of speculation developed such as a presumed stay in the Himalayas. Finally, Sri Aurobindo published a clarification in the *Karmayogin* on 19 March 1910, informing the readers that he was not at all staying with the *mahātmās*[62] in Tibet, but was dwelling among humans and . . .

> as he requires perfect solitude and freedom for his Sadhan for some time, his address is being kept a strict secret. . . . For similar reasons he is unable to engage in journalistic works, and *Dharma* has been entrusted to other hands.[63]

Sri Aurobindo lived very much withdrawn at this period, meeting with few people. In particular he met with and instructed Motilal Roy in *yoga*, as he had expressed this wish. Roy was later to found a small spiritual community named Prabartak Sangha in Chandernagore.[64]

In spite of the intensive efforts of several supporters it became more and more difficult to find proper accommodation for Sri Aurobindo. One of the main reasons may have been that Chandernagore was only a rather small town with a limited scope for anonymity. Some of his friends thought of taking him to France, but at the end of March Sri Aurobindo received once more an *ādeśa* (an inner command) to go to Pondicherry. When a disciple later asked him why this was his choice he answered:

---

62 Legendary immortal sages living in the Himalaya according to the conviction of some Theosophists. Sri Aurobindo however thought them to be "mental formations", as he once said in a talk. See Nirodbaran, *Talks with Sri Aurobindo*, vol. I, 20 (14 December 1938).

63 *Karmayogin*, 461.

64 See Chapter 11 "Pondicherry (1915–1926)".

> I could not question. It was Sri Krishna's Adesh. I had to obey. Later on I found it was for the Ashram and for the Work.[65]

Pondicherry was the centre of the French enclaves in India, a small coastal town in south-east Tamil Nadu, more than 900 miles from Calcutta. In August 1909 Sri Aurobindo had already for the first time begun Tamil studies in connection with his linguistic research and he had even employed a scholar for this purpose. The name Pondicherry was also familiar to him, because around the same time he had met a south Indian named S. Parthasarathy Iyengar who belonged to a group that worked for the independence of India, publishing *India,* a Tamil newspaper.

In September 1909 a correspondent of that paper had met Sri Aurobindo in Calcutta for an interview. The journalist was deeply impressed by Sri Aurobindo's appearance, his eyes, his calm voice and the atmosphere of solid peace. Sri Aurobindo patiently answered several questions regarding his *sādhanā* and announced that there would be great upheavals in politics and society in the years to come, with great changes and new ideas and actions in all fields of life.[66]

When one of the editors of the newspaper in Madras was arrested because of sedition, the editorial team withdrew into the safe territory of Pondicherry, working under the direction of Parthasarathy's brother Srinivasachariar,[67] who had gone to school in the French Colony. Srinivasachariar was a friend of the prominent poet Subramania Bharati who had also been persecuted by the British police and had therefore withdrawn to Pondicherry.

While Sri Aurobindo was staying in Chandernagore, that is to say from mid-February to the end of March 1910, the

---

65 Purani, *Evening Talks*, 571.

66 sriaurobindoashram.org/Research/The "India" Interview (1909).

67 Two other spellings are Srinivasachari, Srinivasacharya.

British authorities in Bengal continued considering plans to take action against him. It was especially the Viceroy Lord Minto, who wished to have Sri Aurobindo removed from the political scene but his plans were resisted by John Morley in London who advocated a more moderate approach regarding the freedom fighters.

The search of the *Karmayogin* office after Sri Aurobindo's departure had not produced any incriminating material, but the authorities decided now to bring a charge of sedition against the responsible printer in connection with Sri Aurobindo's open letter of 25 December 1909 to his countrymen, since the author himself was out of reach. The printer was given a sentence of six months' rigorous imprisonment at first instance, but a little later was acquitted by the appellate court. A judge named Fletcher decreed that although the goals Sri Aurobindo pursued were not in agreement with the wishes of British politics, no British laws had been violated through his text.

This verdict was a veritable debacle for the authorities in Bengal who were now forced to accept another major defeat in court after the *Bande Mataram* trial. At the beginning of 1911 the new viceroy, Lord Hardinge, therefore decreed that henceforth no more similar charges should be brought against the freedom fighters unless a successful trial was virtually assured.

7

Pondicherry
(1910-14)

MOVING into distant Pondicherry required some complicated logistics since everything had to be done secretly. Sri Aurobindo asked his cousin Sukumar Mitra to book a passage by steamer to Pondicherry, while Suresh Chandra Chakravarty should travel there in advance by train in order to inform Srinivasachariar and his circle of the imminent arrival. The departure was planned to take place on the morning of 1 April on-board the *S.S. Dupleix* from Calcutta. The destination of this shipping line was Colombo in today's Sri Lanka, but there would be a stopover in Pondicherry.

Sukumar Mitra received help from a friend named Nagendra Kumar Guha Roy as he himself was under constant observation by informers. He instructed Nagen to deposit two suitcases at his own place and to buy tickets for Sri Aurobindo and for Bijoy Nag who would accompany him. For security reasons both of them were to be registered under false names with Colombo as their destination.

The journey south began on 31 March. Initially a boat took Sri Aurobindo across the Hooghly River to Agarpara where a second boat was waiting that took him downstream to Uttarpara. There a third boat from Calcutta was expected to take him on, but the boats missed each other; it was therefore decided to continue the journey with the second boat from Calcutta. When they arrived, they found none of their contacts receiving them at the wharf and so Sri Aurobindo drove to Sukumar's house with his companions. However, they did not meet Sukumar there and therefore they returned right away to the wharf.

Meanwhile, Nagen had returned to Calcutta with the third boat and was considering their next moves with Sukumar. The latter advised him to fetch Sri Aurobindo's suitcases from the steamer *Dupleix* where they had already been deposited in a reserved cabin. While Nagen was on the way to the steamer, Sukumar was informed that Sri Aurobindo had been at his place and had returned to the wharf. Sukumar passed on this message to Nagen when he returned with the suitcases, whereupon the latter rushed back to the wharf. He had been told on the steamer that the two passengers would require a health certificate for the passage, which was normally issued by a doctor at the wharf, but the doctor had already gone home. When Nagen finally found Sri Aurobindo and Bijoy, he told them about the certificate and they all drove to the doctor's residence. They were in an extreme hurry now, since to travel as planned meant boarding the ship by 11 p.m. After that time there would be no entry.

The doctor examined the two passengers named J.N. Mitter and B.Ch. Bhowmik and was astonished at the high level English of J.N. Mitter. He issued the required certificates. Shortly before 11 p.m. they reached the ship, which departed after midnight. The rather confused situation preceding the voyage was certainly a hidden blessing for Sri Aurobindo, because under regular circumstances he would have had to take the health test in the presence of a police officer at the wharf, and his portrait was well known to the authorities. Thus it was due to the hectic circumstances that he could board the ship unrecognized. All the while it struck his young companions that — unlike themselves — Sri Aurobindo had remained absolutely calm during all these events.[1]

[1] This report is mainly based on sources given in →

Arrival in Pondicherry

Pondicherry is situated some eighty-five miles south of Madras[2] on the Coromandel Coast, the Bay of Bengal. The town has a long history dating back to ancient times. As early as two thousand years ago, there was a port in the area which served as a trading base with the Roman Empire. The place, which was originally named Puducherry ("new village" in the local Tamil language), was in later centuries ruled by several dynasties. In 1673 the French India Company acquired the area from the Sultan of Bijapur and it became a French colony used for purposes of trade and commerce. Over time it became the object of different political and military disputes with the British. It was only in 1816 that it finally became a French possession after having been captured by the British several times in between. The French named their colony Pondichéry; in 1954 its union with India was effected.[3] At the time of Sri Aurobindo's journey the little town was a rather obscure place used as a refuge by many pirates and smugglers. As mentioned above, some freedom fighters had also discovered the place, going there to escape the clutches of the British police. For Sri Aurobindo this remote locality would not only offer protection from the British, but also provide the opportunity to detach himself from political activities and dedicate himself entirely to his yogic path, for which he had been feeling a growing inner need.

→ sriaurobindoashram.org/research/from Chandernagore to Pondicherry. Purani gives a more or less identical account in *The Life of Sri Aurobindo* 135ff., which differs however in a few details.

2 Today, Chennai.

3 In 2006, Pondicherry was renamed Puducherry (English) and Poudouchéry (French), thus returning to the original name before the colonial period. However, according to some reports the new version, decreed by the Government of India, has not yet been widely accepted by the local people.

While Sri Aurobindo's departure from Chandernagore was still being prepared Suresh was sent by train down south to contact the Nationalists in Pondicherry and make arrangements for Sri Aurobindo's accommodation. He was dressed like a European to look Anglo–Indian and to attract less attention in the distant town. Suresh was only eighteen years old and unlike the other activists he had no record with the police yet, therefore he was not under permanent observation. He set off with a little travelling bag and a small amount of money. Sri Aurobindo had given him a letter of introduction to Parthasarathy Iyengar which he was asked to hand over in the office of the newspaper *India*.

The journey proceeded as planned and Suresh arrived in Pondicherry on 31 March. His first impressions of the town were rather disillusioning:

> I had heard people talk about the French, their love of beauty, and of Paris, this magnificent capital, and I thought I might find some reflection of it in Pondicherry. However, there was nothing of the kind. It was an altogether ordinary town, with houses as you find them everywhere, there was nothing that would move you or fascinate you by its poetry.[4]

Speaking neither Tamil nor French, Suresh had a hard time getting along in this unfamiliar place. He did have a reading knowledge of English, but had no practice at all in speaking the language; he could not utter much more than "yes" or "no". Finally he succeeded in finding the office where he met Srinivasachariar, who read Sri Aurobindo's letter and promised Suresh to make all necessary arrangements.

The next three days until the arrival of the steamer were rather unnerving for the young Bengali. Although Srinivasachariar received him as a guest at his place, he treated

---

4 Suresh Chakravarty, *Pondichéry, dernier refuge,* Pondichéry: Sri Aurobindo Ashram, 2006, 65.

him somewhat curtly and refused to talk with him about Sri Aurobindo's accommodation. The reason was that the Nationalists were, even in Pondicherry, shadowed by the British police and therefore wished to handle the matter with extreme caution. Actually, they had apprehensions at the beginning that it might be a trap, although they believed Sri Aurobindo's letter to be authentic. Ultimately Suresh won their confidence more and more. None the less, without his knowledge they contacted a wealthy businessman named Sankara Chettiar who agreed to make some rooms available for Sri Aurobindo on the top floor of his house. In the end Srinivasachariar's group even wanted to arrange a kind of official reception for Sri Aurobindo, but this plan was cancelled when Suresh urged them to accept the fact that Sri Aurobindo was not interested at all in any personal publicity.

Chettiar's House

The *Dupleix* arrived in Pondicherry in the afternoon of 4 April 1910. Due to the low water-level in this region, large ships cannot dock at the pier, they must anchor at some distance away from the coast. Passengers and goods are then transported by small boats to the pier. When Suresh and Srinivasachariar approached the steamer on a launch, Sri Aurobindo and Bijoy Nag stood at the railing and greeted them with joy. After a short while all of them stepped onto French soil and drove in a carriage to Chettiar's house, where Sri Aurobindo examined the rooms rented for him and found them quite suitable for his purpose. Along with Suresh and Bijoy he occupied the entire second floor which was constructed in such a way that it was hardly visible from the street. There was a small air shaft through which food, etc. could be transported upstairs and which made it possible to listen to what was going on below.

Through his servants Chettiar provided the three Bengalis

daily with rice, peas and vegetables from the market. Suresh and Bijoy prepared the lunch, which was served on the floor on banana leaves in the south Indian style. Early in the morning and in the afternoon Chettiar sent Sri Aurobindo a glass of tea, in the evening all of them received *pāyasam*, a sweetened milk rice with ingredients such as almonds and raisins.

Once during this period in Chettiar's house Sri Aurobindo fasted for twenty-three days without discontinuing his usual activities: his *yoga* practices, his literary work as well as his daily eight-hour walking up and down, which had become a special feature of his *sādhanā* thereby illustrating the dynamic aspect of his *yoga*.[5] After fasting he resumed taking his normal food without transition, as had been also the case after the ten-day fast in Alipore Jail. When Nirodbaran once asked him how it could be possible to remain active without food in this way, he answered, "One draws energy from the vital plane instead of depending on physical sustenance".[6]

For three months Sri Aurobindo and his companions remained day and night in Chettiar's house as they wanted to avoid attracting attention. But it was all in vain; detectives from the British police soon traced them as the authorities in Calcutta had been informed that two passengers had boarded the *Dupleix* at the last minute. Therefore they became suspicious and showing a photo of Sri Aurobindo to the doctor who had issued the health certificates, they were able to establish the identity of Sri Aurobindo. Now the police assumed that Sri Aurobindo might try to escape via Colombo to North Africa; their plan was to intercept him when he would change ship. But the detectives in the Madras area somehow found out that he was actually staying in

---

5 There are reports that this permanent walking later left an inch-deep track in the floor at another place.

6 Nirodbaran, *Talks with Sri Aurobindo*, vol. I, 86 (1 January 1939).

Pondicherry and sent a message to Calcutta. Since then — probably from the end of April — Chettiar's house was being observed by informers in civilian dress, all the time.

On the very day that Sri Aurobindo arrived in Pondicherry, the long-planned arrest warrant was issued against him but because of his absence, the printer of the *Karmayogin* was arrested, as mentioned above. Secretary of State for India in London, John Morley was irritated over this new action against Sri Aurobindo as he considered the charge of sedition unfounded. He advised the viceroy in Delhi not to apply for an extradition order from Pondicherry, since he did not expect any co-operation from the French. A debate took place in the British House of Commons in which Labour Party MP Ramsay MacDonald vehemently criticized the Government's action against Sri Aurobindo. Presenting several quotations from his articles, he suggested that Sri Aurobindo had actually disassociated himself from terrorism, therefore the government should treat a man like him with greater prudence and broadmindedness. Otherwise, he predicted, the British would face a dark future in India.[7] Sri Aurobindo later read a report on the debate in the *Hindu* newspaper, published in Madras, and so gathered important information such as the fact of the warrant against him. A return to British India was now out of the question for some time.

He lived a rather withdrawn life in Chettiar's house. The only visitors allowed to see him regularly were Srinivasachariar and the poet Bharati, a highly-gifted literary and intellectual personality whose articles were essential for the success of the newspaper *India*. Inspiring discussions took place with Sri Aurobindo on all sorts of subjects and sometimes Bharati brought along his friend V. Ramaswami Iyengar, who listened

---

7 Debate in the House of Commons, 28 April 1910, reported in the *Times* (London), 29 April 1910.

to their talks with rapt attention. Iyengar had originally contacted Sri Aurobindo in connection with a special occurrence:

In the nineteenth century there had been a wealthy landowner in Tamil Nadu (south India) who had a *guru* named Nagai Japata. Around 1880 the latter felt that he was soon going to die and therefore called all his followers. When asked to whom they should turn as their master in the future, he answered that in thirty years a *yogī* from the north would come as a refugee to the south and practise there an Integral Yoga (*pūrṇa yoga*). He added that this would be one sign of the approaching freedom of India. "He gave three utterances as the mark by which this *yogī* could be recognized and all these were found in the letters to my wife", Sri Aurobindo later wrote on this prophecy.[8] The "three utterances" were interpreted to refer to the three madnesses mentioned in a letter to Mrinalini.[9]

The landowner passed on his *guru*'s words to his son who again informed his sons about it, among them K.V. Rangaswami Iyengar, who resided as a landowner in the delta of the Kāverī River. When Iyengar heard about Sri Aurobindo he became very attentive because he felt this might be the announced *uttara-yogī* — the *yogī* from the north. At first he sent his friend Ramaswami to Sri Aurobindo and after his positive report, requested a meeting for himself. Thereafter he was convinced that Sri Aurobindo was indeed the *yogī* they had been expecting and so decided to give him support. That was easy for him from the financial viewpoint, but he had to proceed with great caution since he had an official function as elected representative of the big Indian landowners, and the British would have been little pleased to learn about his new contact.

---

8 *Letters on Himself and the Ashram*, 78. See also Purani, *The Life of Sri Aurobindo*, 144.

9 See in, "Marriage to Mrinalini Bose" Chapter 3.

During this period Sri Aurobindo was again experimenting with channelling, receiving texts of yogic teachings. It was his impression that behind these messages there was the spirit of the Hindu reformer Raja Rammohun Roy, and he arranged the texts as a little book in nine chapters, titled *Yogic Sadhan*. When Rangaswami Iyengar came to know of it, he offered to pay for the printing and also promised Sri Aurobindo more support, which proved to be very important for his small group. The book was printed in 1911 and appeared in several editions. However, Sri Aurobindo later disassociated himself from the contents and had the distribution stopped, since the mode of receiving the text through "automatic writing" was not in tune with his own standards anymore. It is interesting to note that *Yogic Sadhan* was not published under Sri Aurobindo's name: only "Edited by the Uttara Yogi" was to be found on the cover.

Meeting Paul Richard

In mid-April 1910 there were elections in Pondicherry, which took place every four years, with two candidates competing for a seat in the chamber of deputies in Paris. Often they did not even know Pondicherry, or only came for short visits, and they tried to influence the outcome of the elections by giving money to the local mafia gangs. This time Paul Bluysen won, a journalist from Paris.

A few days later Srinivasachariar and Bharati informed Sri Aurobindo that a French lawyer named Paul Richard had come to Pondicherry in connection with the election and wished to see him. Richard had originally been appointed as one of the two candidates and had therefore travelled to India. Although while in Bombay he learned that another candidate would take his place, he decided none the less to continue his journey to the south.[10]

10 P. Richard, *Without Passport*, 55. Source quoted in *The Lives of* →

Richard was two-year older than Sri Aurobindo, he had grown up in southern France. After serving in the military he had been educated as a priest and then studied Law. He also intensively studied Eastern and Western spirituality, and hoped to meet some genuinely realized Indian *yogīs*. In 1911 he had married Mirra Alfassa, a French artist with Turkish–Egyptian roots, who led a small group of seekers in Paris interested in spirituality and esotericism. Due to her own manifold experiences and studies she had acquired a deep knowledge of the inner worlds and was therefore able to support Richard effectively in his inner search as well as with some literary projects.

Sri Aurobindo was not at all pleased that his friends had spoken to Richard about him when Richard had enquired about *yogīs* in the region. Sri Aurobindo assumed that Richard would merely be a curious tourist with a superficial interest in *yoga*, and therefore declined to meet him. But his two companions Srinivasachariar and Bharati were able to change his mind, referring to their difficult situation and pointing out that one day it may be of great advantage for all of them to know someone as influential as Richard in Paris.

This was an argument Sri Aurobindo could not ignore and so in the end he had two very long meetings with the visitor. It was not planned that the meetings should last several hours, but when Richard told Sri Aurobindo his vita, giving an account of his philosophical and spiritual searching, interest was aroused and Sri Aurobindo felt the encounter had a significance.

Richard asked Sri Aurobindo of the symbolical meaning of the Star of David (*yoga-cakra*) which Mirra had seen several

---

→ *Sri Aurobindo*, 223. However, according to a statement of the Mother he was sent to Pondicherry to help Paul Bluysen in the election campaign. (*Mother's Agenda*, vol. 2, 5 November 1961.)

times in her meditation. This symbol consists of two overlapping triangles pointing upwards and downwards respectively, with a lotus in the centre. Sri Aurobindo explained to him that this symbol (which was later also to become his own) represented the opening of the consciousness to the Divine.

Srinivasachariar was present during their talks as an interpreter, since apparently Sri Aurobindo wanted to speak English only and Richard's knowledge of English was insufficient.[11] However, it has been reported that Sri Aurobindo spoke French fluently with the Tibet expert Alexandra David-Néel when she paid him a visit two years later.[12]

Richard was deeply moved by his meeting with Sri Aurobindo and never missed an opportunity during his travels to praise him as an eminent *yogī* who would lead humanity into a new age. He repeated this in a speech given in Japan, that was later published in his book *The Dawn Over Asia*.

Sri Aurobindo was likewise impressed by Richard and stayed in touch with him through correspondence in which Mirra Alfassa also took part. After some time Sri Aurobindo mentioned her in his circle of young companions as "a French lady from Paris, who was a great initiate . . ."[13] and wrote Motilal Roy in April 1914 that Richard was for him a brother in *yoga*, one who had the same goal in mind of replacing the present European civilization by a spiritual civilization.

> He and Madame Richard are rare examples of European Yogis who have not been led away by Theosophical and other aberrations. I have been in material and spiritual correspondence with them for the last four years.[14]

---

[11] Suresh Chakravarty, *Pondichéry, dernier refuge,* 104.

[12] *The Life of Sri Aurobindo,* 235.

[13] Nolini Kanta Gupta, *Reminiscences,* 75.

[14] *Autobiographical Notes,* 195.

Thus, Richard's visit to Pondicherry was ultimately significant in so far as it became instrumental in establishing contact with Mirra.

Change of Residence

In October 1910 Sri Aurobindo had for the first time received a major amount of money from Rangaswami Iyengar; he was now in a position to rent a flat for himself and his companions. A little earlier Mrinalini's cousin Saurin Bose had joined the small group. Now all of them moved into the house of Sundara Chettiar, a relative of Sankara, situated in the eastern part of town, in the rue de la Pavillon.[15] A month later Sri Aurobindo wrote a letter to the newspaper *Hindu* publicly announcing his stay in Pondicherry. In his statement he said,

> I left British India over a month before proceedings were taken against me and, as I had purposely retired here in order to pursue my Yogic sadhana undisturbed by political action or pursuit and had already severed connection with my political work, I did not feel called upon to surrender on the warrant for sedition, as might have been incumbent on me if I had remained in the political field.[16]

Furthermore, Sri Aurobindo wrote that he was living like a recluse, receiving only a few friends as visitors. His place of stay was well known for a long time to the British government and local people. He did not want to have correspondence on political subjects with anyone, he continued, and would make a decision about his leaving British India only when there was a verdict in the *Karmayogin* case.

As chance would have it, the verdict was published along with Sri Aurobindo's letter in the *Hindu*, the charge of sedition was rejected and the printer acquitted. Sri Aurobindo's

---

15 Now Rue Suffren.

16 *Autobiographical Notes,* 264.

companions in Bengal now hoped he would return to Calcutta, but he decided to stay for another year or two in Pondicherry to further develop his *sādhanā* at some distance from the political scene.

If we wish to visualize Sri Aurobindo's new location in the town, the following "co-ordinates" may help: from the optical point of view, Pondicherry is divided into two districts through a canal that runs more or less parallel to the coast in a north–south direction. The eastern part, situated at the sea-side (in which today there is the Sri Aurobindo Ashram) looks partially European with some stately buildings from the time of the French administration. The western part situated further inland looks more like a typical Indian town with a busy bazaar, streets of shops and dense traffic of cars, rikshaws and bicycles.

In Sri Aurobindo's time the "busy-ness" was rather limited, and he had now moved into the eastern part of town living with his three companions who liked to walk on the beach in the evening, just a few blocks from the sea. After a while they were joined by Nolini Kanta Gupta who had belonged to Barin's group in the Maniktala Gardens, but had been acquitted in the Alipore trial. He was later to become one of the most well-known disciples of Sri Aurobindo, playing an important role in the Ashram life up to the 1980s.

After Sri Aurobindo's place of residence had become public, all kinds of people from all over India, from even distant regions, began arriving to pay him a visit and to have his *darśan*.[17] But Sri Aurobindo was deeply immersed in his *sādhanā* and his studies and was not in the least ready to play the role of an adored idol. He felt quite harassed by the visitors who were often obtrusive and reckless, even climbing up to his window to have a glimpse of him. To put an end to it, he

---

[17] See Glossary.

published another statement in the *Hindu* on 23 February 1911, telling the readers that he did not receive any visitors and that any journey to his place would therefore be purposeless. Furthermore, he clarified, that all reports from pilgrims of supposed talks with him had been freely invented.

Literary Works

Sri Aurobindo had written repeatedly that from the cultural point of view the Western country of his own choice would not have been England, but France,[18] and now he was residing in Pondicherry, on French territory, and he would spend the rest of his life there. Never again would he leave this place where he developed his Integral Yoga and created his most important literary works. England had given him the English language through which he could later reach readers all over the world, and now France granted him protection and security. Through his correspondence with Richard and Mirra he had also established a direct contact with Paris, the centre of European culture. We may say that he was truly a globally-oriented Indian — a *yogī* writing poetry in English, residing on *de jure* French soil, having a preference for subjects related to ancient Greece and studying old Vedic texts in their original.

At this time Sri Aurobindo was working on *Ilion*, an epic poem of nine books with more than 5,000 lines in which he tried to apply quantitative hexameter[19] in the English language. The action is inspired by Homer's *Iliad*, it reports the last day of the Battle of Troy. Tragedy and doom fill the air, while the champion fighter Achilles and the Amazon Penthesilea are wrestling with their own passions and the forces of destiny,

---

18 See, for instance, *Autobiographical Notes*, 35.

19 The hexameter is a metre used by Homer and others. It consists of six (Greek hexa) feet with the quantity -vv (long short short) which may optionally be replaced by — (long long). Below, an original line of Sri Aurobindo will be quoted with the following structure: -vv — -vv -vv -vv —

and the gods and goddesses are watching the scene from lofty Olympus, ultimately determining the course of events through their own decisions.

Richard Hartz, who is doing research in the Ashram Archives, has aptly noted in a commentary on *Ilion*:

> It may seem strange that an Indian mystic, in the midst of the most intensive Yogic *sadhana*, was so captivated by an ancient Greek theme and the possibilities of the Homeric metre that he worked for years on an epic about the Fall of Troy, making it his major literary project until in 1916, when he began to transfer his poetic energies to *Savitri*. But it is hinted in the poem itself that his interest in this subject was not merely literary. He says of the Greek warriors emerging from their tent:
>
> So one can see them still who has sight from the gods in the trance-sleep.[20]

Another clue for explaining Sri Aurobindo's interest in the subject of *Ilion* (which is another name for Troy) is found in his *Thoughts and Aphorisms*. In the section Jnana (knowledge), he says that there are "four very great events in history" and mentions in the first place "the siege of Troy", for it "created Hellas".[21] And in another aphorism we are told, "Athens, not Sparta is the progressive type for mankind".[22] In the city of Troy war and battle took place, but basically it was here that the foundation for the cultural state of Athens was laid down, which created magnificent poetry and philosophy, worked out valuable first approaches for science and research and also gave rise to the political system of democracy which was to play such an important role in the future of humanity. It was

---

20 *Recent Publications*, SABDA, December 2009, 19. The last line: *Collected Poems*, 434.

21 *Essays Divine and Human*, Thoughts and Aphorisms, 427.

22 Ibid., 448.

a crucial epoch from the point of view of the evolutionary philosopher Sri Aurobindo who, as our contemporary, would have gladly noted that the model of Athens was able to prevail over that of the militaristic Sparta. At the time that he wrote his lines this was by no way certain, and Europe was still to find its way through many errors and aberrations.

Below we quote the first lines of the epic *Ilion* as a sample of Sri Aurobindo's English poetry in hexameter:

Dawn in her journey eternal compelling the labour of mortals,
Dawn the beginner of things with the night for their rest or their ending,
Pallid and bright-lipped arrived from the mists and the chill of the Euxine.
Earth in the dawn-fire delivered from starry and shadowy vastness
Woke to the wonder of life and its passion and sorrow and beauty,
All on her bosom sustaining, the patient compassionate Mother.
Out of the formless vision of Night with its look on things hidden
Given to the gaze of the azure she lay in her garment of greenness,
Wearing light on her brow.[23]

Sri Aurobindo was also working at this time on the plays *Eric* and *Rodogune.* The first deals with a king in ancient Norway at the time of the Vikings, whereas the second takes place in ancient Syria and is full of dramatic action in an interplay of love, hatred and jealousy with Princess Rodugune, who has a slightly angelic personality, in the centre.

Sri Aurobindo had already written this play in 1906, but it became lost and he created a second version now. Even before his arrival in Pondicherry he had written *The Viziers of Bassora* and *Perseus the Deliverer;* in 1915 *Vasavadutta* was added. As the plays are a little less important than his main works, we will introduce in the following only one of them in detail. This will enable us to get some insight into this field of his

[23] *Collected Poems*, 113.

literary work which appears to be more related to Shakespeare than to *yoga*, although — as we shall see — elements of the latter can also be traced.

The Play Eric

Young Eric has been elected King of Norway, after King Olaf Thorleikson was killed in battle. His son Svegn too had been very eager to succeed him, but he was defeated by Eric in the struggle for power. Since then the Earl of Trondhjem has spent his time brooding in his fastness in the hills, sowing discord wherever possible, and waiting for his chance to perhaps still gain the upper hand.

To help her brother in his ambition, Svegn's sister Aslaug decides to go to Eric's court disguised as a dancing-girl in order to kill him. Svegn's wife Hertha joins her, but in truth she is intent on reconciling the two inimical parties and wants to try to prevent the worst.

Right after their first meeting Eric and Aslaug feel strongly attracted towards each other. With great excitement Aslaug reports to Hertha:

A mighty man!
He has the face and figure of a God,
A marble emperor with brilliant eyes.[24]

Intuitively, Eric becomes suspicious that Aslaug may have come with other intentions than what she pretends, because her looks and her demeanour appear to be too noble for the role of a dancing girl. He questions her, but she insists on her identity, whereupon Eric confesses,

. . . I am enamoured of thy golden hair,
Thy body like the snow, thy antelope eyes,
This neck that seems to know it carries heaven

[24] *Collected Plays and Stories*, 540.

Upon it easily. Thy song, thy speech,
This gracious rhythmic motion of thy limbs . . .[25]

Now he desires her, he wants to possess her and offers her a necklace as the price. When Aslaug at first rejects the proposal and then accepts it half-heartedly, he offers to present the necklace to her as a gift, if she makes a decision for him out of her own free choice.

Aslaug is now struggling with her conflicting emotions. She still feels the hatred with which she had come to the court to get rid of her brother's rival, but at the same time there is a feeling of steadily growing love. None the less, one night she finally makes up her mind to carry out her original plan and confides this to Hertha, who wants to prevent the attempt on Eric and thus approaches him. She divulges Aslaug's plan, but also negotiates an agreement that Aslaug, Svegn and herself will be spared.

When Aslaug enters Eric's room he pretends to sleep, because he is confident that Aslaug's love for him will prevail in the conflict of emotions. Standing in front of him, she lifts the dagger twice for thrusting it. A classical author would have probably allowed her to carry out her plan, thus adding another tragedy to the innumerable poetic dramas of this world. But Sri Aurobindo sends his inwardly torn heroine an intervening and transforming impulse of the soul. She is facing a very difficult decision now because not to act appears to her to be like her brother's death:

Svegn's death or life and such an easy stroke,
Yet so impossible to lift my hand!
To wait? To watch more moments these closed lids,
This quiet face and try to dream that all
Is different! But the moments are Fate's thoughts

[25] *Collected Plays and Stories*, 549.

Watching me. While I pause, my brother's slain,
Myself am doomed his concubine and slave.[26]

The feeling of love is too strong now, she cannot thrust the dagger, she throws it away and kneels down before Eric who forgives her magnanimously and chooses her as his bride. At first Aslaug resists, as she is full of shame at having betrayed her brother's cause, but then the poet lifts the whole situation to the higher plane of the gods, who effect their action on earth through human beings. So Eric frees Aslaug of her guilt and refers to Freya, the Mother of Heaven who represents love here, while Thor embodies Power:

Aslaug, the world's sole woman! thou cam'st here
To save for us our hidden hope of joy
Parted by old confusion. Some day surely
The world too shall be saved from death by love.
Thou hast saved Svegn, helped Norway. Aslaug, see,
Freya within her niche commands this room
And incense burns to her. Not Thor for thee,
But Freya.[27]

Then Eric and Aslaug marry by exchanging rings and finally — with a great deal of effort — even the rebellious Svegn is won as a partner for the new alliance so that there is now a complete happy end.

When Aslaug arrived at the beginning at Eric's Court in Jara, she sang a song:

When Love desires Love,
Then Love is born.
Nor golden gifts compel,
Nor even beauty's spell
Escapes his scorn.

---

26 *Collected Plays and Stories*, 586.

27 Ibid., 591.

When Love desires Love,
Then Love is born.[28]

Here we already have the central motif of the play: love, transforming love. Actually we find the first suggestion on the subject of transformation, which was later to play an important role in the Integral Yoga of Sri Aurobindo. More precisely, he deals with "psychic transformation" (as he termed it) in which the human vital nature with its often crude reactions is purified through impulses of the soul and taken to a higher plane. This is, in the same way, the case with Eric and with Aslaug although the change is more dramatic with the latter. Furthermore, in the background we also find in this play the ideal of political unity, which was always considered very important by Sri Aurobindo, in this case the unity of Norway re-established through the reconciliation with Svegn.

In contrast to *Ilion* we should not assume that there might be any special significance to places like Syria or Norway. What Sri Aurobindo once wrote with reference to his play *Perseus the Deliverer*, also holds true here:

> In a romantic work of imagination of this type time is more than Einsteinian in its relativity. . . . Fantasy reigns sovereign; the names of ancient countries and peoples are brought in only as fringes of a decorative background.[29]

Linguistic Studies

At this time Sri Aurobindo also continued his Tamil studies and started doing research on "The Origins of Aryan Speech" which however were never completed.[30] Academic Indology

---

28 *Collected Plays and Stories*, 534.

29 Ibid., 328

30 The incomplete study has been published in *The Secret of the Veda*, 551-81, Sri Aurobindo Ashram 1971. In the *Complete Works* it appears in vol. 14, *Vedic and Philological Studies*. On p. →

holds that there is no linguistic relationship between the south Indian Draviḍian languages and the Indo-European tongues such as Sanskrit, Greek, Latin and German. But Sri Aurobindo arrived at the conclusion that there are common roots dating back to a distant past, and he presented some evidence to substantiate his thesis.[31]

It was fifty years later that the two brilliant Russian linguists Wladislaw M. Illitsch-Switytsch and Aaron B. Dolgopolsky presented a similar thesis, establishing the "Nostratic" linguistic theory:

> Nostratic is considered to be the common mother of the Indo-European, the Dravidian languages of South India, the Kartwel languages of the Southern Caucasus, the Uralian family . . . the Altaic languages . . . as well as the Afro-Asiatic family of languages.[32]

After Illitsch-Switytsch (who first founded this line of research) had died in an accident, his colleague Dolgopolsky continued the work at the University of Haifa in Israel. He compiled about 1,600 roots as the original stock of the Nostratic family of languages and has thus continued Sri Aurobindo's linguistic

---

→ 562 Sri Aurobindo writes, also for clarifying the term *arya*: "I base my conclusions on the evidence of the Sanskrit language helped out by those parts of the Greek, Latin and Tamil tongues which are cognate to the word-families of Sanskrit, and by the origins of Aryan speech I mean, properly, the origin of human speech as used and developed by those who fashioned these word-families and their stocks and off-shoots. The significance of the word Aryan, as I use it, goes no farther."

31 Thus, in the Indo–European equation *father, pater, pita,* etc., there is no Tamil equivalent, because in Tamil "father" means *appā*. But there is Sanskrit. *apatya*, son, descendant, and Sri Aurobindo assumed the common root to be *ap*, to originate, create.

32 *Spektrum der Wissenschaft*, Dossier 1/2004, p. 11.

approach in a direction which the latter already delineated half a century earlier with several examples. However, scholars in the field of Indology and Indo–European studies refuse to recognize this theory.[33]

Life in Pondicherry

In April 1911 Sri Aurobindo and his companions moved into a house in the rue Saint Louis. The political situation in the country was less tense now, but in the summer of 1911 an attempt to eliminate a top official, in one of the districts of Madras, was carried out. The authorities found out that the assassin had been trained by V.V.S. Aiyar, a Tamil revolutionary who lived in Pondicherry and who was closely connected to Srinivasachariar and Bharati. There were no investigations concerning Sri Aurobindo, but it was known that he maintained relations with those persons. Therefore, he also was involved though indirectly, and in the *Madras Times* the wish was expressed publicly that action should be taken against the revolutionaries, that they should be deported.

The British intensified the surveillance of the freedom fighters through their agents and followed them wherever they went. There were even plans to kidnap some of them and take them to British India to bring a charge against them there. Sri Aurobindo's companions knew of this threat and therefore guarded him day and night. They kept bottles of acid ready so that they would be able to defend him against an attack in the house (he hardly moved outside at all).

This kind of attack did not take place, but there was a plot against the freedom fighters on the part of a Tamilian named Mayuresan, a citizen of Pondicherry who had been serving the British for a long time as a well-paid informer. He prepared

33 For the reasons, see ibid., 12. (They say that the Nostratic word equations can be explained by mere accidental similarities of words or lean words.)

some faked documents which suggested that the Tamilian and Bengali refugees in the town were planning terrorist attacks there itself. Then Mayuresan put the documents inside a jar, sealed it and had it thrown into the well in Aiyyar's house. It was his plan to give a tip to the French authorities, who would then pull the jar out of the well and uncover those supposed terrorist plans.

But Mayuresan had back luck: one of Aiyyar's servants inadvertently pulled out the jar when fetching water from the well in the morning, and showed it to Aiyyar. The latter consulted with his friends and they decided to ask Sri Aurobindo for advice. He told them they should disclose the whole matter to the French. They did so, and the French sent officers who examined the jar with its obviously faked documents. A magistrate also came to Sri Aurobindo's place to inspect his rooms. But when he saw handwritten notes with Latin and Greek texts he exclaimed incredulously, "he knows Greek, he knows Latin. . . ." The magistrate politely said goodbye and went away. Mayuresan later ran into problems with the French police and had to flee to British India.

The fact that Sri Aurobindo had received financial support from K.V.R. Iyengar did not imply that he could live now in prosperity. His small group had constant expenses for rent and livelihood, but no income whatsoever. Therefore they continued to be short of money and Srinivasachariar and Bharati could not help either. At times there were even desperate situations, as described by Sri Aurobindo in a letter to Motilal Roy, dated 3 July 1912: He has just $1\frac{1}{2}$ Rupees left at this moment and there are no prospects of any improvement of their plight. There is one single person in Pondicherry who may possibly help, but he has gone travelling for an indefinite period of time. A messenger sent to contact him has not yet returned. Even if he arrived soon, it would still be uncertain whether any money would come to him and his small group.

In these extremely tense circumstances, Sri Aurobindo comments on the difficult situation, not without a touch of humour:

> No doubt, God will provide, but He has contracted a bad habit of waiting till the last moment. I only hope He does not wish us to learn how to live on a minus quantity like Bharati.[34]

Sri Aurobindo appeals to Roy to send some money if possible, and perhaps to contact other people who might lend a small or substantial amount. Roy had visited Sri Aurobindo in 1911 for six weeks in Pondicherry to talk about his *sādhanā* and other things. On this occasion he had witnessed for himself the difficult situation of the group. Now he does whatever is in his power to send money from his own (or external) resources. During these years the small community changes its accommodation several times; by the end of 1913 they moved into a house on rue François Martin No. 41 where Sri Aurobindo then lived for nine years in his two rooms on the first floor and where he had many talks with his disciples.

We already know that he was not much affected by adverse external circumstances, but now we see that he also transferred this spirit to his companions. They shared a single towel between five persons and did not complain if their meals sometimes consisted only of rice and chillies with a little oil and salt. Otherwise, they followed the Bengali custom of eating rice and fish, often served with wine (which was very inexpensive in Pondicherry) and they smoked a lot. Sri Aurobindo also had this habit, but he later gave it up immediately when he came to know that the Mother was very much suffering from the cigar smoke.[35] She was on principle against smoking and made this one of the few fixed rules in the Ashram.

---

34 Purani, *The Life of Sri Aurobindo*, 151.

35 *Mother's Agenda*, vol. 6, 14 June 1965. See also Nirodbaran, *Twelve Years with Sri Aurobindo*, 14.

As a compensation for this at times rather austere life, Sri Aurobiindo's companions had the joy of being in his company, living a life full of inspiration. He shared with them his great inner treasures, teaching them Greek, Latin, French and Italian and introducing them into the great works of world literature. He was for them a private tutor, with infinite patience and inexhaustible resources of knowledge. Masterpieces such as Sophocle's *Antigone* or Dante's *Divine Comedy* were studied for instance by Nolini, in the original, with his help and without any previous education in this field. Sri Aurobindo hardly talked with them about *yoga* at this early period in their community, but it was part of his *yoga* practice in daily life to transfer to them his dynamics, widening their inner horizon as a preparation for things that were to come later. Living with him meant to constantly learn and explore.

In the meantime Sri Aurobindo continued working intensively on his manifold literary projects and he made progress on his yogic path. In a letter to Motilal Roy, written shortly after his birthday on 15 August 1912, he informs him of the status of his *sādhanā*. He mentions that his birthday usually marks a turning point in his life, or spiritual path, and then notes:

> This time it has been very important for me. My subjective sadhana may be said to have received its final seal and something like its consummation by a prolonged realisation & dwelling in Parabrahman for many hours. Since then, egoism is dead for all in me except the Annamaya Atma — the physical self which awaits one further realisation before it is entirely liberated from occasional visitings or external touches of the old separated existence.
>
> My future sadhan is for life, practical knowledge & shakti — not the essential knowledge or shakti in itself which I have got already — but knowledge & shakti established in the same physical self & directed to my work in life.[36]

---

36 *Autobiographical Notes,* 177.

We get more clarity on the significance of this letter in some statements which Sri Aurobindo made retrospectively in 1945 to clarify some details of his biography.[37] The first important realization in his *Sādhanā* was the realization of the silent, spaceless and timeless *Brahman*, that is the realization of the static *Brahman*, attained with Lele's help in 1908. This was followed by the realization in Alipore Jail of the dynamic *Brahman*, the cosmic consciousness in which all beings and all that exists is experienced as the Divine. The third realization he calls in the text quoted above "dwelling in *Para-Brahman*", it is "that of the supreme Reality with the static and dynamic *Brahman* as its two aspects . . .",[38] that is to say a combination of the first two realizations on a higher plane of unified vision.

At another place Sri Aurobindo writes on the *Para-Brahman* which means literally "supreme *Brahman*":

> The Divine is supracosmic, the eternal Parabrahman who supports with his timeless and spaceless existence all this cosmic manifestation of his own being and nature in Space and Time.[39]

As a fourth realization followed "that of the higher planes of consciousness leading to the Supermind".[40] He already had some glimpse of this fourth stage in 1912, but not yet any certain and comprehensive knowledge.

An important visitor at the end of 1911 was the Tibetan and Buddhist expert Alexandra David-Néel who belonged to a study group of Mirra Alfassa in Paris; she had gone to see Sri Aurobindo following the suggestion of Mirra. Sri Aurobindo told her about his inner explorations and the French lady was

---

37 *Autobiographical Notes*, 94.

38 Ibid.

39 *Essays on the Gita*, 322.

40 *Autobiographical Notes*, 94.

deeply impressed by the meeting, grateful to have met him.[41]

We had already mentioned above the moving of the small community to rue François Martin where there was a comparatively large accommodation. This became possible through the help of an admirer of Sri Aurobindo named Nagen Nag, a relative of Bijoy Nag with some financial means, who had joined the group. As his personal servant he brought along a cook named Birendra Roy who was, as it turned out, an informer for the British police, receiving payment for his services. One day a certain occurrence made him believe that the group had seen through his role and he therefore confessed everything on his own. The others at first thought it was a joke and merely laughed, but then Birendra showed them the large amount of money he had from the British. With tears in his eyes and sincere repentance he placed the money at Sri Aurobindo's feet, promising that he would never again become involved in such an activity. The group reacted with icy silence, but Sri Aurobindo allowed Roy to remain yet for a while in the community, until he finally returned to Bengal.

One important new contact at this time was a young Tamil named Aravamudachari Iyengar, a friend of V. Rangaswami Iyengar. He joined the community and was later to become a well-known *sādhak* of the Sri Aurobindo Ashram under the name of Amrita. He reported the following impressions of his first meeting with Sri Aurobindo:

> Sri Aurobindo's eyes, it seemed, burned brighter than the lamplight for me; as he looked at me, in a trice all gloom vanished from within me, and his image was as it were installed in the *sanctum sanctorum* of my being. . . . I felt within me that he had accepted me.[42]

---

41 See also "Quotations on Sri Aurobindo and His Work" with Madame David-Néel's personal impressions on their meeting.

42 Nolini Kanta Gupta, *Reminiscences*, 159.

Meanwhile, Sri Aurobindo's *yoga* progressed well. In a letter to Paul Richard dated 20 September 1911 he described the current status of his development as follows:

> My Yoga is proceeding with great rapidity, but I defer writing to you of the results until certain experiments in which I am now engaged, have yielded fruit sufficient to establish beyond dispute the theory and system of Yoga which I have formed and which is giving great results not only to me, but to the young men who are with me. . . . I expect these results within a month, if all goes well.[43]

During these early years in Pondicherry it happened that Sri Aurobindo received through intuition seven mantric Sanskrit lines which for a long period of time became a guide-line for his *sādhanā*. As they contained four main elements each, he called them the *sapta catuṣṭaya* (seven quaternaries). In the following chapter we will present them and his diary of *yoga*, which was discovered long after his departure and whose regular entries begin in 1912.

---

43 *Autobiographical Notes*, 284.

8

Record of Yoga : The Yoga Diary

WE had already mentioned Sri Aurobindo's *yoga* diary once before in connection with his journey to Barisal when he started the entries. These were made from 1909 to 1927, but with a greater regularity mainly from 1912-20. He gave them different names and the most frequent was "Record of Yoga", therefore the editors of the two volumes, which comprise 1,500 pages, chose this title. These records, in notebooks and on loose sheets, were discovered later. In the Sri Aurobindo Ashram there was a controversy regarding the question whether they should be published at all, since Sri Aurobindo himself had not released them for publication. In 2001 they were then first brought out as a book.

For Western readers without knowledge of Sanskrit the records are almost inaccessible because in some sections the frequency of Sanskrit words is enormous. For Indians it is easier, since they have some access to this vocabulary through languages such as Hindi. But there is another difficulty: Sri Aurobindo has used the Sanskrit terms in many cases with his own symbolic or specific meanings in the context of the *yoga* path that he follows at this stage.

Now, fortunately, the Department *Archives and Research* of the Sri Aurobindo Ashram has prepared a glossary for facilitating reading, which has some 200 pages and is very helpful.[1] It explains not only Sanskrit words, but also some

[1] Available through download, see Internet addresses.

special English terms such as *supermind*. To give a little insight into the diary and its style of writing, we present in the following some examples. The first extract belongs to a category of very difficult passages with a high frequency of Sanskrit terms:

> The tendency to ratna in the bhoga continues and there is occasional ratha. The nirananda is mostly in the physical element of the higher anandas where the indriyas are touched. Motions of contact are now commencing in which, starting with the vishaya and the tivra, all the five physical anandas manifest together raudra, vaidyuta and kama following each other or rather developing out of each other.[2]

Now we may ask: what is the purpose of these records? Perhaps we can imagine Sri Aurobindo as a physicist in a laboratory, noting results in connection with certain experiments, and the data he records only make sense to his specialized colleagues, who have acquired specific background knowledge. Sri Aurobindo's subject of research is his own being, and he notes with phenomenal meticulousness the most subtle psycho–physical processes which take place during this particular phase of his *yoga*. His observations include all levels of being, and details on the most different bodily functions, as well as extrasensory experiences, all carefully noted. We can assume that never before, nor thereafter, has a *yogī* reported so comprehensively on his own inner path; probably there are only very few persons who would be able to withstand psychologically such deep, intensive and permanent self-observation.

Behind all this there is a certain programme (which will be introduced below) and the records reflect the measure in which progress was made with reference to various goals. The subject of the passage quoted above is *ānanda* (bliss). As

---

[2] *Record of Yoga*, 65 (24 January 1912).

is well known, we can experience joy on different levels. Thus we know the joy of a good reading (mental) and the feeling of love (vital) and that of a good meal (physical). Furthermore, there is for instance the joy of a good meditation (spiritual). Now Sri Aurobindo has expanded this differentiation on his own working level in various ways; he lives in a world of highly subtilized experiences that appear almost inaccessible to us, even if we succeed in deciphering his specific code language.

But we will attempt to interpret at least the first sentence of the passage: *ratna* carries the meaning "jewel" in Sanskrit, and in Sri Aurobindo's perception the term has the symbolic meaning of joy, delight in the *R̥gveda*, which here applies. If we look it up in the Glossary, we are given a rather complicated explanation.[3] *Bhoga*, the second term in the above passage, means "enjoyment" and is explained in no less than fifteen lines in the Glossary. Finally, we have a look at the third Sanskrit word, *ratha*. In classical Sanskrit it means chariot, also joy. In Vedic Sanskrit, according to Sri Aurobindo's interpretation, it is "the happy movement of the *Ananda*".

At this point we discontinue the exploration of the sentence for it becomes evident that, with or without the Glossary, Sri Aurobindo's *yoga* diary is a book with many seals and every analysis of a Sanskrit term takes us to ever new ramifications. So we can only give some suggestion of what Sri Aurobindo deals with in the quoted passage: basically, the subject is his progress in developing the consciousness in connection with sense contacts and their reception. Because of some of his later statements we know for instance that he was, as a rule, able to transform even pain into a sensation of *ānanda* (bliss).[4]

---

3 It is "the second intensity of each of the three states of *bhukti* called *rasagrahana, bhoga* and *ānanda*".

4 See also p. 192 (bottom) of this present title, and furthermore: Nirodbaran, *Talks with Sri Aurobindo*, vol. I. (11 December 1938). Also see *The Life Divine*, 113. In the chapter "The Delight of →

But there are also more accessible passages in the diary which can be well understood and make the reading fruitful. The following extract belongs to this category, the few Sanskrit terms in this case each carry their classical meanings:

> Yesterday by a sudden opening of faculty Sanscrit prose, even of the Kadambari[5] type, which was until the last reading difficult to understand, troublesome & wearying to the brain, has become perfectly easy & intelligible at the first reading without labour. A similar result is coming in Sanscrit poetry but more slowly. Prakasha[6] & tapas[7] in the brain have increased, tamas[8] is passing away."[9]

Some readers may have had this experience themselves that sometimes, when studying a foreign language, we are as it were blocked, whereas at other times we understand everything effortlessly, because the mind is open and bright. Sri Aurobindo has the latter experience here not only for a moment but permanently, as if a veil has been removed, which makes studies of this category easy henceforth.

For some period, Sri Aurobindo seems to have had even the faculty of realizing the meaning of words without the help of a dictionary. Thus he notes a day later that sometimes "the *vijnanamaya* knowledge manifests . . . with regard to the

---

→ Being : The Solution" he deals with the question of the transformation of conditioned sense-reactions and finally states: "It is equally within our competence to accustom the superficial being to return instead of the mechanical reactions of pleasure, pain and indifference that free reply of inalienable delight which is the constant experience of the pure and vast Bliss-Self within us."

5 The name of a work in Sanskrit prose.

6 Light.

7 Fiery energy.

8 Inertia, darkness.

9 Ibid., 89 (14 July 1912).

meaning of unknown words."[10] And in an entry dated 31 December 1912 he writes on his Tamil studies:

> Today, in the second verse, the difficulties of the Tamil way of writing (sandhi etc.) were overcome by the intuition as well as some of the difficulties of the grammar, but the Bhashashakti[11] which used formerly to give correctly the meaning of unknown words has not recovered its habit of action.[12]

There are only relatively few passages in which Sri Aurobindo does not use any Sanskrit terms at all, as in the following paragraph where he reports on his current *sādhanā* in an altogether accessible language:

> The work now being done is to fix all gains in the lowest physical consciousness so that they may be always secure and not only present during periods, however long, of concentration, illumination or exaltation.[13]

This quotation takes us to the subject of the yogic path which Sri Aurobindo follows during this period, his special *sādhanā* as he himself often calls it in Sanskrit, with a well-known term.

The Sādhanā Programme: Sapta Catuṣṭaya

We had already proposed the image of the physicist who takes measurements in the laboratory. Behind the numberless data he records during his research there is always an objective that structures the whole undertaking. Similarly it is with Sri Aurobindo: he pursues certain goals in *yoga* and notes in his records how far he approaches them, in the process

---

10 Inertia, 91.

11 The faculty of intuitively grasping the meaning of words (*bhāṣā-śakti*).

12 *Record of Yoga*, 171.

13 Ibid., 878 (24 June 1915).

meticulously registering not only success but also obstacles, setbacks and failures. This absolute sincerity with which he records his data gives the diary its great authenticity.

At the starting point of his *sādhanā* are the *sapta catuṣṭaya* (the "seven groups of four" or quaternaries). This refers, as mentioned above, to seven mantric lines in Sanskrit each of which contains four main elements. The respective texts are given in *Record of Yoga* at the beginning of the first chapter, in Devanāgarī script and Latin transcription as well as Sri Aurobindo's detailed commentaries, though without a literal translation. The first quaternary, the *śānti catuṣṭaya*, runs as follows:

> *samatā śāntiḥ sukham hāsyam iti śānticatuṣṭayam* ।

The four elements in this line are *samatā, śāntiḥ, sukham* and *hāsyam.* Sri Aurobindo discusses the first term *samatā* (equanimity) with many differentiations on more than two pages.

> The basis of internal peace is samata, the capacity of receiving with a calm and equal mind all the attacks and appearances of outward things, whether pleasant or unpleasant, ill-fortune and good-fortune, pleasure and pain. . . .[14]

This reminds us of the *Bhagavad-Gītā*, in which mental peace is an important subject. Thus in verse 2.48 it is said, *samatvam yoga ucyate* (equality is *yoga*). Sri Aurobindo has later emphasized in his thousands of letters to disciples, the importance of *samatā* or *samatva* as the foundation of his *yoga.*[15]

The next element is *śānti*, a well-known Sanskrit word that means peace.

---

14 *Record of Yoga*, 3.

15 He often uses in this context the term equality, as a synonym of equanimity.

> Only when samata is accomplished, can shanti be perfect in the system. . . . shanti may be either a vast passive calm based on udasinata[16] or a vast joyous calm based on nati.[17] The former is apt to associate itself with a tendency to inaction and it is therefore in the latter [more dynamically active] that our Yoga must culminate.[18]

As the third element, follows *sukha* (happiness) the contrary of *duḥkha* (misery, suffering, unhappiness). It is the happiness beyond all sorrow, depression and despondency. And finally we have as the last element of this quaternary *hāsya*, whose lexical meaning is laughter, fun. For Sri Aurobindo, *hāsya* is

> the active side of sukham; it consists in an active internal state of gladness and cheerfulness which no adverse experience mental or physical can trouble.[19]

The subjects of the other six *catuṣṭaya*s are *śakti* (force); *vijñāna* (knowledge) and *śarīra* (the body), its health and well-being. In addition there are "three general *catuṣṭaya*s" which Sri Aurobindo names as *karma, brahma* and *yoga*. The latter has the four elements *śuddhi, mukti, bhukti* and *siddhi*, which we may translate as purity, liberation, enjoyment (on the basis of spiritual liberation) and perfection.

> The last or seventh is at once the means, the sum and the completion of all the rest. Its explanation is essential to the full understanding of the others and will be separately treated.[20]

Once more we realize that every subject of the *yoga* diary which we try to explore has many ramifications and grows very complex. Sri Aurobindo's treatise on the *catuṣṭaya*s comprises

---

16 Indifference to the dualities.

17 Submission; acceptance of all things as part of the divine play.

18 Ibid., 5.

19 Ibid., 5-6.

20 Ibid., 23.

twenty pages and could be (as much else, too) the subject for an entire book.

We had already given the text of the first quaternary and may note that all the others have an identical structure. As a sample, we present a literal translation of the first only: "Equanimity, peace, happiness and gladness, this is the quaternary of peace". However, we have to add that this translation does not really make much sense, because every term he uses is for him a specific term with a precise meaning.

As a summary, we may state that Sri Aurobindo's *sādhanā* has been laid down in seven programmed lines, each of which has four Sanskrit terms as basic elements. In other words, there are twenty-eight points of reference which he kept observing as a researcher on his own account. It will be left to future studies to explore whether and how frequently the individual points were referred to in the entries of the diary. In the following we will try to describe roughly which were the goals and purposes of his *sādhanā*.

A first important aspect of his sādhanā is, in tune with the path of Vedānta,[21] purification and spiritual liberation. These are to include the *whole* being (whereas in the Indian tradition, *yogī*s often did not go further than working out an opening to the light on the vital plane for instance, and then remained there). As a second aspect follows the joyful experience of life and its mastery, an aim in the tradition of Tantra. We had already come across this aspect in the first passage quoted above where he spoke of *ānanda* and of *bhoga* (enjoyment) — a term of Tantra.

Vedānta, with its deep looking within, and Tantra with its mastery of the forces of nature, these two in their conjunction already point to the integral character of Sri Aurobindo's *yoga*. They are supplemented by elements of

---

21 See Glossary.

Vaiṣṇavism, with life being ultimately regarded as *līlā* (Kṛṣṇa's play) and the Divine enjoying his own manifestation. Thus Sri Aurobindo arrives at a *yoga* which is close to the world and affirms it. His Integral Yoga, described in detail in *The Synthesis of Yoga*, is here explored and worked out in its basics, which is not to say that whatever he undertakes in this phase will also be adopted in the *yoga* he later lived and taught.

Extrasensory Experiences

In the Indian yogic literature there are many reports of supra-sensuous experiences and faculties, the so-called *siddhis*. Patañjali, the eminent *yoga* author of ancient times, has already presented them in detail 2,000 years ago in the third section of his *Yoga-Sūtras*, the Vibhūti-Pāda.[22] Telepathy, levitation, knowledge of past, present and future, supernatural hearing and seeing all belong to the numerous *siddhis* mentioned in this section.

In the system of the seven *catuṣṭayas*, the *siddhis* are discussed in the section of *vijñāna* (knowledge).[23] Sri Aurobindo mentions for example *dṛṣṭi*, the faculty of direct vision of the Truth, which he is convinced the Vedic *ṛṣis* possessed, or — related to it — the inner hearing of the Truth which is revealed in the form of a *mantra*. Or he writes on *trikāladṛṣṭi* (the vision of the three times), that is the knowledge of events in past, present and future. This, he says, can open up spontaneously through inner seeing or also through a conscious yogic effort, through

> that process which Patanjali calls sanyama [concentration] on the object, — until the mind in the observer & observed [becomes] one . . .[24]

---

22 Here *vibhūti* means "supernatural forces".

23 *Record of Yoga*, 14-22.

24 Ibid., 19.

Now if we study the *yoga* diary, we realize that Sri Aurobindo experiences many of these *siddhi*s himself and describes them in numberless details. Again and again there are messages from the inner worlds, also Sanskrit texts that he notes in Devanāgarī script, with directions and revelations. For some time he has the faculty of predicting the movement of animals that he observes, the direction in which a bird or butterfly will fly away.[25] He foresees that a companion will enter his room or that someone will visit him after a long period of time.[26] Scenes of extremely distant past ages run like a film before his inner eye and he is able to name them exactly in the terminology of the Purāṇas as this or that *manvantara* (age of the ancestor Manu). He describes events with human beings of that time and depicts in detail the outer form of animals that have ceased existing since long.[27]

He reports some incredible experiences in the field of mind–body interaction related to the subject of auto-suggestion (or affirmations, as they are known today). Health and physical beauty (*saundarya*) are part of the programme of his *sādhanā* and he notes on 10 December 1912, "the important point is that the power of the will to change formations in the body has now been physically present beyond doubt or dispute", and adds that the profuse loss of his hair has been steadily diminishing, and that the gloss and smoothness of the hair has been restored. But he also concedes that his efforts in this field are only partially successful and that he is not able to stop all symptoms of progressing age.[28]

In July 1913 he turns his attention to his teeth. Being totally absorbed in his *sādhanā* he has not brushed them for years, with

25 See, for instance, ibid., 72.

26 See, for instance, ibid., 176.

27 Ibid., 1326ff.

28 Ibid., 143-44.

the inevitable consequences. But now he applies his inner, energetic forces (though not a toothbrush, which he actually does not possess) and notes with satisfaction, ". . . for the last two or three days the *siddhi* of self-preservation and whiteness in the teeth has been swiftly recovering its force."[29] The lower teeth are already again quite white, whereas in the upper teeth still some blotches appear. Some of his companions have later confirmed that his teeth remained white and in a good condition.[30]

All this would not make inspiring reading for sceptics or rationalists but even to those it should be evident that Sri Aurobindo records his experiences with great sincerity, unvarnished. If there is failure or only partial success, he never suppresses the respective data in his diary. We get some insight here into rare yogic practices which perhaps other adepts have also known, but did not make public (and we remember that Sri Aurobindo himself did not publish them either). It was only in the late nineteenth century that the West gained some knowledge of the *siddhi*s, at first through a few writings of Swami Vivekananda and then in the twentieth century through Paramahansa Yogananda's *Autobiography of a Yogi* in which he referred to levitation, telepathy, etc.

Many *yogī*s have warned of the *siddhi*s, for they may magnify the ego of the disciples if they are pleased or proud to display their faculties and enjoy the applause of the public, fond of miracles, which may block further progress in their *sādhanā*. However, Sri Aurobindo's approach in dealing with these experiences is masterful, unexcited and scientific. They are not "miracles" for him,

> but powers of Nature, which manifest of themselves as soon as the vijnanapadma[31] in us begins to open, & are no more a

---

[29] See, for instance, Ibid., 276.

[30] K. Amrita, *Old Long Since*, 163. Source given in *The Lives of Sri Aurobindo*, 445.

[31] Lotus of knowledge.

> cause for bragging & vanity than the power of eating & breathing or anything else that is Nature's.[32]

Samādhi

Another connection with Patañjali's *yoga* exists through the numberless references to *samādhi* experiences in the diary. However, Sri Aurobindo uses the term *samādhi* in his own meaning which is not identical with that of Patañjali. The basic meaning of the word is an inward gathering, deep contemplation, ecstasy, experience of unity or a superconscious state. It is derived from the root *sam-a-dha*, that is to turn one's whole attention to a thing. For Patañjali it is the highest stage of his eight-limbed path (*Aṣṭāṅga yoga*) which he discusses especially in *Yoga-Sūtras* 1.17-23 and 3.3. The highest form of *samādhi* in classical *yoga* is the *nirbīja* or *nirvikalpa samādhi*, the *samādhi* "without seeds" (free from subconscious impressions) or "without differentiation of subject and object" (*nirvikalpa*).

From Sri Aurobindo's viewpoint this kind of *samādhi*, marked by a transcendental trance, would ultimately imply a recoil from life, which is out of the question for him. It is with reference to this point that he writes in the *Synthesis of Yoga*:

> It is evident that where our objective includes the possession of the Divine in life, a state of cessation of life cannot be the last consummating step or the highest desirable condition: yogic trance cannot be an aim, as in so many Yogic systems, but only a means, and a means not of escape from the waking existence, but to enlarge and raise the whole seeing, living and active consciousness.[33]

It is interesting to note that some modern *yoga* teachers who refer to the *Yoga-Sūtras* and teach a life-affirming *yoga* take a similar position, defining *samādhi* for instance as "absolute

---

32 Lotus of knowledge, 15.

33 *The Synthesis of Yoga*, 519.

awareness" so that it is not opposed to life as something transcendental, but rather meant to enrich and fulfil it.

In the *yoga* diary, *samādhi* is an element of the *vijñāna catuṣṭaya*, the quaternary of knowledge. Sri Aurobindo defines it as

> . . . the power by dwelling fixedly of the chaitanya[34] on the object to extend the range of knowledge & consciousness through all the three states of waking, sleep & dream, to the realisation of those tattwas [principles, elements] of the Brahman to which the ordinary waking consciousness is blind. . . .[35]

Thus, he says, access to other planes than those of the physical earth and the physical waking consciousness become possible.

The whole text of the diary contains numberless references to many kinds of *samādhi*. Especially frequent is the *svapna* variant, that is the state of sleep in which various forms of vision are seen while dreaming. The above-mentioned *nirvikalpa* is not part of these experiences, but is briefly mentioned in a note in 1926 in which Sri Aurobindo refers to a viewpoint of Vedānta, that a certain ultimate experience of the Absolute can only be realized in absolute trance.[36]

In the practice of Sri Aurobindo's later Integral Yoga, *samādhi* plays only a limited role and perhaps in some phases only. Thus Sri Aurobindo explained in a letter to a disciple:

> Experiences in trance have their utility for opening the being and preparing it, but it is only when the realisation is constant in the waking state that it is truly possessed. Therefore in this Yoga most value is given to the waking realisation and experience.[37]

---

34 Consciousness, awareness.

35 *Record of Yoga*, 22.

36 Ibid., 1338.

37 *The Integral Yoga: Selected Letters of Sri Aurobindo*, Pondicherry: Sri Aurobindo Ashram Trust 1993, 154.

With these notes on a classical subject of *yoga*, we conclude our report on the *yoga* diary and its manifold contents. It offers to scholars an immense mass of material which has yet to be explored in special individual studies, and those readers who dare to go into this difficult text will make many interesting discoveries.[38] It is like a "closeup" which presents to us an early phase of Sri Aurobindo's *yoga* path, with many significant details and important background knowledge for understanding parts of his work *The Synthesis of Yoga*.[39] However we should qualify this by saying that those who refrain from reading the *Record* will not miss anything that would be of essential importance for the practice of Integral Yoga, which has been expounded by Sri Aurobindo over and over again in numberless writings.

The diary at times also refers to external events if they are relevant to his *sādhanā* and inner work; often this included his concentrating on certain events (with varying success) so that they should develop in a certain direction which he considered desirable from the evolutionary viewpoint. But the whole text does not contain, for instance, references to his meetings or correspondence with Paul or Mirra Richard, with the exception of a brief note on 19 January 1912 where he writes, "Letter from P.R." (Paul Richard).

---

38 D. Banerji has published a first detailed study of *Record of Yoga* in 2012 (see Literature).

39 See the detailed notes of the editors of the *Synthesis* (Complete Works): "The system of seven (*sapta*) sets of four elements (*catuṣṭaya*) evidently underlies the structure of Part IV of *The Synthesis of Yoga . . .*" (*The Synthesis of Yoga*, 914).

9

Meeting with Mirra
(1914)

IN the early morning of 29 March 1914 the train approached Pondicherry. When it was still a few miles away, Mirra had the vision of a column of light in the centre of the town, and when she left the train with Paul at the railway station, the intensity of the light continued to increase.[1]

In the afternoon both of them went to see Sri Aurobindo at his place in rue François Martin where he was expecting their arrival. He stood upstairs at the top of the staircase. Mirra had already seen a photo of him which Paul had brought back after his first visit, but perhaps due to its bad quality Mirra did not get any special inner response. It was only now, at this moment, that she knew she had reached her destination:

> As soon as I saw Sri Aurobindo I recognised in him the well-known being whom I used to call Krishna.[2]

The latter was a personality whom she had already met frequently in her inner experiences during her early youth, and with whom she had established a close spiritual relationship.

While Paul talked with Sri Aurobindo, Mirra sat silently on the floor, close to him. However, she did not listen to their talk, but was entirely turned within. Then

---

1 Iyengar, *On the Mother I*, 83.

2 *CWM*, vol. 13, *Words of the Mother* I, 39.

> . . . suddenly I felt within me as it were a great Force — Peace! Silence! massive. It came, did like this (*a gesture of sweeping at the level of the forehead*), descended like that, and stopped here (*the chest*). And when they finished talking, I stood up and left. And then I noticed that I didn't have a thought in my mind — that I knew nothing any more, understood nothing any more, that I was absolutely in a complete blank. Then I gave thanks to the Lord, and thanked Sri Aurobindo in my heart.[3]

Just a little earlier Mirra had briefly told Sri Aurobindo about her problem of not being able to achieve complete silence, and now it had come by itself — Sri Aurobindo had passed on his own realization to her. All the ideas she had developed so far for the social and spiritual welfare of the world and other concepts, had now become invalid. Her life had a new inner opening and base; it was the beginning of a lifelong collaboration with Sri Aurobindo.

In his epic *Savitri* which will be introduced in another chapter, there are some lines which perhaps refer to this first meeting:

> *Here first she met on the uncertain earth*
> *The one for whom her heart had come so far . . .*
> *Attracted as in heaven star by star,*
> *They wondered at each other and rejoiced*
> *And wove affinity in a silent gaze.*
> *A moment passed that was eternity's ray,*
> *An hour began, the matrix of new Time.*[4]

Nolini Kanta Gupta later reported how Sri Aurobindo described Mirra's inner attitude in a talk with his companions:

> He said he had never seen anywhere a self-surrender so

---

[3] Sri Aurobindo Ashram Archives and Research, April 1989, 116.

[4] *Savitri*, 393, 399.

> absolute and unreserved. He had added a comment that perhaps it was only women who were capable of giving themselves so entirely and with such sovereign ease.[5]

Mirra was undoubtedly an extraordinary lady, and remarkable also was her life until now.

Mirra's Life

Maurice Alfassa, a Turkish banker from Adrianople, belonged to the class of those many persons who went to Alexandria, Egypt in connection with the construction of the Suez Canal. There he met Mathilde Ismaloun who was born in Cairo, and married her in 1874. Both were Sephardic Jews by origin, but their religion played no role in their lives, nor in their daughter's, who was born in Paris on 21 February 1878 and was given the name Blanche Rachel Mirra Alfassa. Her parents had moved to France a year earlier and Mirra[6] grew up as a French citizen along with her elder brother Mattéo.

Even at a young age she had significant inner experiences. She found it difficult to speak of them with her mother, who was a staunch rationalist. But she persisted, and followed her spiritual path without any external guidance.

> Between 11 and 13 a series of psychic and spiritual experiences revealed to me not only the existence of God but man's possibility of uniting with Him . . . , of manifesting Him upon earth in a life divine.[7]

Several teachers appeared to her in sleep, giving her instructions, and some of them she later met on the physical plane, too. Among them was also "Krishna" and she felt that

---

[5] Nolini Kanta Gupta, *Reminiscences,* 81.

[6] At a later stage, the name is often spelt "Mira". Both versions are short forms of "Miriam".

[7] *CWM,* vol. 13, *Words of the Mother I,* 39.

one day with him "the divine work was to be done".[8]

Another significant experience she described later in her *Prayers and Meditations*: at the age of about thirteen every night she went out of her body and rose far above the city, clad in a golden robe. Then she saw all kinds of people gathering under the outspread robe, asking for help. In response, the robe extended towards them

> . . . and as soon as they had touched it, they were comforted or healed, and went back into their bodies happier and stronger than they had come out of them.[9]

At the age of fifteen she became a student at the Académie Julien, a renowned Institute of Art in Paris, and learned the classical techniques of painting. In 1897 she married the painter Henri Morisset, a student of Gustave Moreau who was also the teacher of Henri Matisse and Georges Rouault. During this period Mirra lived in a milieu of several world-famous artists, musicians and writers. She and her husband took part in various exhibitions in the salons with their own work. In 1898 their son André was born.

During this epoch there was an active interest in esotericism, and many study groups were exploring all kinds of mystic teachings as well as Far Eastern philosophies. In 1905 Mirra became a member of a "Mouvement Cosmique" which had been founded by the Frenchman Charles Barlet and Max Théon, a Polish Jew. The latter had a deep knowledge of the Kabbalah and various occult traditions. His wife Alma, who hailed from the Isle of Wight, was an expert in occultism.[10]

Mirra helped with the editing of the journal *La Revue Cosmique* and contributed especially a number of wisdom

---

8 *CWM*, vol. 13, *Words of the Mother I*, 39.

9 *CWM*, vol. 1, *Prayers and Meditations*, 81 (22 February 1914).

10 Her civil name was Mary-Christine Woodroff-Ward.

teachings translated from the English language. She was also in-charge of a group named *Idéa*. Various members of society from the fields of culture and politics met in Henri Morisset's studio to discuss questions of life and philosophy. At this time Mirra tried intensively to establish constant contact with the inner Divine and she achieved the realization of the psychic being shortly before the end of 1905.[11]

In 1906 and 1907 Mirra visited Max Théon and his wife in their house in Tlemcen, Algeria, spending a long period of time with them studying occultism and undergoing many inner experiences. During these stays she came to appreciate especially the practical knowledge of Alma. The latter died a year later of pneumonia while travelling on the Isle of Jersey. Subsequently Max Théon discontinued all his activities and withdrew to Tlemcen for the rest of his life, until 1927.

In 1908 the relationship of Mirra and Herni Morisset came to an end and they divorced. Meanwhile, Mirra had met Paul Richard who gave impressive talks at the *Idéa* circle, and they began a partnership, at first with no intention to marry. But Richard, too, had divorced and was required to live in well-ordered circumstances in order to obtain visitation rights for his three children. So he asked Mirra whether they could marry, and she agreed in May 1911, although she was basically not interested in marital relations with him. Rather she had realized that (in spite of his philosophical and spiritual interests) a certain adverse āsuric power stood behind his personality and that it would be her challenge to deal with it and try to convert it, that is to say to turn it towards the Light.[12] Thus it was not a happy relationship, but a constant struggle. However, Richard played a positive role in Mirra's life in so

---

11 "Psychic being" is a term in Sri Aurobindo's Yoga, see Glossary. Also see as a source *Mother's Agenda*, vol. 12, 15 April 1972.

12 *Mother's Agenda*, vol. 2, 5 November 1961.

far as he took her out into the world through his manifold interests and activities — especially, of course, to Pondicherry.

Richard wrote a few books such as *L'ò ther Vivant* (The Living Ether) which — as the Mother later explained — were based in essence on her knowledge which he put into a good French: "I would tell him my experiences, and he would write them down."[13] After he had become a lawyer he entered politics and proved to be an excellent orator who could address an audience very effectively.

After returning from his first visit to Pondicherry in 1910, Paul told Mirra about Sri Aurobindo, but he was mainly impressed by his aspect of knowledge, without being able to appreciate properly his spiritual personality. He told Mirra that he would take her to Pondicherry as soon as possible, and this happened now, four years later.

We can gather from some of Mirra's diary notes how deeply she was touched by the meeting with Sri Aurobindo.[14] Thus she noted on 30 March 1914:

> It matters little that there are thousands of beings plunged in the densest ignorance, He whom we saw yesterday is on earth; his presence is enough to prove that a day will come when darkness shall be transformed into light, and Thy reign shall be indeed established upon earth.[15]

A few days later she adds:

> A great joy, a deep peace reign in me, and yet all my inner constructions have vanished like a vain dream. . . . It seems to me that I am being born to a new life and all the methods,

---

13 *Mother's Agenda*, vol. 2, 5 November 1961.

14 She had started the diary in 1912 when she noted down her inner experiences regularly after her morning meditation. Extracts from it were published in 1932 under the title *Prières et Méditations* (Prayers and Meditations).

15 *CWM*, vol. 1, *Prayers and Meditations,* 113.

> the habits of the past can no longer be of any use. It seems to me that what I thought were results is nothing more than a preparation.[16]

Founding the Journal Arya

Paul Richard had come to Pondicherry to run for a seat in the Paris Chamber of Deputies but in the end he got only 231 votes, whereas the winner — Paul Bluysen — won more than 33,000 votes. Sri Aurobindo had tried through letters to Motilal Roy to promote Richard's campaign but it was in vain, as Richard could not reach any specific section of the population. Moreover the elections were manipulated in various ways, as usual.

Now the question was whether he would depart with Mirra. But they decided to stay. Richard proposed to Sri Aurobindo a joint project: the publication of a journal that was to be named *Arya*. If we look up the word *ārya* in a Sanskrit dictionary, we find meanings such as "venerable, honourable man" and not the later ideologically disfigured re-interpretation of the word Aryan. Sri Aurobindo explains its true significance as follows:

> The word in its original use expressed not a difference of race, but a difference of culture. For in the Veda the Aryan peoples are those who had accepted a particular type of selfculture, of inward and outward practice, of ideality, of aspiration.

The Aryan in Sri Aurobindo's sense strives to overcome obstacles which block human progress, "for in everything he seeks truth, in everything right, in everything height and freedom".[17]

The journal was published in English in Pondicherry; there was an identical parallel edition in French brought out under

---

16 *CWM*, vol. 1, *Prayers and Meditations*, 114-16 (1 April 1914, 3 April 1914).

17 *Essays in Philosophy and Yoga*, 441-43.

the title *Revue de la Grande Synthèse,* with Paul and Mirra translating from the English text. The aims of the journal were described in a brochure as follows: its purpose was "a systematic study of the highest problems of existence . . ." as well as "the formation of a vast synthesis of knowledge, harmonising the diverse religious traditions of humanity, occidental as well as oriental". Another objective was ". . . the unification of intellectual and scientific disciplines with those of intuitive experience."[18]

It was planned to publish studies on philosophy and comparative religion: Sri Aurobindo's translations of passages from the *Ṛgveda* and the Upaniṣads and wisdom texts and contributions on the growth of consciousness based on each author's own research and on ancient traditions. Since his arrival in Pondicherry, Sri Aurobindo had written articles and studies on numberless subjects in several notebooks, which served now as a basis for his contributions. However, rather than editing these texts, he rewrote them from scratch.

The first edition was published on 15 August 1914, Sri Aurobindo's birthday. There is even a small entry in the *yoga* diary in which he notes the active interest of the subscribers.[19] He contributed around 90 per cent of the texts, and in the earlier editions there was additionally a series by Paul Richard titled "The Eternal Wisdom". Mirra looked after the management of the journal and was doing the major part of the French translations for the *Revue*. The office was in the same house which Sri Aurobindo inhabited with his companions at rue François Martin, with Saurin officially in-charge of it.

With the exception of *Savitri,* all the major works of Sri Aurobindo were published in the *Arya* in their first versions, which were later often edited and enlarged for the book

---

18 Iyengar, *On the Mother I,* 106.

19 *Record of Yoga,* 600.

publications. We may especially mention *The Life Divine*, *The Synthesis of Yoga*, *The Secret of the Veda*, *The Ideal of Human Unity* and *The Human Cycle*.[20] There are some other titles such as *The Future Poetry* and *The Foundations of Indian Culture* which are also based on contributions first published by Sri Aurobindo in the *Arya*.

Two weeks before the publication of the first edition of the journal, on 28 July 1914, the First World War broke out. Paul was drafted for military service, but he was somehow able to evade it. However, due to his contact with Sri Aurobindo and his circle he found himself in the bad books of the British, who still considered the Nationalists as dangerous revolutionaries. Therefore, the British put pressure on the French, so Paul Richard was forced to leave Pondicherry on 22 February 1915, one day after Mirra's birthday. She would have liked very much to remain with Sri Aurobindo, but perhaps he believed that the right moment for a close collaboration with Mirra had not yet come, and therefore he did not hold her back.

The revolutionaries in Pondicherry too came under pressure as a result of the war, since the French authorities were urged by the British to deport them. That is why some of them, like Bharati, were considering emigration to Algeria and made this proposal to Sri Aurobindo at the end of 1914. However, he rejected it with the brief commentary: "I am not going to budge an inch from Pondicherry".[21]

When one day he somehow learned that the danger of his deportation was becoming serious, he informed Mirra in Paris. Now as chance would have it, her brother Mattéo worked at the colonial office and was responsible for such matters. So she contacted him

---

[20] The latter book was originally published under the title *The Psychology of Human Development*.

[21] Purani Talks, Manuscripts. Quoted in *The Lives of Sri Aurobindo*, 258.

> . . . and he got the ratification paper in his hands — he put it at the bottom of his drawer. It disappeared completely, and we never heard of it again.[22]

This deliberate inactivity of her brother was, in Mirra's eyes, the most important official act he ever performed in his life; it was of great consequence for Sri Aurobindo's future.

Meanwhile, before his departure, Paul Richard transferred all rights concerning the *Arya* to Sri Aurobindo; now the 64 pages of the journal had to be prepared by him alone every month. But the French edition was stopped in February 1915. Moreover, Paul and Mirra left behind some manuscripts for serial publication, with Mirra contributing a compilation with spiritual maxims from various sources. Sri Aurobindo was to continue this work for another six years, until January 1921.

For Mirra the departure from Pondicherry is a difficult, unbearable blow. On 3 March 1915 she notes on board the Japanese ship *Kaga Maru*:

> Solitude, a harsh, intense solitude, and always this strong impression of having been flung headlong into a hell of darkness! Never at any moment of my life, in any circumstances, have I felt myself living in surroundings so entirely opposite to all that I am conscious of as true, so contrary to all that is the essence of my life.

Mirra turns to her inner Master, invoking him,

> O Lord, what have I done that Thou hast thrown me thus into the sombre Night?[23]

Before describing the further course of events, in the following chapter we will introduce those main works of Sri Aurobindo which originated from the *Arya*.

---

22 *Mother's Agenda*, vol. 10, 4 January 1969.

23 *CWM*, vol. 1, *Prayers and Meditations*, 294.

10

The Main Works

The Life Divine

The earliest preoccupation of man in his awakened thought and, as it seems, his inevitable and ultimate preoccupation — for it survives the longest periods of scepticism and returns after every banishment — is also the highest which his thought can envisage. It manifests itself in the divination of Godhead, the impulse towards perfection, the search after pure Truth and unmixed Bliss, the sense of a secret immortality.[1]

The soul is not bound by the formula of mental humanity; it did not begin with that and will not end with it; it had a prehuman past, it has a superhuman future.[2]

The body will be turned by the power of the spiritual consciousness into a true and fit and perfectly responsive instrument of the Spirit. This new relation of the spirit and the body assumes — and makes possible — a free acceptance of the whole of material Nature in place of a rejection.[3]

. . . For Ananda [bliss] is the very essence of the Brahman, it is the supreme nature of the omnipresent Reality.[4]

---

1 *The Life Divine*, 3.

2 Ibid., 790.

3 Ibid., 1022.

4 Ibid., 1025.

THE *Life Divine* is generally known as Sri Aurobindo's main philosophical work, which is true, although in a special sense: it is not philosophy for its own sake with which he is occupied, but he has used an elevated philosophical language for expressing his spiritual vision of the world. Preceding the individual chapters, there are short quotations from the Vedas, the Upaniṣads or the *Bhagavad-Gītā* which show that the seers of ancient times had already touched in essence certain ideas and insights. These are in tune with Sri Aurobindo's own vision and he now takes them up, reformulates them for our modern mentality and at times develops them considerably further.

Many of these quotations had often been interpreted differently in the Indian tradition, but in the light of his own vision he reveals their true and original significance. Thus he builds a bridge from Vedic times and demonstrates to his readers that he is not moving in vacant space with his expositions, but rather picking up the thread of something that had already been worked out and realized, at least partially, in a first attempt.

His language is at times difficult to follow, with long involved phrases more frequently found in Latin or high level German than in modern American English or in the common English of today. Therefore some readers consider certain texts as hardly accessible. But Sri Aurobindo is a seer with a global vision. When he writes on a subject, he has an eye on every aspect of it and treats it as comprehensively as possible in our verbal language, which sometimes results in rather complex sentence constructions.

The Life Divine is the proper book for intellectual readers who ask deep questions on the meaning of existence, on the sense of the world, who are looking for well-founded answers. For such readers the book with its 1,000 pages is a unique work that ascends to rare heights in its discourse; it gets to the bottom of the depths of human existence as well. But it is throughout a *spiritual* philosophy, which might be one of the reasons why it only rarely attracts attention in our Western universities. For instance: Sri Aurobindo makes a case for belief in reincarnation; he assumes that the individual soul of humans is reborn again and again, developing itself through many births and different kinds of existences. So on this point, and many others, he holds a position which appears somewhat foreign to Western philosophy and its methods. None the less there have been great personalities of our hemisphere who have recognized and appreciated the importance of his work, and it was especially due to this eminent book that he was twice nominated for the Nobel Prize in literature.[5]

Below we shall attempt to briefly summarize its content. To facilitate this effort, we will avoid complex issues in our exposition (which there are in great number) and only present in simple language some basic statements of Sri Aurobindo on humanity, the universe and the destiny of mankind.

This world, humanity, are part of a great plan: the supreme Divine Being has created the universe for his own joy and self-experience. The earthly existence is initially marked by inconscience and inanimateness, but irrevocably implanted in it are lines of development that move towards their realization through evolution over immensely long periods of time. At first the evolution progresses very slowly, starting with the principle of Matter from which Life and then Mind develop. This process becomes possible because whatever unfolds, is already involved in the seed. In this context Sri Aurobindo speaks of an involution that precedes evolution.

But the principle of Mind is not the final destination in evolution. It can only receive a limited Light and is, in its perception of the world, characterized by fragmentary vision and action and is accompanied by conflict and struggle. Higher

---

[5] See Chapter 14.

stages of consciousness and a blossoming of the soul on the heart level awaits human beings. It is their destiny to attain the "supramental consciousness" which enables them to live, to act, here in this world in tune with the highest Truth and thus to participate in the joy of a truly divine life on earth. For neither liberation into a transcendent bliss, connected with a rejection or contempt for life on earth, nor a soul-less abiding in material wealth and progress are for Sri Aurobindo the goal of the journey.

For the individual, evolution proceeds through reincarnation: the soul is not really imprisoned in this world (as often believed in the Indian tradition) but rather it develops through numberless experiences whose essences it assimilates, and through which it progresses lifetime to lifetime. At a certain stage humans reach a point where they become aware of their true destiny and consciously take charge of it. At this moment the deliberate spiritual path begins through which evolution is accelerated, and in which course humans experience different forms of "transformation", resulting in a higher and wider consciousness and ultimately in a physical being freed from illness and decay, open to the divine Force and able to receive it.

If a great number of beings develop in this way, an evolution of society becomes possible, which in turn generates new forms of community. Truth, harmony, love and beauty are values which would dominate in this kind of society, according to Sri Aurobindo's vision. But in our "real" world, as it is at present, humans are facing pain and suffering. For evolution progresses through a thick crust of Ignorance which often resists our aspirations, and at times even creates an impression that there is a standstill, or a backward movement. Sri Aurobindo comprehensively discusses this subject of suffering in the world, pointing out that it is the Divine himself who suffers in humans taking pain upon himself. However, there will be future stages of evolution, Sri Aurobindo says, in which the development proceeds from Light to greater Light and not from Ignorance to Knowledge. He concludes with this statement:

> Our evolution in the Ignorance with its chequered joy and pain of self-discovery and world-discovery, its half-fulfilments, its constant finding and missing, is only our first state. It must lead inevitably towards an evolution in the Knowledge, a self-finding and selfunfolding of the Spirit, a self-revelation of the Divinity in things in that true power of itself in Nature which is to us still a Supernature.[6]

So far our summary of the contents of *The Life Divine*. It is a book with a bold vision, marked by a multiplicity of perspectives. The vision is basically optimistic, but subjects such as ignorance, darkness and falsehood are not ignored. Sri Aurobindo actually dedicates some complete chapters to these subjects. Often he also discusses in great length other philosophical positions, especially that of Śaṅkara for instance, in order to reject them if they disagree with his own perception, or, to elevate them to a higher level.[7] Some of these sections are no doubt more relevant to Indian readers than to Westerners. As a rule, the latter need not be persuaded, for example, that a spirituality focused on the Beyond and despising the world is not the right approach, whereas in India this was a subject of great importance.

At times the reading is also difficult because Sri Aurobindo creates his own terminology which is not familiar even to those who are well-acquainted with Indian philosophy. Thus we find

---

6 See Chapter 14, 1070.

7 The great philosopher Śaṅkara (788–820) taught Māyāvāda (Illusionism), which from Sri Aurobindo's viewpoint has led the thinking of many Indians into a wrong direction, resulting in a disdain of life and the world, as it was ultimately considered as unreal. However, Śaṅkara's followers have rejected this criticism.

new words such as *overmind* or *supermind* and also meet unfamiliar compounds like Real-Idea, Conscious-Being or Knowledge-Force. But those who overcome these difficulties can discover a great wealth of spiritual insight in Sri Aurobindo's magnificent work. The Sanskrit vocabulary is limited to some 150 terms such as *atman* and *brahman* which are commonly found in Indian spiritual literature and explained in many glossaries.

After the first serial publication of the text from August 1914 to January 1919 in the *Arya*, the book was brought out in two volumes and three parts in 1939-40. For this edition Sri Aurobindo added a few chapters and revised some others. In 1949 an American edition appeared in a single volume, and in the current edition of the *Complete Works* the text is brought out in volumes 21-22.

The Synthesis of Yoga

> All life is Yoga[8]
>
> For the sadhaka of the integral Yoga it is necessary to remember that no written Shastra, however great its authority or however large its spirit, can be more than a partial expression of the eternal knowledge. He will use, but never bind himself even by the greatest Scripture. Where the Scripture is profound, wide, catholic, it may exercise upon him an influence of the highest good and of incalculable importance. It may be associated in his experience with his awakening to crowning verities and his realisation of the highest experiences.[9]
>
> . . . But knowledge is not complete without works; for the Will in being also is God and not the Being or its self-aware silent existence alone, and if works find their culmination in knowledge, knowledge also finds its fulfilment in works. And,

---

[8] *The Synthesis of Yoga*, 8.

[9] Ibid., 55.

> here too, love is the crown of knowledge; for love is the delight of union. . . . Therefore to approach God by love is to prepare oneself for the greatest possible spiritual fulfilment.[10]

In his work *The Life Divine* Sri Aurobindo has dealt mainly with basic questions of life such as the meaning of existence, the destiny of humans and their potential to develop. In some chapters, as for example "The Triple Transformation",[11] he outlines the stages of spiritual evolution of man, and here we also find some hints relevant to *yoga*. But it is left to *The Synthesis of Yoga* to go deeper into this subject. In this work too, the language is elevated and demanding and we do not find any simple instructions that can be easily put into practice.

Sri Aurobindo explains the reasons in a note in the *Arya*:

> As in *The Life Divine*, he is more concerned ". . . with a deep study of the principles underlying the methods rather than with a popular statement of methods and disciplines. But without this previous study of principles the statement of methods would have been unsound and not really helpful. There are no short cuts to an integral perfection."[12]

In the context of contemporary yogic literature the *Synthesis* would be classified as "yogic philosophy" and can be considered as the most important and comprehensive work in this field. There are also many hints of the practice of *yoga*, but they are found in a more concrete form in *Letters on Yoga*. It is the great merit of the *Synthesis* that the essence of all yogic paths and their secrets are worked out with great clarity and depth.

The book has four parts: the first three deal with the *trimārga* of the *Bhagavad-Gītā*, that is the threefold path of works, knowledge and love (*karma, jñāna* and *bhakti*). In the section

---

10 *The Synthesis of Yoga*, 546-47.

11 *The Life Divine*, 922.

12 *Essays in Philosophy and Yoga*, 104.

on knowledge Sri Aurobindo also discusses other paths of the Indian tradition, such as *haṭha-yoga* and *rāja-yoga*. The subject of the fourth part is his own specific contribution: Integral Yoga, the *yoga* of self-perfection. In the last chapter of this part, higher stages of consciousness, for instance the intuitive mind or supermind are treated.

Sri Aurobindo, in referring to paths of the Indian tradition, first describes their conventional meaning and working; he then proceeds to explain their use in the context of an Integral Yoga, in some cases giving them, to a certain extent, a new role and orientation in tune with his own vision. To analyse this in detail will not be possible here. But we can describe some essentials of his philosophy of *yoga*, finding an important source for this purpose in the 11th chapter of Part Four, "The Principle of the Integral Yoga", in which Sri Aurobindo himself recapitulates, in a kind of synopsis, the most important points of his work.[13] Following is a brief summary especially based on this text:

Classical *yoga* basically proceeds by taking up a particular aspect of our being such as thinking, feeling, the will or body as a starting point for achieving union with the Divine by offering this specific part to Him through an appropriate discipline.

> In an ordinary Yoga one main power of being or one group of its powers is made the means, vehicle, path. In a synthetic Yoga all powers will be combined and included in the transmuting instrumentation.[14]

The most well-known paths of the Indian tradition are *haṭha-yoga* and rāja-yoga, the triple path of the *Bhagavad-Gītā* and tāntric *yoga*. *Haṭha-yoga* starts with the body, regulating the physical and nervous currents of energy through certain postures (*āsana*s) and breathing techniques (*prāṇāyāma*). The

---

[13] *The Synthesis of Yoga*, 609 f.

[14] Ibid., 609.

awakening of the *kuṇḍalinī,* the hidden serpent-power and its ascent through the *cakra*s (subtle-physical centres) culminating in the experience of the divine consciousness, is also part of this path.

Rāja-yoga starts with the mind, it purifies and stills its movements, bringing about a great inward gathering and concentration, also supported by *āsana*s and *prāṇāyāma*. In this process the mind of a person may develop extraordinary capacities of will and knowledge, but the highest goal here, too, is union with the divine consciousness.

In the triple path the systematic use of purified reason and concentration (*jñāna-yoga*) ultimately brings about knowledge and the vision of the Divine. In the path of works the individual will is turned to the will of the Supreme and thus gradually union with the Lord and Master of the universe is achieved. In the path of devotion and love (*bhakti-yoga*) the feelings are turned towards the Divine, they are purified more and more until union with the divine Being is realised.

In this process, each type of *yoga* is marked by the means it uses,

> thus the Hathayogic process is psycho-physical, the Rajayogic mental and psychic, the way of knowledge is spiritual and cognitive, the way of devotion spiritual, emotional and aesthetic, the way of works spiritual and dynamic by action.[15]

Furthermore, there is the tāntric discipline which in its essence is a synthesis:

> It has seized on the large universal truth that there are two poles of being whose essential unity is the secret of existence, Brahman and Shakti, Spirit and Nature, and that Nature is power of the spirit or rather is spirit as power. To raise

15 *The Synthesis of Yoga*, 610.

> nature in man into manifest power of spirit is its method and it is the whole nature that it gathers up for the spiritual conversion.[16]

In Tantra there is, as in *haṭha-yoga*, the ascent of the *kuṇḍalinī* and the awakening of the *cakra*s, and, as in *rāja-yoga*, the purification of the mind, meditation and concentration as well as elements of the triple path. But another essential element is added: while the other paths traditionally focus on *mukti* (spiritual liberation) and ultimately strive for a transcendent goal, for the tāntric *yogī*s there was also the aspect of a joyful experience of the force of the Spirit here in life itself,

> . . . which the others may take incidentally on the way, in part, casually, but avoid making a motive or object. It is a bolder and larger system.[17]

Now, in his synthesis, Sri Aurobindo takes up all these *yoga* paths but does not simply content himself with putting them together by way of addition. There is also, in the process of connecting them, a fundamental new orientation. His Integral Yoga

> starts from the method of Vedanta to arrive at the aim of the Tantra. . . . Our synthesis takes man as a spirit in mind much more than a spirit in body and assumes in him the capacity to begin on that level, to spiritualise his being by the power of the soul in mind, opening itself directly to a higher spiritual force and being. . . .[18]

Therefore, in Sri Aurobindo's *yoga* there is not an ascent of the awakened *śakti* upwards from the lowest *cakra*, but the process is changed into a descent:[19]

---

16 *The Synthesis of Yoga*, 611.

17 Ibid., 612.

18 Ibid.

19 See also Satprem's comprehensive discussion of this point in his title *Sri Aurobindo or the Adventure of Consciousness*, chapters 4 and 5.

> To arrive by the shortest way at the largest development of spiritual power and being and divinise by it a liberated nature in the whole range of human living is our inspiring motive.[20]

Methods of *haṭha-yoga* may be optionally applied, those of *rāja-yoga* are brought into play as "an informal element". Of central importance is self-surrender: the comprehensive self-giving of a human being to the Divine who, through his Light and inner direction, guides each one gradually towards the integral spiritual life. The spiritual liberation of the Indian tradition remains an important step in this system but it is only a first step, a pre-condition for the second step: the joyful experience of the cosmic Oneness of the Divine.

Finally, there is the culmination in the third stage, with human beings dynamically realizing divine oneness with all beings, therefore participating actively and with intuitive understanding in the Divine's intention for humanity.

> The individual Yoga then turns from its separateness and becomes a part of the collective Yoga of the divine Nature in the human race. The liberated individual being, united with the Divine in self and spirit, becomes in his natural being a self-perfecting instrument for the perfect outflowering of the Divine in humanity.[21]

This *yoga* aims at development, at an elevation of the mental into the full spiritual and supramental nature. "Therefore this Integral Yoga of knowledge, love and works has to be extended into a *yoga* of spiritual and gnostic self-perfection." Thus the triple path "becomes a keynote of the whole *yoga*", for it enables the soul to ascend to its highest intensities and divine oneness.[22]

---

20 *The Synthesis of Yoga*, 613.

21 Ibid., 614.

22 Ibid.

This is, roughly, Sri Aurobindo's yogic philosophy in *The Synthesis of Yoga*. It is a work that remained incomplete (which, however, we hardly note in view of its great volume of 900 pages). We know from a statement in one of Sri Aurobindo's letters that he originally intended to write more chapters after "The Yoga of Self-Perfection" but did not find time to do so.[23] Some parts of the text were revised in different periods from the 1920s up to the 1940s and at times also enlarged. In the *Complete Works*, the book has been brought out as volumes 23-24 and it contains, as compared to earlier editions, some additional material as for example an incomplete chapter on "The Supramental Time-Consciousness".

The Ideal of Human Unity

> . . . and such possibilities as the proposed United States of Europe.[24]

One of the many mantric words of wisdom of the Indian seers of ancient times is *ekam advitīyam brahma:* the *Brahman* is one without a second.[25] This motif of the One we find frequently in the sacred writings of India. For Sri Aurobindo, oneness was an important subject to which he referred not only in the context of *yoga* in the sense of the individual becoming one with the Divine, but he extended the idea also to politics and society where for millennia we have often been experiencing the contrary, that is to say national egoism, conflict, war and division. Or, if there was unity, then all too often it was enforced through the oppression of a more or less brutal empire.

---

23 *The Synthesis of Yoga*, 913-14.

24 *The Human Cycle,* 336 fn.

25 *Chāndogya Upaniṣad*, VI.2.1.

In *The Ideal of Human Unity,* Sri Aurobindo tries to explore the possibilities of a progressive-minded humanity in the future. To write on such a subject necessarily implies referring to current historical events, taking them as a starting-point for a look into the future. But history never stands still. In the decades following the writing of the text some fundamental changes took place which Sri Aurobindo could no longer consider, although in later revisions during the 1930s and 1940s he reformulated some of his statements. The political world of his time was especially marked by the dominant position of powerful empires such as England, Germany and France, whereas other nations such as Russia and America played, for the time being, only side roles.

But apart from these analyses with a temporal background, there are also basic ideas expressed in a context of the philosophy of history, which are of great value even today, for Sri Aurobindo expounds with great force his vision of a humanity that overcomes division and nationalistic fragmentation, that develops into a free grouping in the framework of a world union. However, a mere outer union in the form of uniting empires, for instance, would not be the real goal, but might result in a mighty state machinery, oppressive to the individual. It is only when human beings are given a social setting enabling them to live a happy, self-determined and fulfilled life that the ideal of unity would be really worthwhile.

At the end of the book Sri Aurobindo concludes by stating that a true realization of this ideal can only take place on a spiritual basis. What is required is the growing knowledge "that there is a secret Spirit, a divine Reality, in which we are all one".[26] Humanity should make efforts

---

[26] *The Human Cycle,* 577.

> to live out this knowledge and bring about a kingdom of this divine Spirit upon earth. By its growth within us oneness with our fellow-men will become the leading principle of all our life, not merely a principle of cooperation but a deeper brotherhood, a real and an inner sense of unity and equality and a common life.[27]

In the end there would be a spiritual unity "which would create a psychological oneness not dependent on any intellectual or outward uniformity", always ready "to enrich its secure unity by a free inner variation and a freely varied outer self-expression".[28]

But Sri Aurobindo is sufficiently realistic to know that humanity is still far from such a stage of development. Therefore he concedes that in a preliminary stage the development has to progress through "mechanical means" which probably refers to processes of unification, as they took place after the Second World War in Europe, when a gradual progress was achieved in the fields of economic and political co-operation. In a footnote that was added at a later revision, he actually mentions the possibility of the "United States of Europe"[29] and points out that in the present stage a world union would not be conceivable. Rather we would have to assume that, for the time being, there would be several smaller agglomerations such as the Commonwealth.

The text was already published in 1919 as a book and a second revised version was brought out in 1950. The revision was done mainly before the Second World War, but even after that, Sri Aurobindo still added a few updating footnotes and a supplementary chapter, for considering more recent developments.

---

27 *The Human Cycle,* 577.

28 Ibid., 578.

29 See quotation at the beginning of this section.

The Human Cycle

The Human Cycle was first published under the title *The Psychology of Social Development*. The occasion of the series in the *Arya* was Sri Aurobindo's reading of a newspaper article in which the theses of Karl Lamprecht (1856–1915, a German professor of history) was discussed. Lamprecht had developed a new type of historiography in which he abandoned the traditional descriptive method. In his approach he tried not merely to report events exactly, but to look deeper and discover patterns that underlie the growth of nations. Then he arrived at the thesis that peoples develop in certain stages of cultural ages which come into being in connection with the economic development. He called these stages symbolism, typism, conventionalism, individualism and subjectivism. The latter represents, for example, individual commerce and money economy after about CE 1700.

Although Sri Aurobindo could not accept any kind of interpretation that forces history and its course into a corset of particular fixed sequences, he found Lamprecht's genetic approach basically interesting and took it as a starting-point for his own independent deliberations on the philosophy of history.[30] Focusing on ancient India, he calls the Vedic age "symbolic".

> The religious institution of sacrifice governs the whole society and all its hours and moments, and the ritual of the sacrifice is at every turn and in every detail . . . mystically symbolic.[31]

Next follows the "typal" stage,

---

30 In Germany, there was much resistance against Lamprecht and his ideas, some of his academic colleagues vehemently rejected his new approach. However, the reception was much friendlier in countries such as France and the US.

31 *The Human Cycle*, 7.

> predominantly psychological and ethical. . . . Religion becomes then a mystic sanction for the ethical motive and discipline. . . . This typal stage creates the great social ideals which remain impressed upon the human mind even when the stage itself is passed.[32]

And third is the "conventional" stage.

> The conventional stage of human society is born when the external supports, the outward expressions of the spirit or the ideal become more important than the ideal, the body or even the clothes more important than the person.

This is the period when the caste system is formed, a distortion of the original system in which birth was not the main factor of the social order, ". . . for faculty and capacity prevailed."[33]

Then followed the "individualistic" age in Europe, marked by "a revolt of reason, in its culmination a triumphal progress of physical science".[34] In this epoch democratic rights such as the equality of all humans and equal opportunities are established, the individual is not considered anymore a mere cog in the wheel but achieves a status as a person with a soul, and an individual mission in life. This age was arising and spreading especially in Europe, " . . . the East has entered into it only by contact and influence, not from an original impulse."[35]

Finally, in the fifth stage there is the "subjective" age in which humans try to look deeper and to know what is behind the surface.

> It is a step towards self-knowledge and toward living in and from the self. . . . Everything depends on how that step

32 *The Human Cycle*, 11.

33 Ibid., 11-12.

34 Ibid., 16.

35 Ibid., 15.

> is taken, to what kind of subjectivity we arrive and how far we go in self-knowledge; for here the dangers of error are as great and far-reaching as the results of right seeking.[36]

In this section Sri Aurobindo also discusses in detail the cultural path of the Germans and analyses the errors that brought about their disaster in the first half of the twentieth century. He points out that the true goal of every society should be

> first to provide the conditions of life and growth by which individual Man, — not isolated men or a class or a privileged race, but all individual men according to their capacity, — and the race through the growth of its individuals may travel towards this divine perfection.[37]

At this point we observe that Sri Aurobindo returns once more to his basic motif of an evolutionary development towards the Divine, upon which he then proceeds to elaborate. The subjective age, he says, will turn into a spiritual and ultimately perhaps even "gnostic" period, that is to say supramental progression, with humans developing the capacity to be guided by a divine Light in whatever they think and do.[38]

The Foundations of Indian Culture

In the Indian philosophical tradition there existed a highly developed culture of debate. Thus we know of Śaṅkara: even at a young age he went to see the most renowned scholars of his country to discuss the Vedic writings and their commentaries. In a certain way, Sri Aurobindo was able to go back to this tradition when he decided to cross swords with the well-known English cultural critic, William Archer. Due to his education in England, the art of debating as taught at British universities and in parliament was also quite familiar to him.

---

36 *The Human Cycle*, 56.

37 Ibid., 65-66.

38 Ibid., 181.

Archer was one of those Englishmen who used to look down on Indians, on their religion and society, with snootiness, although in politics his positions were rather progressive and he was in favour of India to soon be granted independence. But Sri Aurobindo believed that his broadsides against the country and its society, published under the title "India and the Future", should be countered. At first John Woodroffe,[39] a British author friendly towards India, had responded to Archer; now Sri Aurobindo too joined the debate with his article "Is India Civilized", vehemently defending the essence of Indian culture and using the stylistic device of polemics.

It was his purpose to restore self-confidence in his countrymen, as they were often overly impressed by the glamour of the British colonial power with its contempt of Indian culture. He raises the question,

> Why are a certain class of Indians still hypnotised in all fields by European culture and why are we all still hypnotised by it in the field of politics? Because they constantly saw all the power, creation, activity on the side of Europe, all the immobility or weakness of a static inefficient defence on the side of India. But wherever the Indian spirit has been able to react, to attack with energy and to create with *éclat*, the European glamour has begun immediately to lose its hypnotic power.[40]

Thus, in this series of essays written as a reaction to Archer the objective is not merely a rejection of his criticism, but also a dynamic reformulation of the foundations of Indian culture, through which we are given an impressive and comprehensive portrait of the Indian cultural history as well as its achievements in the fields of religion, spirituality, art, literature and politics. Sri Aurobindo comments in a central statement:

---

39 In the West, he became well known through his tāntric studies.

40 *The Renaissance in India,* 62.

> Indian culture recognises the spirit as the truth of our being and our life as a growth and evolution of the spirit. It sees the Eternal, the Infinite, the Supreme, the All; it sees this as the secret highest Self of all, this is what it calls God, the Permanent, the Real, and it sees man as a soul and power of this being of God in Nature. The progressive growth of the finite consciousness of man towards this Self, towards God, towards the universal, the eternal, the infinite, in a word his growth into spiritual consciousness by the development of his ordinary ignorant natural being into an illumined divine nature, this is for Indian thinking the significance of life and the aim of human existence.[41]

Among the sections that are especially worth reading are his comments on Indian literature, the great creations in the Sanskrit language that ". . . stand very evidently in the front rank among the world's great literature."[42] With his thorough knowledge of the subject, Sri Aurobindo proceeds to reveal the great value of literary works such as the Vedas and the Upaniṣads, the epics *Mahābhārata* and *Rāmāyaṇa* as well as the brilliant poetic creations of Kālidāsa, introducing us to the wide range of Indian culture with powerful inspiration and flowing language.

Added to this writing is an essay on "The Renaissance of India" in which Sri Aurobindo refers to the comments of the Irish poet James H. Cousins in an article with the same title, pointing out that a cultural awakening of India is of great importance for the country itself and for the world. But India, he says, must solve her problems in her own way, "through solutions arising out of her own being and from her own deepest and largest knowledge".[43]

The essays in this work were published from 1918 to 1921

---

41 *The Renaissance in India*, 214.

42 Ibid., 314.

43 Ibid., 43.

in the *Arya* and later revised by Sri Aurobindo. They first appeared as a book in 1953. In the Indian editions the book was first brought out under the title *The Foundations of Indian Culture* with the addition "And the Renaissance of India", as was also the case in volume 14 of the *Sri Aurobindo Birth Centenary Library* (1972). However in the *Complete Works of Sri Aurobindo*, vol. 20, the title has been changed into *The Renaissance in India*, with the sub-title "And Other Essays on Indian Culture".

The Future Poetry

Poetry has accompanied Sri Aurobindo throughout his life. Even as a young student in England he composed verses and at the end of his life he turned his energies once more to the epic *Savitri*. In the second half of the nineteenth century when he was born, poetry had still a higher ranking in European society than today (with the exception of the Baltic countries where the print runs of lyric volumes are still very high). The terrors of the two world wars have swept away the mood for romance and idealism.

Sri Aurobindo considered the Muse poetry as an important aspect of the new creation and spiritual world which he envisioned. In its true form he believes it to be closely connected with the term *mantra*, the inspired word received from the higher planes of consciousness.

> For neither the intelligence, the imagination nor the ear are the true or at least the deepest or highest recipients of the poetic delight, even as they are not its true or highest creators; they are only its channels and instruments: the true creator, the true hearer is the soul. The more rapidly and transparently the rest do their work of transmission, the less they make of their separate claim to satisfaction, the more directly the word reaches and sinks deep into the soul, the greater the poetry.[44]

[44] *The Future Poetry*, 12.

The true poet is the one who feels in his creation the creative joy, bliss (*ānanda*) which reflect the universal joy of the creation of the universe and its hidden rhythms, and who is able to share this joy with his readers. Evidently, this definition of poetry is miles away from the common modern understanding of the term. Actually, the title *The Future Poetry* under which his essay is published in this book is not to be interpreted as a prophecy of future developments, but rather as a pre-vision of developments as they should take place, from Sri Aurobindo's viewpoint, in a spiritual age that leads mankind to its true evolutionary future.

The occasion of his writing was a book by the Irish poet James H. Cousins titled *New Ways in English Literature* which was sent to Sri Aurobindo in 1917 for the purpose of a review in the *Arya*. But he liked it so much that in the end he published a series of thirty-two articles in his journal instead of a review. In this series he introduces his own concept of an intuitive mantric poetry and analyses under this aspect the works of well-known English and Irish authors. At the same time there are also numberless references to other eminent poets such as Goethe, Tagore, Whitman, Dante and Homer.

Some of the most important sections deal with the essence of English poetry, a subject with which Sri Aurobindo was deeply familiar. In his opinion, the English language has not always created the greatest or most perfect poetry, but "the unfettered play of poetic energy and power has been here the most abundant and brought forth the most constantly brilliant fruits". However, he concedes

> that English poetry and literature have been a far less effective force in the shaping of European culture than the poetry and literature of other tongues. . . .[45]

---

45 *The Future Poetry*, 48.

Then he proceeds to show what were the contributions of ancient Greece and Rome, of Italy, France or Germany for the cultural enrichment of Europe.

Sri Aurobindo analyses very deeply the works of poets like Keats, Shelley or Byron and discusses their creations from a spiritual viewpoint. Thus he writes of Shelley:

> The spiritual truth which had possession of Shelley's mind was higher than anything opened to the vision of any of his contemporaries, and its power and reality which was the essence of his inspiration can only be grasped, when it is known and lived, by a changed and future humanity. Light, Love, Liberty are the true godheads in whose presence his pure and radiant spirit lived; but a celestial light, a celestial love, a celestial liberty.[46]

Among German poets he mentions Goethe (to whom he has dedicated a poem) and Schiller, Heine and Nietzsche. On the latter he notes that

> . . . Nietzsche does not think, but always sees, turbidly or clearly, rightly or distortedly, but with the eye of the seer rather than with the brain of the thinker.[47]

Poets of the twentieth century like Rilke are not mentioned, since Sri Aurobindo did not read many books after moving to Pondicherry and was therefore not very much acquainted with the more recent developments in European cultural history. With reference to India, he remarks that

> the religious poetry of the later Indian tongues has for us fervours of poetic revelation which in the great classics are absent, even though no mediaeval poet can rank in power with Valmiki and Kalidasa.[48]

---

46 *The Future Poetry*, 143.

47 Ibid., 34.

48 Ibid., 39.

The Future Poetry was not published as a book during Sri Aurobindo's lifetime, as he had plans for a thorough revision which were never realized. Only a few minor word changes were made, over time, in most chapters. In an editor's note, mention is made of Sri Aurobindo's original intention that

> . . . in particular he wished to write a chapter or chapters on contemporary poetry, and was considering a treatment of the metaphysical poets of the seventeenth century.[49]

By the middle of 1950 he actually ordered some books of great authors of the twentieth century in order to write a chapter on them, but it was already too late. However, Nirodbaran has noted that he was able to read out to Sri Aurobindo some texts of a few works of modern authors whose books were found in the small Ashram library.[50]

The Secret of the Veda

Sri Aurobindo had learned Sanskrit on his own and also studied intensively the older Vedic Sanskrit, which has a great wealth of grammatical forms and whose words often carry several meanings. It is a special feature of this older language that the meanings are less fixed than in classical Sanskrit, and for this reason *R̥gveda* translations often vary considerably.

Sri Aurobindo's studies convinced him that the hymns of the *R̥gveda* had a hidden meaning which should be explored beyond the ritualistic or naturalistic interpretations. He believed that the authors expressed spiritual experiences in verses that were in agreement with his own inner exploits. As evidence he especially quoted the last verse of a hymn of the R̥ṣi Vāmadeva:

> All these are secret words that I have uttered to thee who

---

[49] *The Future Poetry*, 399.

[50] *Twelve Years with Sri Aurobindo*, 271.

> knowest, O Agni, O Disposer, words of leading, words of seer-knowledge *that express their meaning to the seer*.[51]

In *The Secret of the Veda* Sri Aurobindo shows on the basis of many passages how, according to his vision, certain terms are used with a symbolical meaning. Thus the term *go* (cow) represents rays of light or *soma* (wine), the divine bliss.[52] Gods like Indra or Agni too represent certain psychological or spiritual functions. These interpretations have no doubt a subjective element and are rarely recognized in the Western academic field. But in India some dissertations have been written on this subject which investigate, for example, whether Sri Aurobindo's symbolic meanings result in a convincing translation in all the relevant passages.

Sri Aurobindo has also translated several hymns, some of which were published in *The Secret of the Veda*, others in the supplementary volume *Hymns to the Mystic Fire*. These are not literal renderings, but rather very free translations through which he expresses his specific interpretations, giving them a powerful spiritual character. The poet Subrahmania Bharati (who studied the Vedas with Sri Aurobindo) once asked him how he had arrived at his understanding of the verses. Sri Aurobindo answered briefly, "it was shown to me".[53] And at another place he says:

> Sri Krishna has shown me the true meaning of the Vedas, not only so but he has shown me a new Science of Philology showing the process and origins of human speech so that a new Nirukta [science of etymological interpretation] can be formed and the new interpretation of the Veda based upon it.[54]

---

51 *Ṛgveda* IV.3.16. *The Secret of the Veda*, 210 (italics, W.H.).

52 M.P. Pandit has compiled all the symbolical meanings in his title *Key to Vedic Symbolism*, Dipti Publications, 1971.

53 Sri Aurobindo Circle, No. 37, 61. Quoted in S. Mishra, *Sri Aurobindo and Sanskrit*, Sri Aurobindo Society, 2000, 20.

54 *SABCL*, vol. 27, *Supplement*, 433.

Sri Aurobindo's essays on the Vedas and his translations which were published during 1914-17 and in 1920 in many editions of the *Arya* were not brought out as a book during his lifetime. We know that in this case too he had in mind a revision, with some enlargements never realized.[55] The first book edition came out in 1956 and in the *Complete Works* the title has been published as volume 15, followed by *Hymns to the Mystic Fire*.

The Īśa and Kena Upaniṣad

The Indian tradition knows 108 Upaniṣads, but only a small number of them are considered as important. The Vedāntic philosopher Śaṅkara has recognized sixteen as authentic Vedic revelations and commented on ten of them. Sri Aurobindo has also treated the same texts, by translating them and writing commentaries on several of them.

Even during his stay in Baroda he had studied intensively the Upaniṣads and written many translations and essays. In the *Arya* he took up this subject once more, revising the texts or entirely rewriting them. At first his articles on the *Īśa Upaniṣad* appeared in 1915-16, followed by the *Kena, Kaṭha* and other Upaniṣads. His treatise on the *Īśa Upaniṣad* with translation and commentary is the most important. He wrote comprehensive notes on those eighteen verses, with philosophical comments in clear and quite accessible language.

Even in the first verse there is the grandiose image of a universe formed by the Divine:

> All this is for the habitation by the Lord, whatsoever is individual universe of movement in the universal motion.

And in the second verse it says,

> Doing verily works in this world one should wish to live a hundred years.[56]

[55] *The Secret of the Veda*, 602.

[56] *Īśa Upaniṣad*, 4.

What is remarkable is the world-affirming position of the ancient author which is in tune with Sri Aurobindo's own thought. In his commentary he notes:

> Thus, the third movement of the Upanishad is a justification of life and works, which were enjoined upon the seeker of the Truth in its second verse. Works are the essence of Life. Life is a manifestation of the Brahman.[57]

The *Kena Upaniṣad* dates back to a more ancient period and enquires of the deeper, hidden plane behind our thought, life and perception. It leads to "That which is unexpressed by the word, that by which the word is expressed" — the *Brahman*.[58] In his commentary on this Upaniṣad Sri Aurobindo points out that the *Īśa* and *Kena* both treat the same subject, namely achieving the state of immortality and growing into the divine consciousness. But while the *Īśa* "is concerned with the whole problem of the world and life and works and human destiny in their relation to the supreme truth of the *Brahman* . . ." the *Kena Upaniṣad*

> . . . approaches a more restricted problem, starts with a more precise and narrow inquiry. It concerns itself only with the relation of mind-consciousness to Brahman-consciousness and does not stray outside the strict boundaries of its subject. The material world and the physical life are taken for granted, they are hardly mentioned.[59]

This commentary on the *Kena* too is very comprehensive and full of profound insights.

Sri Aurobindo's texts on the Upaniṣads appeared in the *Centenary Edition* in 1972 as volume 12 *The Upanishads*. In the new edition of the *Complete Works* they have been brought out

---

57 *Īśa Upaniṣad*, 63.

58 4th verse.

59 *Kena and Other Upanishads*, 15.

as volume 17 *Isha Upanishad* which includes ten incomplete commentaries of very different length, and volume 18 *Kena and Other Upanishads*.

Essays on the Gita

Sri Aurobindo's close relationship with Kṛṣṇa has already been mentioned several times in connection with certain experiences. Kṛṣṇa's dialogue with Arjuna in the *Bhagavad-Gītā* appeared to him as "one of the very great events in history".[60] No wonder then that he also wrote a comprehensive commentary on the *Gītā*, as has traditionally been done by numberless *yogī*s and saints in India. Here the objective is not really to work out the historical truth as immanent in the text; the authors mainly take the *Gītā* as an occasion for supporting their own thoughts and teachings, with the help of the verses of the *Gītā*.

Sri Aurobindo had been studying the *Gītā* intensively since his time in Baroda and felt attracted to this work because on one hand it advocates doing works in this world, and on the other it presents a synthesis of the paths of love, works and knowledge. In the first chapter he points out that it would hardly be possible

> to extract from the Gita its exact metaphysical connotation as it was understood by the men of the time. . . . But what we can do with profit is to seek in the Gita for the actual living truths it contains . . ., to extract from it what can help us or the world at large . . .[61]

In his treatise Sri Aurobindo discusses many subjects such as the historicity of Kṛṣṇa (which he affirms), the teaching of Sāṁkhya, Yoga and Vedānta, the significance of the sacrifice and the *avatāra* and the importance of equanimity, to which he

---

60 *Essays Divine and Human*, 427.

61 *Essays on the Gita*, 5.

dedicates an entire chapter. The basic lines of the three above-mentioned *yoga* paths are worked out as well as the truth of the godhead, inhabiting everything. The idea of transformation which plays a great role in Sri Aurobindo's system is referred to when he explains:

> But the egoistic mind and life we now and apparently are, must first surrender itself for transmutation into the hands of that inmost secret Divinity within us.[62]

In one of the last chapters Sri Aurobindo addresses "the supreme word and most secret thing of all":

> The Spirit and Godhead is an Infinite free from all dharmas and though he conducts the world according to fixed laws and leads man through his dharmas of ignorance and knowledge, sin and virtue, right and wrong . . . , yet the Spirit and Godhead transcend all these things, and if we too can cast away all dependence on dharmas, surrender ourselves to this free and eternal Spirit . . ., then that is the truest, the greatest release . . .[63]

In the original text of the *Gītā* (18.66) it says:

sarvadharmān parityajya mām ekaṁ śaraṇaṁ vraja

> Abandon all *dharma*s, take refuge in Me [Kr̥ṣṇa] alone.

Srinivasa Iyengar reports how *Essays on the Gita* long ago found a prominent reader:

> From beyond the shores of India came Miss Margaret Woodrow Wilson [into the Ashram], daughter of the wartime American president. She had read Sri Aurobindo's *Essays on the Gita* in the New York Public Library in the late nineteen twenties, and that effected the "decisive turn" in her life. She first acquired the habit of inward concentration, and learned

---

62 *Essays on the Gita*, 310.

63 Ibid., 558-59.

> to open herself to the psychic and the spiritual, and at last she was permitted to make the "passage to India" and join the Ashram.[64]

There she stayed until the end of her life and helped with the typing and proof-reading of *The Life Divine* and other works such as *The Ideal of Human Unity.*

Anilbaran Roy, a disciple of Sri Aurobindo, has published with Sri Aurobindo's permission a complete translation of the *Bhagavad-Gītā* with commentary, based on the texts in *Essays on the Gita*. This book was brought out in 1938 and is still available.[65]

---

64 Iyengar, *Sri Aurobindo*, 559.

65 *The Message of the Gita.* With Text, Translation and Notes as interpreted by Sri Aurobindo, Sri Aurobindo Ashram, 1972.

11

Pondicherry
(1915-26)

To pick up the thread of the action: After the departure of Paul and Mirra Richard, Sri Aurobindo now faced the task of editing the *Arya,* month by month, on his own. This implied not only keeping new texts ready all the time, but also going through proofs from the printing press and all the other responsibilities.

In a letter to a follower in 1935 Sri Aurobindo made an interesting remark on his inner state during this period, until the return of the Mother:

> It is not clear what your Guru meant by my sitting on the path; that could have been true of the period between 1915 and 1920 when I was writing the *Arya,* but the Sadhana and the work were waiting for the Mother's coming.[1]

At least the journal was financially successful, "it paid its way with a large surplus".[2] All the same the overall situation remained critical; the money they had was just sufficient for their subsistence, they could not afford to buy good clothes nor to renovate their accommodation. This fact was not changed by Motilal Roy's support, which they received regularly.

---

1 *Letters on Himself and the Ashram,* 269.

2 *Autobiographical Notes,* 102.

Sri Aurobindo lived rather casually together with his young companions at rue François Martin No. 41. He treated them as equals, allowing them so much freedom that Motilal was once shocked during a visit, observing their chaotic living conditions. Sri Aurobindo had more quiet now during the time of the war, because travelling had become difficult. It was only on rare occasions that he stepped out of the house, but he regularly received Bharati for joint *Ṛgveda* studies.

One of the few other visitors was the Danish painter Johannes Hohlenberg who arrived in the spring of 1915 and made a sketch for a portrait of Sri Aurobindo, which he painted a little later. Sri Aurobindo still remembered the painter twenty-five years later and remarked,

> At the end of every meditation, he used to say, "Let us now talk of the Ineffable".[3]

There was also a photographer who came during these years and to whom we owe the well-known picture of Sri Aurobindo sitting at the writing table with a pen in his hand.

At the end of 1918 Sri Aurobindo was visited by Ambalal Purani, an activist of the independence movement in Gujarat. Since his youth he had felt inspired by Sri Aurobindo and had laid the foundation for a revolutionary movement along with his elder brother C.B. Purani, who had met Sri Aurobindo already in 1908. When in 1914 Ambalal read in a newspaper of the publication of the *Arya*, he at once registered as a subscriber. Now, at the age of twenty-four, he visited his idol in Pondicherry to consult with him regarding further actions.

Purani arrived in Pondicherry in December and was informed that he could meet Sri Aurobindo at 3 p.m.

> Sri Aurobindo was sitting in a wooden chair behind a small

---

3 Nirodbaran, *Talks with Sri Aurobindo*, vol. I, 321 (27 December 1939).

> table. . . . I felt a spiritual light surrounding his face. His look was penetrating. He had known me by my correspondence. I reminded him about my brother having met him at Baroda, he had not forgotten him.[4]

Purani told Sri Aurobindo that his group was ready to start revolutionary activities. Sri Aurobindo remained silent for a while and then, changing the subject, he enquired about the state of Purani's *sādhanā*. Purani described his efforts and added: "Sadhana is all right, but it is difficult to concentrate on it so long as India is not free". "Perhaps it may not be necessary to resort to revolutionary activity to free India", Sri Aurobindo replied and pointed out that it would therefore be better to concentrate on *yoga*.[5] Other persons would be found to work out the goal of freedom for the country. But those who had a call for *yoga* should give priority to it. He said that he was not in a position to agree to the revolutionary programme, but Purani would of course be free to choose that path none the less.

Purani retorted with amazement that it was Sri Aurobindo himself who had originally proposed and inspired these activities. But Sri Aurobindo explained to Purani that he had observed the negative development they often take:

> Young men come forward to join the movement, driven by idealism and enthusiasm. But these elements do not last long. It becomes very difficult to observe and extract discipline. Small groups begin to form within the organisation, rivalries grow between groups and even between individuals.[6]

Then, finally, the government would succeed in infiltrating the movement and there could be all kinds of quarrels, he added.

---

4 Purani, *Evening Talks,* 16.

5 Ibid., 16-17.

6 Ibid., 17.

Purani told Sri Aurobindo that he felt a strong call to work for the freedom of India and he could not sleep properly as long as this goal was not realized. Sri Aurobindo replied after a few minutes of silence: "Suppose an assurance is given to you that India will be free?" When Purani asked who could give this assurance, Sri Aurobindo replied, "Suppose I give you the assurance?" Purani immediately accepted this and noted, "My work was over — the purpose of my visit to Pondicherry was served".[7]

Purani joined the Ashram in 1923 and became a well-known disciple of Sri Aurobindo. Later in his life he also travelled to Europe and America giving lectures. The *Evening Talks with Sri Aurobindo,* recorded by Purani, also contains talks from the early period from 1923 which are not included in Nirodbaran's *Talks with Sri Aurobindo.* The latter comprises only the period before and after the Second World War.

Finally, in 1919, the painter Mukul Chandra Dey came to visit Sri Aurobindo. He made portraits of prominent Indians for a book project and wanted to include Sri Aurobindo in his collection. Dey reports that Sri Aurobindo enquired how long the session would take and then sat patiently for an hour, "he did not move even a bit, nor did I see him bat an eyelid even once".[8]

Mirra in France and Japan

Mirra and Paul Richard had travelled by steamer to Marseille via Colombo and on to Paris by train. Then Paul started his military service in Lunel near Montpellier. Later they moved to Marsillargues, where they met Mirra's son André. But Mirra had a very difficult time in France, she could hardly bear the

---

7 Purani, *Evening Talks*, 17-18.

8 M. Dey, *My Darshan of Sri Aurobindo at Pondicherry,* 26-28. Quoted in *The Lives of Sri Aurobindo,* 317.

separation from Sri Aurobindo and India. Later she once remarked in a talk, full of pain:

> He did not keep me, what could I do? I had to go. But I left my psychic being with him, and in France I was once [in Lunel] on the point of death: the doctors had given me up.[9]

Sri Aurobindo kept contact with her through correspondence and she received his first letter in Marsillargues. Evidently, it had been proposed to him to seek refuge at a safer place than Pondicherry, and he replied:

> The whole earth is now under one law and answers to the same vibrations and I am sceptical of finding any place where the clash of the struggle will not pursue us. In any case, an effective retirement does not seem to be my destiny. I must remain in touch with the world until I have either mastered adverse circumstances or succumbed or carried on the struggle between the spiritual and physical so far as I am destined to carry it on. . . . One needs to have a calm heart, a settled will, entire self-abnegation and the eyes constantly fixed on the beyond to live undiscouraged in times like these which are truly a period of universal decomposition.[10]

In October 1915 Paul Richard was found to be unfit for military service and thus released, so he and Mirra returned to Paris. Paul wanted to leave France and finally succeeded in getting appointed as a foreign trade representative of the government, travelling to Japan with Mirra in connection with some mission. Here she could live in better conditions which at least appealed to her artistic sense, although the spirituality of India was missing. "Four years, from an artistic point of view, I lived from wonder to wonder."[11]

---

9 Sri Aurobindo Circle, 33, 64. Quoted in Nilima Das, *Glimpses of the Mother's Life,* I, 160.

10 *Autobiographical Notes,* 285.

11 *CWM,* vol. 4, *Questions and Answers 1950-51,* 307.

Mirra made contacts with spiritual persons, she painted a lot, adopted the Japanese style of living and was wearing the *kimono* with natural grace. In January 1919 Japan was struck by a terrible epidemic which resulted in numberless deaths. Mirra at first protected herself through her occult force, but when inwardly she started wondering what was behind the epidemic, she herself caught the infection and was bed-ridden, with a high fever. She refused all medical treatment as she wanted to carry out the battle from within. While that battle went on she felt a powerful āsuric being attacking her, but after a long struggle with all her might she was able to repulse the asura's attempt to kill her. A little later a Japanese friend came to see her and told her that the epidemic was suddenly under control.[12]

In 1919 Mirra met Rabindranath Tagore in Japan and resided in the same hotel with him for a while. He invited her to be in charge of his cultural institution Shantiniketan, but she did not accept the proposal, since she knew that her destiny would be elsewhere.

Mrinalini's Death

The same epidemic that had ravaged Japan had also struck India some time earlier and Sri Aurobindo's wife Mrinalini was one of its victims. Again and again there were plans for her moving to Pondicherry, but Sri Aurobindo wrote her that she could only come when he had a secure financial status. Then the war broke out and travel was not possible anymore. But in December 1918 her father had taken her to Calcutta, to arrange for her journey to Pondicherry. In the big town she quickly became infected with the virus and died, within two days. A letter of Sri Aurobindo to his father-in-law shows how deeply affected he was by the loss:

---

12 *CWM*, vol. 5, *Questions and Answers* 1953, 181-83.

> I have not written to you with regard to this fatal event in both our lives: words are useless in face of the feelings it has caused.... God has seen good to lay upon me the one sorrow that could still touch me to the centre. He knows better than ourselves what is best for each of us, and now that the first sense of the irreparable has passed, I can bow with submission to his divine purpose. The physical tie between us is, as you say, severed; but the tie of affection subsists for me. Where I have once loved, I do not cease from loving.... I should be glad if you would send me two or three of her books, especially if there are any in which her name is written. I have only of her, her letters and a photograph.[13]

Mirra's Return

In March 1920, at the end of a five-year stay, Paul and Mirra Richard left Japan accompanied by Dorothy Hodgson, an English friend whom Mirra had previously met in France. They travelled to Colombo and booked a passage to Pondicherry arriving on April 24. At some distance from the Indian coast Mirra had an extraordinary experience:

> I was on the boat, at sea, not expecting anything ... when all of a sudden, abruptly, about two nautical miles from Pondicherry, the quality, I may even say physical quality, of the atmosphere of the air, changed so much that I knew we were entering the aura of Sri Aurobindo. It was a *physical* experience....[14]

Now again there were daily meetings between Paul and Mirra Richard with Sri Aurobindo, but the situation had changed: Mirra had realized that she could not transform Paul's nature and told him that their relationship was finished.[15] At the same time she was opening more and more to Sri Aurobindo,

13 *Autobiographical Notes*, 148.

14 *CWM*, vol. 4, *Questions and Answers 1950-51*, 223.

15 *Mother's Agenda*, vol. 2, 5 November 1961.

intensifying her spiritual relationship with him. When Paul felt that Mirra really wanted to separate from him, he challenged her and tried to change her mind. Several times he was in a riot in their rented accommodation and one day even tried to strangle her. However, she remained calm and called Sri Aurobindo inwardly.

> I saw him[16] come, like that (*gesture enveloping Mother and immobilizing everything*). Then Richard's hands loosened their grip.

The Mother later summed up,

> It was certainly Sri Aurobindo's power that made Richard decide to leave.[17]

He soon left Pondicherry, travelled for some time in India but later went on to America, where he founded a centre for Asian studies.

Mirra and her friend Miss Hodgson were at first staying in guest houses and later in a house on rue St. Martin. When in November 1920 the roof of a godown had collapsed during a tempest, Sri Aurobindo came to know that the house in which they were staying was also not safe; he invited Mirra and Miss Hodgson to move into his own house. From that time onward Mirra and Sri Aurobindo had always lived in the same house.

Sri Aurobindo's Letter to Barin

At the beginning of 1920 Barin had been released from imprisonment in the Andamans islands and contacted his brother through several letters. It was only in April that Sri Aurobindo found time to answer, sending Barin a long letter in Bengali. This letter is significant in so far as Sri Aurobindo

---

16 Sri Aurobindo.

17 Ibid.

gives his brother an update on current events, and we learn how he judges his own development and the political processes of that time. Moreover, he discusses some basic ideas of his spiritual philosophy and his *yoga* in a rather concrete manner. In fact, certain sections almost read like a commentary on some of his writings published in the *Arya*.

Sri Aurobindo begins by pointing out that he considers his experiences with Lele, or in Alipore prison, etc. as only a preliminary stage, as a seeking, as a testing of different paths. Only after having moved to Pondicherry "the indwelling *guru* of the world indicated my path to me completely, its full theory". This development took place during the last ten years and Pondicherry is "the appointed place for the fulfilment of my *yoga*".[18] But the centre of the work was Bengal; he hoped it would extend to the whole of India and to the whole world in the future.

Then he makes some remarks on the special feature of his *yoga*, the union of Spirit and life.

> What the Divine wants is for man to embody Him here, in the individual and in the collectivity — to realise God in life.[19]

The old systems of *yoga* had not achieved this goal, had weakened India's vitality through illusionism and disdain of the world, which resulted in decay. Body, life, mind, supermind and bliss-existence are the five stages of the Spirit, and

> . . . the higher we climb, the nearer comes a state of highest perfection of man's spiritual evolution. When we rise to the Supermind, it becomes easy to rise to the Bliss. The status of

---

18 sriaurobindoashram.com/E-Library/Writings in Bengali Translation/A Letter of Sri Aurobindo to his Brother, 359-60.

19 Ibid., 360.

> indivisible and infinite Bliss becomes firmly established. . . . This endeavour is the central clue of my yogic path, its fundamental idea. But it is not an easy thing. After fifteen years I am only now rising into the lowest of the three levels of the supermind and trying to draw up into it all the lower activities. But when the process is complete, there is not the least doubt that God through me will give this supramental perfection to others with less difficulty. Then my real work will begin.[20]

Sri Aurobindo criticizes his brother's attitude who looks upon his body as "a corpse". This is the old ascetic position, he says, the path of *nirvāṇa*. Rather there should be joy and bliss in the body and in the mind. For

> . . . the body is made of consciousness, the body is a form of God. I see God in everything in the world. . . . Concrete waves of this bliss flow even through the body. In this condition, filled with spiritual feeling, one can live the worldly life, get married or do anything else. In every activity one finds a blissful self-expression of the divine.[21]

He then touches on a subject which we had already mentioned in the chapter on his *yoga* diary, that is to say his dealing with sense experiences and their transformation:

> I have for a long time been transforming on the mental level all the objects and experiences of the mind and senses into delight. Now they are all taking the form of supramental delight. In this condition there is the perfect vision and experience of Sachchidananda — the divine Existence, Consciousness and Bliss.[22]

Next Sri Aurobindo refers to the Bengali newspaper *Prabartak*

---

20 sriaurobindoashram.com/E-Library/Writings in Bengali Translation/A Letter of Sri Aurobindo to his Brother, 361.

21 Ibid., 367.

22 Ibid., 367.

which is edited by Motilal Roy, and notes that readers find it very difficult to follow the articles. But

> . . . there is the same complaint about the *Arya*: people can't understand it. Who wants to give so much thought and consideration to his reading?

Then he proposes a new interpretation of India's weakness:

> It is my belief that the main cause of India's weakness is not subjection, nor poverty, nor a lack of spirituality or religion, but a diminution of the power of thought, the spread of ignorance in the birthplace of knowledge. Everywhere I see an inability or unwillingness to think. . . .[23]

This, he says, is different in Europe where there is a great culture and discipline of thought, and a striving for knowledge which brought about its power. He is also optimistic regarding its future:

> People say that Europe is rushing into the jaws of destruction. I do not think so. All these revolutions, all these upsettings are the first stages of a new creation.

It is only in the spiritual field where Europe has deficits and where ". . . her thought-power stops working." But here too efforts are made to surmount even this limitation.[24]

At the end of the letter Sri Aurobindo refers to Barin's idea that the country would require emotional enthusiasm for the political work. But Sri Aurobindo has been very much disillusioned regarding this activity and points out:

> We did all that in the political field during the Swadeshi period; everything we did has fallen in the dust. Will there be a more auspicious outcome in the spiritual field? I don't

---

[23] sriaurobindoashram.com/E-Library/Writings in Bengali Translation/A Letter of Sri Aurobindo to his Brother, 369.

[24] Ibid., 370.

> say there has been no result. There has been; every movement produces some result. But it is mostly in an increase of possibilities.[25]

Evidently Sri Aurobindo sees the spiritual work now as a foundation for a stable political development; unshakeable equality is an essential element. On this basis, he wants "the radiation of the sun of knowledge". For this purpose he does not require tens of thousands of disciples, but it would be enough if 100 men, free from petty egoism, would dedicate themselves to God's work. As for his personal role,

> I do not want to be a guru. What I want is for someone, awakened by my touch or by that of another, to manifest from within this sleeping divinity and to realise the divine life. Such men will uplift this country.[26]

External Contacts

Sri Aurobindo had been living a very withdrawn life since 1914 with few contacts to the external world, as he was entirely focused on his inner work and his literary activities. This changed during the year 1920 when he started laying the foundation of his future spiritual community and again started taking interest in the country's political events.

A well-known visitor in 1921 was Motilal Roy from Chandernagore, who had regularly given financial support to Sri Aurobindo in the past years. Around 1915 he had founded a spiritual community named Prabartak Sangha[27] which was intended to be an experiment in collective spiritual life under Sri Aurobindo's guidance. Motilal hoped that Sri Aurobindo would return to Bengal in the not too distant future and

---

25 sriaurobindoashram.com/E-Library/Writings in Bengali Translation/A Letter of Sri Aurobindo to his Brother, 372.

26 Ibid., 372-73.

27 "Pioneer Community".

choose, as the main place for his activities, the centre in Chandernagore with himself playing a leading role in realizing Sri Aurobindo's ideas.

Now Sri Aurobindo had invited him for talks about his *sādhanā* and his progress. But Motilal could not properly make use of his stay, as his thoughts were focused on the centre in Chandernagore which was not yet very well established, and to which he was attached. He received letters from there urging him to return home and finally even a telegram from his most important co-worker. This caused him to leave Pondicherry before the birthday of Sri Aurobindo (15 August) and against the latter's will.

Another problem for Motilal was the changed circumstances in Pondicherry. Barin had returned, and Motilal sensed that his own leading role in Bengal might be endangered as Sri Aurobindo had entrusted various tasks to Barin. Moreover, Motilal did not fail to notice the important role Mirra played in Sri Aurobindo's household, which irritated him (as well as some other followers). After his return to Chandernagore Motilal continued his activities in the centre but his approach and attitude were not quite in agreement with Sri Aurobindo's ideas any longer, therefore Sri Aurobindo disassociated himself from the community in 1926, cutting all connection with it.

He later explained the deeper reasons in a talk:

> Anyway, I wanted to give it a trial and gave that idea to Motilal. Then he took up the idea and, as you know, he took it up with all his vital being and in an egoistic way. So the vital forces found their chance. They tried to take possession of the work and of the workers. It is after several such lessons that I had to give up the idea of rushing into work. This Yoga is not a cut-out system. It is a growth by experience.[28]

[28] Purani, *Evening Talks*, 158-59.

In 1921 there was a visit from A.B. Purani who described the daily routine in Sri Aurobindo's house at that time as follows:

> A breakfast of tea, three slices of toast and butter at 7.00; before 11.30 everyone to take his bath. Sri Aurobindo taking his after all the others; lunch between 11.30 and 12.30; afternoon tea, prepared by the inmates of the house in turn, at 3.30; dinner, generally consisting of fish curry, rice, curd and bread, at 9.30. On 1 January 1922 the Mother took entire charge of the management of Sri Aurobindo's house, including the kitchen. There was a complete change in the routine. Arrangements were made upstairs for Sri Aurobindo's bath.[29]

The Mother later also made a change in the diet, introducing vegetarian food, but she admitted some exceptions.

Purani joined the community in 1923 and made notes on the evening talks with Sri Aurobindo. On the procedure of the talks he writes:

> As years passed the evening sittings went on changing their time and often those disciples who came from outside for a temporary stay for sadhana were allowed to join them. . . . Members of the household would gather every day at the fixed time with some sense of expectancy and start chatting in low tones. Sri Aurobindo used to come last and it was after his coming that the session would really commence. He came dressed as usual in dhoti, part of which was used by him to cover the upper part of his body. . . . How much these sittings were dependent on him may be gathered from the fact there were days when more than three-fourths of the time passed in complete silence without any outer suggestion from him, or there was only an abrupt Yes or No to all attempts at drawing him out in conversation. And even when he participated in the talk one always felt that his voice was that of one who does not let his whole being

---

29 Purani, *The Life of Sri Aurobindo*, 181-82.

flow into his words; there was a reserve and what was left unsaid was perhaps more than what was spoken. . . .

The whole thing was so informal that one could never predict the turn the conversation would take. The whole house therefore was in a mood to enjoy the freshness and the delight of meeting the unexpected. There were peals of laughter and light talk; jokes and criticism. . . . These sittings, in fact, furnished Sri Aurobindo with an occasion to admit and feel the outer atmosphere and that of the group living with him. It brought to him the much-needed direct contact of the mental and vital make-up of the disciples, enabling him to act on the atmosphere in general and on the individual in particular. . . . Far more important than the actual talk and its content was the personal contact, the influence of the Master, and the divine atmosphere he emanated; for through his outer personality it was the Divine Consciousness that he allowed to act.[30]

In 1923 Sri Aurobindo began — against his original intention — to accept the role of a *guru*. From the viewpoint of his own nature, he would have preferred to allow things to develop in a kind of free evolution, to intervene as little as possible, but he realized more and more that there were also disadvantages connected with this way of proceeding. Thus, some people took up what they thought to be Sri Aurobindo's *yoga* and wrongly believed they were on the right path, although actually they were misled and ended up having big problems.[31]

During the following years he received a large number of letters in which he was asked for all kinds of help and instruction, but he answered only those which were written, in his perception, by serious spiritual seekers and sent his

30 Purani, *The Life of Sri Aurobindo*, 183-84.

31 Purani Talks manuscripts 3:255. *The Lives of Sri Aurobindo*, 338.

guidance with the help of Barin, Purani or Amrita. There were also some enquiries from American readers of the *Arya*. When it was proposed to him that he should arrange lectures and courses (as was done by the Kriyā Yogī Paramahansa Yogananda) he refused to do so, since this kind of method would not work for his path:

> It has to be received personally, it has to be lived, the seeker, *sadhaka*, has to change by a difficult aspiration and endeavour his whole consciousness and nature, his mind, heart, life . . . into a greater Truth than anything the normal life of man can imagine.[32]

By the middle of 1926 some fifteen to twenty members lived in two houses in his community. Occasionally, Sri Aurobindo informed them in the evening talks about the state of his *sādhanā*, especially on his birthday, 15 August 1923. When a disciple enquired about his *yoga*, Sri Aurobindo replied:

> I am at present engaged in bringing the Supermind into the physical consciousness. . . . The physical is by nature inert and does not want to be rendered conscient. It offers much greater resistance as it is unwilling to change.

It was a kind of "digging the earth", as the Vedic *ṛṣi*s called it, and

> so long as Matter is not Supramentalised the mental and the vital also cannot be fully Supramentalised. The physical is therefore to be accepted and transformed. It is this birth after birth on every plane that makes the process complex.[33]

In a talk dated 11 November 1925 Sri Aurobindo pointed out the importance of equanimity and common sense in *yoga* and remarked on himself:

---

32 Undated letter draft of Sri Aurobindo, published in the *Bulletin of Sri Aurobindo International Centre of Education*, **28**(3): 48.

33 Purani, *Evening Talks*, 504.

> A perfect yoga requires perfect balance. . . . That was the thing that saved me all through, I mean the perfect balance. First of all I believed that nothing was impossible, and at the same time I could question everything.[34]

The Overmind

In the evening talks Sri Aurobindo had been stating since 1926 that it would be important to have an intermediate stage between the supermind and mind. Sri Aurobindo called it "Overmind" and has described this plane in detail in *The Life Divine* as the world of the gods and many possibilities:

> The Overmind releases a million Godheads into action, each empowered to create its own world, each world capable of relation, communication and interplay with the others. . . . In the Supermind all this would be held together as a harmonised play of the one Existence. . . .

In Overmind, however, the One Consciousness

> is separated into many independent forms of consciousness and knowledge; each follows out its own line of truth which it has to realise. . . . Overmind thus gives to the One Existence-Consciousness-Bliss the character of a teeming of infinite possibilities which can be developed into a multitude of worlds or thrown together into one world. . . .[35]

Furthermore, Sri Aurobindo explains,

> In its nature and law the Overmind is a delegate of the Supermind Consciousness, its delegate to the Ignorance. Or we might speak of it as a protective double, a screen of dissimilar similarity through which Supermind can act indirectly on an Ignorance whose darkness could not bear or receive the direct impact of a supreme Light.[36]

---

34 Purani, *Evening Talks*, 168.

35 *The Life Divine*, 294-95.

36 Ibid., 293.

At the beginning of 1926 the possibility of a descent of a higher consciousness was mentioned several times in the evening talks, and several disciples had the impression that something special was due to happen soon. It also struck them that Sri Aurobindo came late to the evening talks more and more: instead of at 4:30 p.m. it was at 6 p.m. or much later, once even as late as 2 a.m. Purani writes that the guidance of the disciples had already been increasingly transferred to Mirra since the beginning of 1926. Some female disciples — their number was perhaps three or four — had started going to her for meditation.[37] Finally, Purani reports as an eyewitness what happened on 24 November:

> From the beginning of November 1926 the pressure of the Higher Power began to be unbearable. Then at last the great day, the day for which the Mother[38] had been waiting for so many long years, arrived on 24 November. The sun had almost set, and everyone was occupied with his own activity some had gone out to the seaside for a walk — when the Mother sent round word to all the disciples to assemble as soon as possible in the verandah where the usual meditation was held. . . . By six o'clock most of the disciples had gathered. It was becoming dark. In the verandah on the wall near Sri Aurobindo's door, just behind his chair, a black silk curtain with gold lace work representing three Chinese dragons was hung. The three dragons were so represented that the tail of one reached up to the mouth of the other. . . . We came to know afterwards that there is a prophecy in China that the Truth will manifest itself on earth when the three dragons (the dragons of the earth, of the mind region and of the sky) meet. Today on 24 November the Truth was descending. . . . There was a deep silence in the atmosphere after the disciples had gathered there. Many saw an oceanic flood of Light rushing down from above.

37 Purani, *The Life of Sri Aurobindo*, 211, 214.

38 Mirra.

> Everyone present felt a kind of pressure above his head. The whole atmosphere was surcharged with some electrical energy.[39]

Then came the Mother and Sri Aurobindo and a meditation began which lasted about three quarters of an hour. Thereafter the disciples bowed before the Mother, while Sri Aurobindo held his right hand behind the Mother's to indicate that his blessings for the disciples were there behind hers. Some disciples had significant spiritual experiences during this event and all of them felt its special importance. After Sri Aurobindo and the Mother had withdrawn, Datta spoke into the silence, "The Lord has descended into the physical today".[40]

Sri Aurobindo gave an explanation in two letters in 1935:

> [24th November 1926] was the descent of Krishna into the physical. Krishna is not the supramental Light. The descent of Krishna would mean the descent of the Overmind Godhead preparing, though not itself actually, the descent of Supermind and Ananda. Krishna is the Anandamaya; he supports the evolution through the Overmind leading it towards Ananda.[41]

Present during this event were twenty-four disciples, several of whom later became well-known followers such as Pavitra (a Frenchman with the birth name Phillipe Barbier Saint-Hilaire), Purani, Champaklal and Pujalal. Two days later Sri Aurobindo said to his brother Barin who was also present that he should inform all of them:

> Mirra is my Shakti. She has taken charge of the new creation. You will get everything from her. Give [your] consent to whatever she wants to do.[42]

---

39 Purani, *The Life of Sri Aurobindo*, 215-16.

40 Ibid., 217. Datta is Miss Hodgson.

41 *Letters on Himself and the Ashram*, 273, 272.

42 Sri Aurobindo, reported oral remarks, notation of 27 →

Thereafter Sri Aurobindo withdrew and Mirra alone had constant access to him. She was now guiding the disciples spiritually as well as in daily matters; it was a great change in the Ashram life. So Mirra began to play "officially" her role as the Mother, as Sri Aurobindo's *śakti,* his effective power. While he would open up new fields of consciousness in the inner worlds, it was up to her to keep in touch with the external world and try to pass on to the community some part of what Sri Aurobindo worked out. "Transformation" was the keyword and this project was now started on a solid foundation.

Henceforth, Sri Aurobindo remained invisible for his disciples (with one or two exceptions) but they could see him three times a year on *darśan* days: on 21 February, the Mother's birthday; on his birthday, 15 August, and on 24 November, known as Siddhi Day.[43] Later, in 1939, 24 April was added as the day of the Mother's final arrival in Pondicherry. These *darśan* days are still celebrated today in the Sri Aurobindo Ashram, and its members as well as visitors are allowed to go to the rooms of Sri Aurobindo or the Mother.

→ November, 1926. Haradhan Bakshi Papers, notebook 3, 240. Quoted in *The Lives of Sri Aurobindo*, 345.

43 *Siddhi* here means successful completion (of the descent of Kṛṣṇa into the physical).

12

Pondicherry
(1927-38)

In 1926 Sri Aurobindo began calling Mirra "the Mother" for the first time, which soon became the standard, although he continued at times to call her Mirra Devi or Mira Devi.[1] In Europe Mirra and Mira are short forms of the Hebrew name Miriam, while Devi is appended to Indian female names as a sign of respect. The name "Mira" is also known in India, especially through Mīrā Bāī, a famous Kṛṣṇa devotee and poet (1547–1614) whose songs are popular even today.

Sri Aurobindo instructed his followers henceforth to be guided by the Mother in their *yoga*; he did not accept any exceptions, for

> . . . there is no difference between the Mother's path and mine; we have and have always had the same path, the path that leads to the supramental change and the divine realisation; not only at the end, but from the beginning they have been the same.[2]

We can conclude from some statements in Sri Aurobindo's letters that several of his disciples found it hard to accept the new circumstances, and over time a few of them left. Additionally the new disciplined style of living, upon which the Mother insisted, did not suit them.

---

1 *The Lives of Sri Aurobindo*, 352.

2 SABCL, vol. 26, *On Himself*, 456.

Sri Aurobindo was able now to concentrate entirely on his inner work, while the Mother looked after the community and its needs, and thus the collective *yoga* made rapid progress. As the Mother later said in a talk, there were even spectacular developments:

> Suddenly, immediately, things took a certain shape: a very brilliant creation was worked out in extraordinary detail, with marvellous experiences, contact with divine beings, and all kinds of manifestations which are considered miraculous . . .[3]

Then one day the Mother went to Sri Aurobindo to report the current progress with some enthusiasm. But he looked at her and said that it was a creation of the overmind, no doubt interesting and effective and the Mother would become famous through it, she would be able to turn events on earth topsy-turvy. But:

> . . . it is not success that we want; we want to establish the Supermind on earth. One must know how to renounce immediate success in order to create the new world, the supramental world in its integrality.[4]

The Mother understood at once what he meant and so she withdrew, and dissolved the whole creation, to restart on a new foundation.

However, this had only become necessary because the *sādhakas* were not able to assimilate properly the descending force. While some disciples had brilliant experiences and were perceiving this period like a permanent wonder, others lost their inner balance and could not stand the pressure. As a consequence, there was an invasion of hostile forces, otherwise the *yoga* could have progressed further and the way would

3 *CWM*, vol. 9, *Questions and Answers 1957-58*, 148.

4 Ibid., 149.

have been paved for a supreme action of the divine Force. But as it was, "the Mother had to push the Divine Personalities and Powers, through which she was doing the action, behind a veil and come down into the physical human level and act according to its conditions . . ." Thus, the rapid progress was slowed down and there was instead a phase with great difficulties, with "struggle, illness, ignorance and inertia".[5]

The community was quickly growing now. In 1926 there were only twenty-five members, at the end of the next year thirty-six, and in 1928 already eighty and by 1934 the number had reached 150. This meant that constantly new accommodations had to be rented and soon a house was acquired for the first time, which is part of today's Ashram main building. The new members came from all parts of the country, a majority from Bengal and Gujarat, a few from Europe and America. Sri Aurobindo was hesitant to use the term "Ashram" which commonly refers to a community assembled around the *guru*, because the word appeared to be too much associated with traditional ideas. But eventually he did accept it, as there was no better alternative term.

In his concept the Ashram was a field of experimentation where the descent of a higher spiritual force into human life was attempted. To make this endeavour successful it was necessary that the members represented various types of human beings with their difficulties as well as their possibilities. It was intended to be a "microcosm" which symbolized in a certain way the world and its problems, and aimed for their far-reaching solutions. This implied that there would be tension and conflict among the members, for the Ashram was a "laboratory" for a *yoga* of transformation and the latter

[5] *Letters on Himself and the Ashram*, 331 (for further elucidation, see the whole passage, 330-32).

> has to deal with all sorts of elements favourable and unfavourable. . . . If only sattwic[6] and cultured men come for yoga, men without very much of the vital difficulty in them, then, because the difficulty of the vital element in terrestrial nature has not been faced and overcome, it might well be that the endeavour would fail.[7]

In another letter Sri Aurobindo further clarified the point:

> To deal with a few exceptional types would hardly solve the problem. And would they consent to follow my path — that is another question? And if they were put to the test, would not the common humanity suddenly reveal itself — that is still another question.[8]

Letters on Yoga

Sri Aurobindo had withdrawn externally, therefore his letters played a role of increasing importance. Before his withdrawal, he had written letters only occasionally, but now he found more time so that his correspondence grew more and more. Since 1930 he had started encouraging a few individual *sādhaka*s to write letters to him, but after a while he opened this possibility to all of them. As a result, quickly a real flood of letters arrived in his room which meant he had to dedicate ten to twelve hours daily for answering them. Between 1930 and 1938 he wrote thousands of letters on all conceivable theoretical and practical problems. Out these, initially a few small books originated such as *Bases of Yoga* and *The Riddle of this World*, later on an edition in several volumes.

Already in 1928 he had published the little book *The Mother* which is based on the text of four letters from summer 1927 as well as a message to his disciples dated 21 February 1927 (the

---

6 Peaceful, balanced.

7 SABCL, vol. 22, *Letters on Yoga*, 856.

8 *Letters on Himself and the Ashram*, 599-600.

birthday of the Mother). In this writing, which is one of his most well-known texts, he describes the personalities of the divine Mother and their respective functions, furthermore some important basic principles of his integral path: personal effort and surrender to the Divine, the right inner attitude and egoless action. The central passage of the text deals with the four main aspects of the Mother: Māheśvarī (comprehending wisdom), Mahākālī (invincible force), Mahālakṣmī (beauty and harmony) and Mahāsarasvatī (flawless work and exact perfection in things).[9]

The complete edition of the letters as a book was a great challenge due to the voluminous material available; inevitably a selection had to be made. In the end it was decided to arrange a compilation with reference to the subjects treated in the letters. The advantage of this procedure was that the respective extracts could be clearly arranged, but there was also the disadvantage of the letters being presented only partially. For instance, Sri Aurobindo may have treated half a dozen different subjects in one letter and now the passages on peace and silence appeared at one place whereas those on devotion or meditation from the same letter appeared at another. However, those readers who are interested in following a complete correspondence may study the publication of Nirodbaran, who has brought out Sri Aurobindo's letters to him along with his own questions in two volumes.[10]

In all these writings we get a very living experience of Sri Aurobindo, we can observe his infinite patience of answering again and again similar questions (sometimes even penned in a seemingly provoking or angry tone), his humour, his large vision and his universal knowledge. The following example reveals how informal was the style of exchange at times,

---

9 *The Mother with Letters on the Mother*, 17ff.

10 *Nirodbaran's Correspondence with Sri Aurobindo*, 2 vols., Pondicherry, Sri Aurobindo Ashram.

although only with a limited number of disciples who were as close to Sri Aurobindo as Nirodbaran who is here complaining over an uninspired phase of his *sādhanā*:

> At present I am only sleeping and sleeping, no aspiration, no will, nothing — shunyam, *void*! *Have I set the devil in my track by my boasting*? *Please* save me from this Dilipian despair.
>
> Which boasting? But why hug despair without a cause — Dilipian[11] or other? Come to your senses and develop a Nirodian jollity instead. . . .
>
> The Overmind seems so distant from us, and your Himalayan austerity and grandeur takes my breath away, making my heart palpitate!
>
> O rubbish! I am austere and grand, grim and stern! every blasted thing that I never was! I groan in un-Aurobindian despair when I hear such things. What has happened to the common sense of all you people? In order to reach the Overmind it is not at all necessary to take leave of this simple but useful quality. Common sense by the way is not logic (which is the least commonsense-like thing in the world), it is simply looking at things as they are without inflation or deflation — not imagining wild imaginations — or for that matter despairing "I know not why" despairs.[12]

A very recommendable short version of the letters is the title *The Integral Yoga: Sri Aurobindo's Teaching and Method of Practice — Selected Letters of Sri Aurobindo* in which the letters have been arranged according to twelve groups of subjects.[13] So it becomes easily possible to know what Sri Aurobindo has written on his *yoga* and other systems, on details of the transformation or obstacles on the path, etc. and we often get

---

11 This refers to Dilip Kumar Roy, a disciple well known for his changing moods.

12 *Nirodbaran's Correspondence with Sri Aurobindo*, 156-57.

13 Sri Aurobindo Ashram, 1993. In the *Complete Works*, the letters are published as vols. 28-31.

more concrete comments here than in *The Synthesis of Yoga*. In the following example Sri Aurobindo discusses the subject of physical transformation, a very advanced stage of Integral Yoga requiring a great deal of preparation. The Mother was attempting this in the final phase of her life on earth.

> The change of the consciousness is the necessary thing and without it there can be no physical siddhi. But the fullness of the supramental change is not possible, if the body remains as it is, a slave of death, disease, decay, pain, unconsciousness and all the other results of the ignorance. If these are to remain the descent of the supramental is hardly necessary — for a change of consciousness which would bring mental–spiritual union with the Divine, the overmind is sufficient, even the Higher Mind is sufficient. The supramental descent is necessary for a dynamic action of the Truth in mind, vital and body. This would imply as a final result the disappearance of the unconsciousness of the body; it would no longer be subject to decay and disease.[14]

Another aspect of the correspondence was Sri Aurobindo's guidance to his disciples concerning their writing of poetry. They attempted, as part of their *sādhanā*, to write mantric verses as he did, inspired by the "overhead" planes or received from the heart level. "Overhead" refers to what is beyond the mind and which has access to the Light of the Truth in a more or less intensive grade. In Sri Aurobindo's system there are the higher mind, the illumined mind and the intuitive mind as preliminary stages of the overmind.

Some disciples of Sri Aurobindo (for instance K.D. Sethna, himself a poet of repute) sent their creations to him. He examined them carefully, making corrections of the text and even informing them from which level the inspiration had been received. Thus a comprehensive correspondence developed on poetry in general, on metre and rhythm, or on

---

[14] SABCL, vol. 24, *Letters on Yoga*, 1229. *The Integral Yoga*, 235.

well-known authors and their ranking in world literature.

While reading these letters, we notice how much Sri Aurobindo is at home in this subject and how much he enjoys the correspondence. While Sri Aurobindo was furthering the *sādhanā* of his disciples in the literary field, the Mother was supporting them — apart from practical work — in the fields of art and music. Many *sādhaka*s experienced a flourishing of their talents after having joined the Ashram, and some of them dedicated much time to the arts. While some had previous knowledge, others were beginners to whom the Mother introduced painting and musical techniques from scratch. One of them was Huta who, at a later period, prepared a large number of illustrations for Sri Aurobindo's *Savitri* in the 1960s. In the field of music Sunil Bhattacharya became well known; he put *Savitri* to music and annually composed New Year Music, continuing over a long period of time. It was especially his composition of 1972 on the occasion of the Centenary of Sri Aurobindo that appealed to many listeners.[15]

Autobiographical Writings

Through his letters, notes and clarifications Sri Aurobindo has left behind a great volume of autobiographical material. In the Sri Aurobindo Birth Centenary Library this material was published under the title *On Himself.* In the new, enlarged edition of the *Complete Works*[16] it has been brought out in the two titles *Letters on Himself and the Ashram* and *Autobiographical Notes and Other Writings*. The latter contains notes in which Sri Aurobindo corrected statements made by biographers and other writers about his life as well as various other material of historical importance.

The historical material includes personal letters written

---

15 See the sound files under sriaurobindoashram.org/Music.

16 Vols. 35 and 36.

> before 1927 (as well as a few written after that date), public statements and letters on national and world events, and public statements about his ashram and system of yoga.[17]

Letters on Himself and the Ashram incorporates letters written between 1926 and 1950 and has been arranged in several sections, such as his outer and inner life, his writings, his role as a spiritual teacher or his Ashram and the *sādhanā* practised there. The last part contains *mantra*s and messages written for the benefit of the disciples. The following lines give more insight into the title:

> What makes this book special? First, about one third of the letters are "new" — new in the sense that they were not published in the Sri Aurobindo Birth Centenary Library. . . . In the forty years since then, many new letters have come to light and are presented here.
>
> Second, whenever possible and appropriate, the question or comment of the disciple is given along with Sri Aurobindo's reply. It also makes the reading more enjoyable. Through the question-and-answer exchanges we catch a glimpse of the relationship between Guru and disciple. We see the Master at work, dealing with each disciple differently, guiding each in his own way through the vicissitudes of *sadhana.*[18]

In fact, we may say that this is a most remarkable publication in the field of Sri Aurobindo's letters, full of significant material. In the following we will present a few extracts from various sections.

In the chapter "Heredity, Past Lives, Astrology" there are some letters printed from disciples who asked about his past lives. Names such as Julius Caesar, Virgil, Dante or Vālmīki

17 *Autobiographical Notes,* vii.

18 Bob Zwicker, "Ashram Archives", in *SABDA — Recent Publications,* June 2012, p. 3.

were proposed as candidates. But Sri Aurobindo either disclaimed any such connections, or else he kept silent, or gave evasive answers. This is also true of a letter dated 1 April 1932 where he seems to have preferred to remain silent only regarding Homer, whose name a correspondent had mentioned among many others. He notes critically that "these historical identifications are a perilous game and open a hundred doors to the play of imagination", following up with many other interesting observations.[19]

In the section "Remarks on Spiritual Figures in India" commentaries are found on Ramakrishna, Vivekananda, Ramaṇa Maharṣi and others. His notes on the Maharṣi are particularly captivating; they throw much light on the famous sage of Tiruvannamalai who resided in his Ashram a few hours away from Pondicherry. In one of his letters Sri Aurobindo tells a disciple that he has no objection to his visiting the Maharṣi:

> I have always encouraged people to go even in long past years when the Maharshi was unknown except to a few and I even sent several there who wanted to come here. Even if anyone wished to leave me and go to him, I would be the last person to interfere. Everyone has the right to choose his own Guru . . .[20]

Sri Aurobindo respects him as a *yogī* with the classical Vedānta realization, but he points out that the Maharṣi does not believe in his own idea of a "descent" of divine Force, etc. — a line of experience that is also difficult to follow for some contemporary spiritual teachers. In the following commentary Sri Aurobindo refers to this issue:

> "The Divine is here, from where will He descend?" is [the Maharshi] argument. But the Divine is everywhere, he is

[19] *Letters on Himself*, 56.

[20] Ibid., 166.

> above as well as within, he has many habitats, many strings to his bow of Power, there are many levels of his dynamic Consciousness and each has its own light and force. He is not confined to his position in the heart or to the single cord of the psycho-spiritual realisation. He has also his supramental station above the heart-centre and mind-centres and can descend from there if He wants to do so.[21]

Several other passages in his letters discuss the different kinds of approach in the two *yoga* paths, and Sri Aurobindo explains that "each path has its own aim and direction and method and the truth of one does not invalidate the truth of the other".[22]

Again and again we note that Sri Aurobindo looks with great detachment at his role as a spiritual teacher; we had already mentioned that he accepted the role of a *guru* only reluctantly. Actually, we learn from some of his statements that his vision went beyond the traditional concept. In an early letter, dated November 1929, he says:

> It is not usual to use the word Guru in the supramental yoga, here everything comes from the Divine himself. But if anybody wants it he can use it for the time being.

The direct relation with the Divine, he adds in another letter a few weeks later, is "a greater and more intimate relation than that of the human *guru* and disciple, which is more of a limited mental ideal". The soul should not be bound by that ideal and the latter should not limit "the inflow of other relations with the Divine and larger forms of experience".[23]

---

21 *Letters on Himself*, 172 (3 March 1937).

22 Ibid., 174.

23 Ibid., 395. Compare this with the Mother's statement, "I am not eager to be the Guru of anyone. It is more spontaneously natural for me to be the universal Mother and to act in silence through love." — *The Mother : A Short Biography*, 2.

Likewise, in the correspondence on "The Question of Avatarhood" we gain the impression that Sri Aurobindo has no great inclination to figure publicly as an *avatāra*. His focus is always on the work that is to be done, he does not seek personal glorification. Thus in a letter dated 7 March 1935 he states:

> Let me make it clear that in all I wrote I was not writing to prove that I am an Avatar. . . . I am seeking to manifest something of the Divine that I am conscious of and feel — I care a damn whether that constitutes me an Avatar or something else.[24]

Very enlightening also are Sri Aurobindo's statements in the section "The Ashram and Religion". His is a very dynamic outlook; he regards

> the spiritual history of mankind and especially of India as a constant development of a divine purpose, not a book that is closed, the lines of which have to be constantly repeated. Even the Upanishads and the Gita were not final though everything may be there in seed.

It is very far from his intention

> to propagate any religion new or old for humanity in the future. A way to be opened that is still blocked, not a religion to be founded, is my conception of the matter.[25]

Therefore, in his Ashram there is no place "for rigid orthodoxy, whether Hindu, Mahomedan or Christian. . . . Those who cling to it, lose hold on life and go under. . . ." He rejects all narrow-minded sectarian thinking and discourages looking upon Hinduism as the only true path.

> If this Ashram were here only to serve Hinduism I would not be in it and the Mother who was never a Hindu would

24 *Letters on Himself*, 419.

25 Ibid., 696.

> not be in it. What is being done here is the preparation of a Truth which includes all other Truth but is limited to no single religion or creed. . . .[26]

Actually, Christians (both Indian and foreign), Buddhists, Jains, Muslims, Jews, Sikhs and Parsis have lived amicably in the Ashram almost from the beginning.

Sri Aurobindo wants to bring down the supramental Truth and for this purpose he needs receptive seekers from all over India, all over the world and with different cultural backgrounds. Only if the multiplicity of the world is to some extent reflected in his Ashram can the work of transformation be fully achieved. All the same it is, of course, a fact that for various reasons he received a more active response from the Hindu community in India.

The Poems : Rose of God

Apart from his correspondence, Sri Aurobindo also composed a large number of mystical poems in the 1930s reflecting inner experiences, which he was constantly having. However, to appreciate them we require a spiritual "antenna" as is also the case with *Savitri*. Without that, we may not have access to his poetry, we may perhaps consider it outdated, as do some modern critics. But those who are open to his verses regard many of them as timeless creations. Here we will only briefly introduce two poems; we present first of all three stanzas from *Rose of God,* written in 1934 and considered by many readers a masterpiece:

Rose of God, vermilion stain on the sapphires of heaven,
Rose of Bliss, fire-sweet, seven-tinged with the ecstasies seven!
Leap up in our heart of humanhood, O miracle, O flame,
Passion-flower of the Nameless, bud of the mystical Name.

---

[26] *Letters on Himself,* 697-98.

Rose of God, great wisdom-bloom on the summits of being,
Rose of Light, immaculate core of the ultimate seeing!
Live in the mind of our earthhood; O golden Mystery, flower,
Sun on the head of the Timeless, guest of the marvellous Hour.

Rose of God, damask force of Infinity, red icon of might.
Rose of Power with thy diamond halo piercing the night!
Ablaze in the will of the mortal, design the wonder of thy plan,
Image of Immortality, outbreak of the Godhead in man.[27]

"It is a pure mystic cry of the soul, and the triune capacity of the inspired word to *utter* Being, to *name* and *thank* the Holy . . . breaks out as *mantra*, and rhythm, form and phrase and meaning coalesce perfectly into an utter and absolute harmony", comments Professor of Literature Srinivasa Iyengar. He further points out — as does Dante — that the rose is the highest symbol of the essence and the efflorescence of God. Bliss, Light, Power, Life and Love are, in the five stanzas of the poem, the respective essences which in their conjunction make up the integral perfection of the Divine.

> In every stanza, the first half names a Power above and the second half invokes that Power to inhabit, inform and re-create the corresponding instrument below.[28]

Very impressive is also the poem *Transformation* (around 1934). It suggests how deeply Sri Aurobindo is filled with the divine Presence even to the physical being. Very significant is the importance of the breath which, as in some Indian traditions like *kriyā yoga*, plays a decisive role in the spiritualization of the being, and we especially note his mentioning of "illumined cells". Here is the first stanza:

My breath runs in a subtle rhythmic stream;

---

27 *Collected Poems*, 564.

28 Iyengar, *Sri Aurobindo*, 614-15.

It fills my members with a might divine:
I have drunk the Infinite like a giant's wine.
Time is my drama or my pageant dream.
Now are my illumined cells joy's flaming scheme
And changed my thrilled and branching nerves to fine
Channels of rapture opal and hyaline
For the influx of the Unknown and the Supreme.[29]

Sri Aurobindo's Sādhanā

A few letters exist from the 1930s in which Sri Aurobindo gives hints of the state of his work and his *sādhanā*. These are especially found in the chapter "General Remarks on the Sadhana of the 1930s" in *Letters on Himself and the Ashram.*[30] In a letter dated April 1935 Sri Aurobindo, in a general statement, comments that he does not seek the supramentalization for himself, since personally he does not need anything.

> If I am seeking after supramentalisation, it is because it is a thing that has to be done for the earth-consciousness and if it is not done in myself, it cannot be done in others.[31]

In November 1933 he noted that the supermind had not yet descended into the body or into matter, but he said that he had reached a stage where this kind of descent had become not only possible, but inevitable.[32] In May 1936 he writes in a letter to a disciple:

> No, it is not with the Empyrean that I am busy: I wish it were. It is rather with the opposite end of things; it is in the Abyss that I have to plunge to build a bridge between the

---

29 *Collected Poems,* 561.

30 *Letters on Himself and the Ashram,* 277-97.

31 Ibid., 283.

32 Ibid., 326.

two. But that too is necessary for my work and one has to face it.[33]

That Sri Aurobindo was busy with the lower end of things becomes also evident from a letter which Nirodbaran sent him in August 1935:

> *Some time back you wrote to me: "Never has there been such an uprush of mud and brimstone as during the past few months. However, the Caravan goes on and today there was some promise of better things." What about the uprush of mud? Has it settled down, and are people now floating in the flood of the Supramental?*
>
> It is still there, but personally I have become superior to it and am travelling forward like a flash of lightning, that is to say zigzag but fairly fast. Now I have got the hang of the whole hanged thing — like a very Einstein I have got the mathematical formula of the whole affair (unintelligible as in his case to anybody but myself) and am working it out figure by figure.
>
> As for people, no! they are not floating in the supramental — some are floating in the higher mind, others rushing up into it and flopping down into the subconscient alternately, are swinging from heaven into hell and back into heaven . . ., some are sitting in the mud and dreaming dreams and seeing visions. . . . But console yourself — these things, it seems, are inevitable in the process of great transformations.[34]

In March 1937 Nirodbaran enquires whether the *sādhaka*s would not start tumbling one by one once the supermind comes nearer. "Then with whom will you enjoy your Supramental? Night and day you are soaring and soaring." But Sri Aurobindo rejects this idea, widespread among his disciples, that he is climbing glorious summits above, whereas they are

---

33 *Letters on Himself and the Ashram*, 360.

34 *Nirodbaran's Correspondence with Sri Aurobindo*, 287-88.

wrestling below with all kinds of blockages. "Romantic one! I am not soaring and soaring — I am digging and digging."[35]

In August 1935 Sri Aurobindo had sent a disciple some lines from his poem "A God's Labour", still unpublished at that time, for illustrating this same matter:

> *He who would bring the heavens here,*
> *Must descend himself into the clay*
> *And the burden of earthly nature bear*
> *And tread the dolorous way.*[36]

In a letter written by the middle of 1935 he states in very clear terms that he is well acquainted with the "hard realities", that he knows everything, "hardship and semi-starvation in England", all kinds of difficulties and perils.

> My life has been a battle from its early years and is still a battle: the fact that I wage it now from a room upstairs and by spiritual means as well as others that are external makes no difference to its character.[37]

At another place he mentions that he, too, has had the experience of dull phases in his *sādhanā*. If they come, *sādhaka*s should take a positive attitude, refusing to be overcome by a mood of defeat; ideally ". . . one has only to get through them as soon as possible and get back into the sun."[38]

In August 1936 Sri Aurobindo informs a correspondent with satisfaction that the *darśan* of 15 August was quite good and that there was general progress.

> A thing has been done which had long failed to accomplish itself and which is of great importance. . . . But it gives a sort

35 *Nirodbaran's Correspondence with Sri Aurobindo*, 852.

36 *Letters on Himself and the Ashram*, 284.

37 Ibid., 44.

38 Ibid., 376.

> of strong practical assurance that the thing will be done.[39]

Similarly, he had written already in December 1934:

> This is, however, certain that a number of souls have been sent to see that it shall be now. That is the situation.[40]

Occasionally, the subject of the descent of the supermind was also treated with humour. Thus Nirodbaran enquired in May 1937 on behalf of a follower outside (named Chand) what the situation was regarding the descent, whether the "tail of the supermind" was already in view — in which case Chand would "give a gorilla jump to Pondy". Sri Aurobindo's brief answer:

> Of course [it is in sight]. Coming down as fast as you fellows will allow.[41]

In fact, humour was an important aspect of Sri Aurobindo's nature and Nirodbaran has even published a whole book on it.[42]

The Accident and Talks with Sri Aurobindo

The day before the *darśan* of 24 November 1938 had passed happily and the *sādhaka*s had gone to take rest.

> Over the Ashram reigned an atmosphere of deep peace and silence. Only one light was burning in Sri Aurobindo's corner room facing the street and keeping a vigil over the pervasive darkness. The Mother too had retired early leaving Sri Aurobindo at his work. He was perhaps busy with *Savitri* now that the "avalanche of correspondence" had been arrested due to Darshan work. Thus the small hours were reached. Then in Purani's room the light was switched

39 *Letters on Himself and the Ashram*, 360.

40 Ibid., 334.

41 *Nirodbaran's Correspondence with Sri Aurobindo*, 590.

42 Nirodbaran, *Sri Aurobindo's Humour*, Pondicherry: Sri Aurobindo Ashram.

> on; it was 2 a.m. He had to prepare hot water for the Mother's bath. At 7.30 a.m. the Darshan would start.[43]

This is Nirodbaran's description of the situation on the night of 23 to 24 November. Then suddenly the emergency bell rang from the Mother's room. When Purani rushed upstairs, she told him that Sri Aurobindo had fallen down, stumbling over a tiger skin on his way to the bathroom. He felt a sharp pain and could not transform it into the sensation of *ānanda* as he was otherwise able to do. When he realized that he could not get up, he lay quietly. The Mother intuitively felt in her sleep that something had gone wrong with him, got up and rushed into his room. She at once suspected he had suffered a fracture and therefore rang the bell.

She asked Purani to call Manilal, a prominent doctor from Gujarat who had come for *darśan*. He arrived quickly and examined the leg. Sri Aurobindo's right knee was flexed and "his face bore a perplexed smile as if he did not know what was wrong with him".[44] The diagnosis was shocking: it was a fracture of the thigh bone. A team of attendants was formed with Manilal, three Ashram doctors including Nirodbaran, his personal attendant Champaklal, Purani and the dentist Satyendra.

Sri Aurobindo's leg was plastered and then he was carefully taken to his bed. A message was sent to Rao, director of a hospital in Cuddalore (a nearby town) who was the friend of a *sādhak* in the Ashram. When he arrived in the morning Rao proposed consulting an orthopaedic surgeon from Madras, a friend of his. The latter arrived in the evening, a little later followed by a radiologist with his machine. The pictures revealed a complicated fracture requiring a long treatment which consisted in exerting a steady traction of the leg by means of splints.

---

43 Nirodbaran, *Twelve Years with Sri Aurobindo*, 4-5.

44 Ibid., 4.

Meanwhile, Sri Aurobindo remained "calm and unperturbed as if nothing had happened to him. No questions about his condition, no anxiety, no complaint of any sort, quiet acceptance of the doctor's direction".[45] However, the members of the Ashram and visitors who had come for *darśana* were quite depressed upon hearing the news. But in the evening the Mother gave *darśan* to all of them, to encourage them.

Sri Aurobindo's accident had brought about a deep change in his outer circumstances. His life of withdrawal was finished now, for helpers had to be constantly present; they used the opportunity for asking him questions. Nirodbaran reports:

> When everything had settled down and our work had fallen into a regular pattern, the "famous" talks started, in the evening to begin with. Sri Aurobindo, lying on his back, used to speak in a low voice to the assembly crowded near the bed. Naturally on that occasion all of us except Purani who stood at a distance, would rally round to listen to his finely cadenced voice and his utterances on various topics made in an intimate tone. He would rarely look at anybody while talking.[46]

The talks were continued even after Sri Aurobindo's recovery, which took several months. Nirodbaran and Purani recorded them by making notes (which do not necessarily render the texts literally). Nirodbaran's *Talks with Sri Aurobindo* cover the period from December 1938 to September 1941, supplemented by two talks from later years. All kinds of subjects were being discussed such as *yoga* and its practice, medicine, literature, philosophy and occultism, frequently livened up by Sri Aurobindo's humorous remarks.

As a sample here is a little excerpt from a talk on inner silence:

---

45 Nirodbaran, *Twelve Years with Sri Aurobindo*, 10.

46 Ibid., 14.

N: Can one do work with the silence intact? Does not the silence get disturbed?

Sri Aurobindo: Certainly one can do work. By silence I mean inner silence. It is perfectly possible to carry on any amount of activity in that state. I told you about my experience which is still with me. It has not been disturbed by any activity.

Dr B: Is silence dynamic or static?

Sri Aurobindo: It is not the silence that is dynamic but you can have full dynamic activity out of the inner silence. Also you can remain without doing anything. People who are kinetic in the vital or mental way cannot remain like that.

Some Marathas came to see me here and inquired what I was doing. I replied: "Nothing." One of them remarked that it was a great thing to do nothing. This is true."[47]

In a talk dated 7 January 1939 Sri Aurobindo referred to his accident and mentioned that after the experience of silence and *nirvāṇa* he had to work incessantly to establish them in every part of his being:

> You know what is equanimity? It means that nothing stirs under any condition. Till last August I was successful. This accident was perhaps the last test to my equanimity. In that way one has to go on working things out till one reaches the central point in the subconscient which is the seed one has to cut out.
>
> It is while working in this way that I came to notice many gaps that had not been filled up. It may be due to those gaps that the accident took place. When one has conquered that subconscient seed a force will be established in the world-action and those who embody it will be able to throw it around them like waves for the change.[48]

---

47 Nirodbaran, *Talks with Sri Aurobindo*, vol. I, 92 (2 January 1939).

48 Ibid., 141.

In an earlier talk Sri Aurobindo had thrown light on another aspect of the accident:

> The hostile forces have tried many times to prevent things like the Darshan, but I have succeeded in warding off all their attacks. At the time the accident to my leg happened, I was more occupied with guarding the Mother and I forgot about myself. I didn't think the hostiles would attack me. That was my mistake.[49]

As mentioned above, again and again there were humorous remarks and laughter. Thus one day Sri Aurobindo enquired with Manilal about his practice of meditation. "Not successful, Sir!" answered the doctor. Sri Aurobindo retorts: "How? I saw you grim and powerful, wrestling your way towards the Brahman." Loud laughter followed this.[50] A few days later they spoke about Tilak, Sri Aurobindo's comrade during the period of the freedom movement, who had also written a commentary on the *Gītā*. When Manilal wants to know Sri Aurobindo's opinion of the book, the latter answers: "I must say I haven't read it." M: "But you have reviewed it." Sri Aurobindo: "Then I must have reviewed it without reading it." More loud laughter.[51]

Over time, when the danger of the Second World War becomes evident, the talks naturally become more serious. In a talk dated 20 December 1938 the subject of Hitler and his nature comes up and Sri Aurobindo sees the expansive "Hitlerian vital, catching hold of other people in its grip".[52] On 8 January 1939 he is told that Gandhi has written that some people in Germany had tried non-violence, though

---

49 Nirodbaran, *Talks with Sri Aurobindo*, 33 (14 December 1938).

50 Ibid., 30 (14 December 1938).

51 Ibid., 46 (18 December 1938).

52 Ibid., 50.

without success, "because it has not been so strong as to generate sufficient heat to melt Hitler's heart". Sri Aurobindo comments,

> It would have to be a furnace in that case. The only way to melt his heart is to bomb it out of existence.[53]

His position regarding Hitler is from the first to the last day uncompromising, he decides to support the Allies and closely follows all developments during the war.

---

[53] Nirodbaran, *Talks with Sri Aurobindo*, 143.

13

The Second World War
(1939-45)

ALTHOUGH Sri Aurobindo had withdrawn from politics after his arrival in Pondicherry in 1910, he kept an eye on it, informing himself about world events through reading newspapers. His attention became intensive when there were the first signs of fatal developments in Europe. At an early stage he had become aware of the new German "Führer" and already in 1936 mentioned "Hitler and his howling tribe" in a letter to Nirodbaran.[1]

It is also Nirodbaran to whom we owe a detailed account of Sri Aurobindo's inner work before and during the Second World War. In his title *Twelve Years with Sri Aurobindo* he has dedicated a long chapter called "War and Politics" to this subject. He shows how Sri Aurobindo was now — during the late 1930s — turning his attention once more to politics, although in his own way, through work on the hidden planes of consciousness. He was convinced that not only on the physical plane, but also in the inner worlds there is an interconnection and that a *yogī* may have an impact on events in the world through the power of thought, even from his seclusion at a distant place. This becomes possible due to the inner freedom he has realized by not floating more or less helplessly on the waves of thought, but rather controlling and directing them himself. Using such power is only legitimate if

[1] Nirodbaran, *Twelve Years with Sri Aurobindo*, 151.

the *yogī*, free from ego, acts and is in tune with the divine Will. Otherwise it would be "magic".

From Sri Aurobindo's viewpoint an āsuric power (hostile force) stood behind Hitler, a mighty personality that tried to block Sri Aurobindo's efforts for a new creation on earth. Nirodbaran reports:

> Long before Hitler's actual invasion of Poland, long before any other person, Sri Aurobindo had seen this dark Asuric Power rising in Germany and striding over Europe, making Hitler its demoniac instrument. . . . Therefore he supported the Allies and warned India of the forthcoming peril, much to the chagrin and indignation of our blind countrymen.[2]

The battle against Hitler was now his most important project until the end of the war.

Winston Churchill

> In the following "black days" of the Second World War after the defeat of France, Churchill, with his stubbornness and his rousing speeches, became the motor of British resistance against Hitler and the symbol of British persistence.[3]

Working on planes of consciousness alone remains ineffective in this world if there are not also those who receive the impulses, and put them into action in the physical world. Sri Aurobindo found his "partner" (without the latter's knowledge) during the Second World War in Winston Leonard Spencer Churchill (1874–1965), a British statesman with special qualities and an extraordinary vita. Sri Aurobindo supported him in his own invisible yogic way wherever it was possible. Thus Nirodbaran reports, for instance, that at a certain stage of the war news via radio was transmitted to Sri Aurobindo's

---

2 Nirodbaran, *Twelve Years with Sri Aurobindo*, 131.

3 ®Microsoft Encarta Enzyklopädie, 2005, "Winston Churchill" tr. into English from the original German text by the author.

room, so that he could follow all developments close to the time of their occurrence. When Churchill was once suffering from pneumonia, he "listened carefully to the health bulletins . . . and, we believe, even helped him with his Force to recover."[4]

At another place Nirodbaran quotes the report of a *sādhak* who — as many others — did not understand Sri Aurobindo's supporting the Allies and rejected it. Finally, there is a talk with the Mother who asks the *sādhak*,

> Do you not see the difference between the forces that are fighting for the Divine and those for the Asuras?

The *sādhak* answered,

> Yes, Mother, I do see; only what baffles me is that Churchill, whom you and Sri Aurobindo have chosen as your direct instrument, wants today India's help for his own country's existence; and yet says that His Majesty's government has no intention of liquidating its Empire!

Then the Mother said,

> But leave all that to the Divine. Churchill is a human being. He is not a yogi aspiring to transform his nature. Today he represents the Soul of the Nation that is fighting against the Asuras. He is being guided by the Divine directly and his soul is responding magnificently.[5]

Churchill was a warrior type of man, a *kṣatriya*, as you would say in India. Even at a young age he voluntarily took part in many battles, which were always taking place somewhere in the British Empire, and he survived them without injuries. During the Boer War he was taken prisoner as a war correspondent, but he managed to escape through a spectacular flight over a distance of 300 miles that took him into freedom.

---

4 Nirodbaran, *Twelve Years with Sri Aurobindo*, 133.

5 Ibid., 137.

In the decades to come he held almost all ministerial offices that were available in British politics. But then he suffered some failures and during the 1930s he touched bottom, due to certain developments. However, with great alertness he continued to follow political events and his attention was more and more focused on Hitler. While war-worn England tried to keep the German dictator at bay through a policy of appeasement, Churchill realized the danger and warned his countrymen indefatigably, though in vain.

The American author and historian William Manchester has written a brilliant work[6] on this period and we will refer to it in the following report to compare Sri Aurobindo's statements with ascertainable data and accounts of historiography. In this context, we will also investigate whether Churchill had a kind of feeling that he was receiving invisible help "from above" and why he was so specifically qualified to play this particular role in the battle against Hitler.

In his biography, which has the sub-title *Alone*,[7] Manchester presents Churchill as a personality with many gifts. He is not only the courageous warrior, but has also great reverence for all creatures, sentiments which would seem to approach ascetic Jainism.[8] In his free time he likes to paint; once a police inspector had observed him for some time during a visit and reported,

> So I would think that the man's inner spirit is superbly calm and that he paints from it, never from the mind or intellect.[9]

---

6 *The Last Lion: Winston Spencer Churchill — Alone 1932-1940*, Little, Brown & Co., 1988. (The second volume of a trilogy on Churchill, the third has currently not yet been published.)

7 *Alone*, because for many years Churchill was alone in warning against Hitler.

8 *The Last Lion*, 20.

9 Walter Henry Thompson, *Assignment Churchill*, New York 1955, 94.

This reminds us of Sri Aurobindo and his writing from the silent mind.

During a lecture in 1934 Churchill warned for the first time against the danger of German rearmament and demanded that his own country should immediately take steps to strengthen its defence. However, the only reaction of the audience was roaring laughter. Even while he was seeing through Hitler and his intentions with an unerring judgement, his countrymen fell victim, in great numbers, to Hitler's charisma. The latter had opened the doors to English politicians after he had become chancellor, and his guests used to return from their visits glowing with optimism and convinced that Hitler was really seeking a political settlement with other nations.[10]

In this context we may quote a statement that Sri Aurobindo made when seeing a photo of Hitler, Goebbels and Goering:

> Hitler gives the impression of the face of a street-criminal. In his case it is successful ruffianism with a diabolical cunning. . . . He is possessed by some supernatural Power and it is from this Power that the voice, as he calls it, comes. Have you noted that people who at one time were inimical to him come into contact with him and leave as his admirers? It is a sign of that Power. It is from this Power that he has constantly received suggestions and the constant repetition of the suggestions has taken hold of the German people.[11]

Churchill refuses to support the proponents of an appeasement policy, and this refusal at first blocks his career. But later it was to become a great advantage that he was not associated with the wrong approach: "Now one can see how lucky I was. Over me beat the invisible wings."[12] Here we have a hint that

10 *The Last Lion,* 81.

11 *Twelve Years with Sri Aurobindo,* 152.

12 Winston S. Churchill, *The Second World War: The Gathering Storm,* Houghton Mifflin, 1948, 178.

Churchill himself felt he had had some protection "from above" in making his decisions.

However, he was also a reactionary man in several aspects of his nature, living rather in the nineteenth than the twentieth century, dreaming of the old world of the glorious Empire from which he could not detach. All this contributed to not being taken seriously by his political colleagues.

But his virtue, of a fearless warhorse of the Empire, was exactly what was needed now in facing the satanic Hitler with his āsuric nature. According to the Indian tradition the *asura*s were originally divine beings who had turned away from the One and became Lords of Darkness. In the *Mahābhārata*[13] they are called "the elder brothers of the gods" and the Mother has explained that at the beginning there were four *asura*s as the first individual beings in the universe. Out of them one was converted (that is to say, returned to the Truth) while another had been dissolved into his origin. But

> . . . two are still living and these two are more ferocious than the others. . . . And as long as these two beings exist, there will be difficulties.[14]

Meanwhile, Hitler too became aware that he had a powerful opponent. When Reich Finance Minister Count Schwerin von Krosigk met a British general, he reported that "Churchill is the only Englishman Hitler is afraid of."[15] During this period Sri Aurobindo and the Mother often spoke of a battle between the forces of light and of darkness. Thus Sri Aurobindo wrote in a letter to a disciple:

> You should not think of it as a fight for certain nations

---

13 *Mbh.* 3.92.6, Pune Critical Edition.

14 *CWM*, vol. 4, *Questions and Answers 1950-51*, 188. The "two beings" are the Lord of Falsehood and the Lord of Death. See also *Mother's Agenda*, vol. 2, 5 November 1961.

15 Quoted in *The Last Lion*, 428.

> against others or even for India; it is a struggle for an ideal that has to establish itself on earth in the life of humanity, for a Truth that has yet to realise itself fully and against a darkness and falsehood that are trying to overwhelm the earth and mankind in the immediate future."[16]

Churchill's vision was similar. Manchester notes that he used to divide those about whom he wrote in his studies into white hats and black hats.

> But that is how he saw life, as a struggle between the forces of light and the powers of darkness.[17]

He was aware of the role he would play in the battle to come and believed that he alone could save his country.[18]

When the situation became very serious and Great Britain had to declare war on Germany, Churchill at last gained recognition for his uncompromising attitude. In 1939 he was appointed First Sea Lord and on 10 May 1940 he replaced Chamberlain as prime minister. Now there were no more restrictions in his battle against Hitler, which appeared rather desperate at times. "And in moments of crises he sought guidance not by reasoning but by intuition", notes Manchester.[19]

We had already mentioned that from Sri Aurobindo's viewpoint Hitler was possessed of an āsuric power. There are some reports about his behaviour which might be interpreted as evidence for this judgement. Thus Manchester notes that the diary of German Colonel-General Jodl was full of phrases

> describing Hitler's loss of selfcontrol, his terror that he might lose his gamble, how he was always trembling on the verge of hysteria and sometimes plunged into it.[20]

16 *Letters on Himself and the Ashram*, 211-12.

17 *The Last Lion*, 434.

18 Ibid., 473.

19 Ibid., 664.

20 Ibid., 640.

Sri Aurobindo, who had no access to such sources at this time, all the more so since Hitler's weaknesses were kept hidden by his attendants as much as possible, wrote a poem in October 1939 titled *The Dwarf Napoleon — Hitler* in which he analyses the dictator's nature and his possession with an amazing insight:

> *In his high villa on the fatal hill*
> *Alone he listens to that sovereign Voice,*
> *Dictator of his action's sudden choice,*
> *The tiger leap of a demoniac skill.*
> *An energy his body cannot invest, —*
> *Too small and human for that dreadful guest,*
> *A tortured channel, not a happy vessel, —*
> *Drives him to think and act and cry and wrestle.*[21]

As for Churchill's insight, Manchester makes a very significant statement at the end of his biography:

> He [Churchill] had come to power because he had seen through Hitler from the very beginning — but not, ironically, because his inner light, the source of that insight, was understood by Englishmen. *Churchill's star was invisible to the public and even to most of his peers.* But a few saw it.[22]

Among them was the Oxford philosopher Isaiah Berlin who pointed out that Churchill had succeeded in impressing his own imagination and will on his countrymen with such intensity "that in the end they approached his ideal and began to see themselves as he saw them".[23]

Whether Sri Aurobindo really played any part in all this, is a matter of personal faith. However, we may mention that it was exactly part of his work, on the level of consciousness, to focus unswervingly on the idea of victory for the forces of

---

21 *Collected Poems*, 641 (italics, three lines, W.H.).

22 *The Last Lion*, 687 (italics, W.H.).

23 Ibid.

Light, in spite of the dark reality of the moment, and keep this image alive until the war was won by the Allies.

We also know from some sources[24] that he and the Mother tried to inspire from distant Pondicherry Churchill's speeches whose style and vocabulary often comes close to his own. Thus we discover an almost mantric sound in a speech of his, dated 18 June 1940, one day after Marshall Pétain began his armistice negotiations with Germany. Churchill declared that, on the battle to come, would depend the survival of the Christian civilization:

> *Hitler knows that he will have to break us on this island or lose the war.*
> *If we can stand up to him all Europe may be free*
> *and the life of the world may move forward*
> *into broad, sunlit uplands.*
> *But if we fail, then the whole world*
> *including the United States,*
> *including all we have known and cared for,*
> *will sink into the abyss of a new Dark Age . . .*[25]

We may compare this with a statement of Sri Aurobindo, contained in a letter to the governor of Madras on the occasion of Sri Aurobindo sending a donation to the war funds, written at the time of the collapse of France and the menacing danger of the break-down of Great Britain:

> We feel that not only is this a battle waged in just self-defence and in defence of the nations threatened with the world-domination of Germany and the Nazi system of life, but that it is a defence of civilization and its highest attained social, cultural and spiritual values and of the whole future of humanity.[26]

---

[24] See, for instance, *Twelve Years with Sri Aurobindo*, 142.

[25] Winston S. Churchill on 18 June 1940. See the complete speech with the original soundtrack under www.historyplace.com/speeches/churchill-hour.htm.

[26] *Autobiographical Notes*, 453.

Later he declared in a letter to a disciple, dated 3 September 1943:

> The victory of one side [the Allies] would keep the path open for the evolutionary forces; the victory of the other side would drag back humanity, degrade it horribly and might lead even, at the worst, to its eventual failure as a race. . . . Even if I knew that the Allies would misuse their victory or bungle the peace or partially at least spoil the opportunities opened to the human world by that victory, I would still put my force behind them. At any rate things could not be one-hundredth part as bad as they would be under Hitler. The ways of the Lord would still be open — to keep them open is what matters.[27]

As for Churchill, he was aware of some hidden support. Thus, in a speech on 31 October 1942 he said:

> I sometimes have a feeling, in fact I have it very strongly, a feeling of interference. I want to stress that I have a feeling sometimes that some guiding hand has interfered. I have the feeling that we have a guardian because we serve a great cause, and that we shall have that guardian so long as we serve that cause faithfully.[28]

The Course of the War

Sri Aurobindo has sketched the further course of the war in the last four lines of his already mentioned poem *The Dwarf Napoleon:*

> *Thus driven he[29] must stride on conquering all,*
> *Threatening and clamouring, brutal, invincible,*
> *Until he meets upon his storm-swept road*
> *A greater devil — or thunderstroke of God.*[30]

---

27 *Autobiographical Notes*, 466-67.

28 W.S. Churchill, *The End of the Beginning*: *War Speeches by the Hon. Winston S. Churchill*, 1943, 207.

29 Hitler.

30 *Collected Poems*, 641.

A major weakness of the *asuras* is their lack of unity. If they unite, their power can be immense, but since they have turned away from the Supreme One and the law of divine harmony, they do not succeed in forging long-term alliances. Sooner or later some personal ambition erupts in one of them and he wants to be the sole sovereign ruler. In the present situation Sri Aurobindo and the Mother believed that humanity might be saved if Hitler and Stalin, who had signed a secret non-aggression pact in 1939, would confront each other in war as soon as possible.

Accordingly, they became active in the inner worlds and worked towards Hitler attacking Russia, which he did in June 1941. When the Mother was later asked how things may have developed if Russia and Germany had worked together instead, she answered:

> Then there would have been no hope for the world. It is by our *coup de maître*[31] that they were on opposite sides. This is divine diplomacy. It is very successful.[32]

Nirodbaran comments in his report on this subject,

> But the world does not know that a Supreme Force had worked for its deliverance."[33]

In the fourth and last part of *Talks with Sri Aurobindo* the discussion more and more predominantly focuses on current military and political developments. Especially significant is a passage dated end of May 1940 concerning Dunkirk. In this French town on the Atlantic coast some 300,000 troops of a British expeditionary corps as well as French forces were surrounded by the Germans without any real hope of escape. But for reasons which have never been conclusively clarified

---

31 That is to say, influencing Hitler to attack Stalin.

32 *Twelve Years with Sri Aurobindo*, 149-50.

33 Ibid., 150.

Hitler ordered the advance of his tanks to be stopped, thus enabling the Allies to start an enormous evacuation through which a major part of the troops could be brought to England via the Channel.

On 31 May 1940 Sri Aurobindo comments on this development: "So they are getting away from Dunkirk!" P: "Yes. It seems the fog helped the evacuation." Sri Aurobindo: "Yes. Fog is rather unusual at this time." And Nirodbaran adds, ". . . by saying this, it seemed Sri Aurobindo wanted to hint that the Mother and he had made this fog to help the Allies."[34]

Cripps' Mission

At first India was not directly affected by the war, but here too some problems arose. The leaders of the Congress were irritated that the British viceroy had not consulted them before declaring that India was at war. Therefore they withdrew their ministers from those provincial governments which they had headed since 1938. As a consequence the Muslim League, which pursued separatist goals, gained influence as its representatives remained active in those parts of the country where Muslims had a majority, that is in the north-west and eastern India. They even passed a resolution demanding that independent Muslim states should be established in those regions — a first pre-announcement of the later Pakistan.

When Japan entered the war in December 1941 and advanced via the Philippines and Bangkok up to Singapore and Rangoon, India too found itself in the danger zone. It was of great importance now for England to assure the loyalty of the different forces in India, and therefore Churchill sent Stafford Cripps to Delhi in spring 1942 in order to make a proposal that would grant India at first the status of dominion (like Canada or Australia). This would not yet be complete independence, but a decisive step towards the desired

[34] Nirodbaran, *Talks with Sri Aurobindo*, vol. II, 681.

freedom. Cripps negotiated with the leaders of the Congress and with Mohammed Ali Jinnah, the representative of the Muslim League, and then turned to the Indian population in a radio address on 30 March 1942 to explain his proposal.

Sri Aurobindo listened to the broadcast and at once sent a telegram to Cripps in which he welcomed the proposal

> as an opportunity given to India to determine for herself, and organise in all liberty of choice, her freedom and unity, and take an effective place among the world's free nations.[35]

Cripps answered a little later by telegram, thanking Sri Aurobindo for supporting his mission and for his message

> . . . allowing me to inform India that you who occupy unique position in imagination of Indian youth, are convinced that declaration of His Majesty's Government substantially confers that freedom for which Indian Nationalism has so long struggled.[36]

Sri Aurobindo also cabled two persons whom he knew who were active in the Congress, and he sent a messenger to Delhi who pleaded for accepting Cripps' proposal. But the Congress, led by Gandhi, rejected it so that the initiative failed. Sri Aurobindo and the Mother were convinced that the divine Grace stood behind the proposal which — had it been accepted — might have prevented the later partition of the country. Similarly, the *Oxford History of India* describes the consequences of the rejection of Cripps' initiative as follows:

> So the golden moment passed and with it the last real chance of establishing a united independent India. The rejection of the offer was the prelude to the partition.[37]

---

35 *Autobiographical Notes*, 469.

36 *Autobiographical Notes*, 469 fn. It is to be noted that Cripps wrote this text as a telegram.

37 *The Oxford History of India*, 828. Quoted in *The Mother : A Short Biography*, 78.

Sri Aurobindo later clarified in a talk dated 7 August 1943 that from the beginning he was little optimistic regarding the chances of Cripps' mission. But he said that he would have sent his messenger to Delhi even if he had known with certainty that the action was in vain. There was a deeper purpose in the overall "play of forces" as he called it, but pointed out that it would be difficult to explain this to the rational mind.[38]

Churchill did not play a luminous role in this case. He had undertaken this action due to pressure from President Franklin D. Roosevelt (who wished for more self-determination for India) but was not really interested in a success of the mission. On 10 November 1942 he declared in a speech that he had not become prime minister "to preside over the liquidation of the British Empire".[39] Moreover, Cripps was considered as his political rival; many observers thought him to be his potential successor in office. Therefore, it could not be very much in Churchill's own interest that Cripps returned home with a successful completion of his mission. The latter explained to his circle of friends that personally, he would have liked to grant India complete independence right away, but Churchill did not admit it, whereas Gandhi demanded it.[40]

Meanwhile the war brought about difficulties for the Ashram also, since the supply of basic foods was reduced to a minimum due to general restrictions. This problem was aggravated because some followers from the north-east, which was threatened by an invasion of the Japanese, had taken their children and families to the Ashram for protection. The Mother opened her doors to them and for the first time admitted children to the Ashram life. On 2 December 1943 a school was

---

38 Purani, *Evening Talks with Sri Aurobindo*, 769.

39 *yourdictionary.com/quotes/empire.*

40 See as a source: H. Kulke, D. Rothermund, *Geschichte Indiens*, Kohlhammer 1982, 324.

founded with twenty children initially, but their number constantly grew.

Another problem during war time was the wrong attitude of some members of the Ashram. Due to their hatred of the British rulers they wished for Hitler's victory, which meant a great danger for the Ashram on French territory. Finally, Sri Aurobindo sent them a message in which he pointed out the risk of a dissolution of the community and stated that "Hitlerism is the greatest menace that the world has ever met".[41]

At times there were also bomb alerts in connection with possible attacks by the Japanese Air Force. Several times all the lights in the town had to be turned off, but an attack never took place. In the end, the victory of the Allies in the Second World War meant the fulfilment of an important aspect of Sri Aurobindo's work; Nazism was the most dangerous force opposing his evolutionary goals and it had been defeated.

---

41 *Twelve Years with Sri Aurobindo*, 167.

14

Literary and Other Activities
(1939-50)

WHEN after several months Sri Aurobindo had recovered from the fracture of his leg and was able to resume walking, his followers felt it would be too long to wait until the next *darśan* on 15 August 1939. Therefore, a new *darśan* date was established (and kept) on 24 April, the day of the final arrival of the Mother in Pondicherry. But while formerly a *darśan* could take up to seven hours, all *sādhaka*s and visitors were advised now to stand only for a moment before Sri Aurobindo and the Mother, and then to proceed.

Sri Aurobindo resumed his work now and took up the book edition of *The Life Divine*, since the Arya Publishing House in Calcutta had enquired about it. He wanted to revise the text and write a few new chapters. Nirodbaran observed him as a witness and looked with great attention at his master setting about the work:

> There he was, then sitting on the bed, with his right leg stretched out. I was watching his movements from behind the bed. No sooner had he begun than followed line after line as if everything was chalked out in the mind, or as he used to say, a tap was turned on and a stream poured down. Absorbed in perfect poise, gazing now and then in front, wiping the perspiration off the hands — for he perspired profusely — he would go on for about two hours.[1]

---

1 *Twelve Years with Sri Aurobindo*, 36.

When the first part of the book was published in November 1939, the war had already begun.

The revision of the Second Part was more thorough: he cancelled eight chapters and wrote twelve anew, especially the last six in which he described the planes between mind and supermind. This portion appeared in Calcutta in July 1940. The book also found its way to England after some time and was reviewed on 17 January 1942 by Sir Francis Younghusband in the Literary Supplement of the *Times.* Younghusband was an officer who had been born as the son of a British family in India and had made his name as an important explorer in China and in north-west India. In his review he appreciated especially Sri Aurobindo's world-positive view:

> Aurobindo does not look upon life on earth as a preparation for life in some distant heaven above the clouds. He would make heavens on earth. He would raise men to the Divine level. . . . The kingdom of God without will have to be built upon the kingdom of God that is within us. And in awakening that spirit the philosophy of Aurobindo may play a striking part.[2]

Younghusband, who himself wrote books on mystical subjects, proposed Sri Aurobindo in 1943 for the Nobel Prize in Literature and his nomination, supported by the Royal Society of Literature, was accepted by the Swedish Academy.[3] However no award in literature was presented in that year. There was to be a second nomination in 1950, this time supported by the Nobel Prize winners Gabriela Mistral and Pearl S. Buck. The Chilean Mistral wrote in her statement that Sri Aurobindo was someone ". . .

---

2 F. Younghusband, "An Indian Seer: The Philosophy of Sri Aurobindo", *Times Literary Supplement,* 17 January 1942. Quoted in *The Lives of Sri Aurobindo,* 388.

3 Several sources given in *The Lives of Sri Aurobindo,* 388, fn. 116.

who belongs to the family of seers and sages of the world."[4] The proposal was supported by thirty-six Indians who held eminent positions in the political and cultural life of the country and a signed memorandum was sent to the Swedish Academy. However, there were thirty-four nominations in that year and the jurors favoured another candidate.

After this work Sri Aurobindo intensively dedicated himself again to his epic *Savitri,* which he considered as his most important literary creation.[5] Furthermore, a compilation of his poems and plays was published under the title *Collected Poems and Plays,* reviewed in 1944 by the Indian author R. Shahani in the literary section of the *Times* with a somewhat reserved appraisement. Shahani did, however, acknowledge Sri Aurobindo as an eminent literary critic and scholar and called *The Life Divine* "one of the master-works of our age".[6]

Originally, Sri Aurobindo was not inclined to allow biographies to be written about himself, because he felt that his real life was not on the surface for others to see.[7] But then over time a number of Indian biographies were published with some fanciful assertions and statements, and it was especially his political life that was presented in a wrong and disfigured manner. Therefore he agreed to read the manuscripts of the south Indian Professor of English Literature, K.R. Srinivasa Iyengar, and the French Professor Gabriel Monod-Herzen (who lived in the Ashram), thus clarifying through some detailed comments the facts of his political work in India. Iyengar later enlarged his biography which became a book of more than 800 pages, published in 1972.

---

4 *Sri Aurobindo, Tributes,* 18. Quoted in Otto Wolff, *Sri Aurobindo,* Rowohlt Verlag 1995, 148 (re-translated into English).

5 It will be introduced in the next chapter.

6 R. Shahani, "A Philosopher of Modern India: Aurobindo the Reconciler", *Times Literary Supplement*, 8 July, 1944, 330.

7 *Autobiographical Notes,* 11.

India's Independence

By the middle of 1945 Sri Aurobindo was once more drawn into politics; in England the Labour Party had come to power whereas Churchill and the Conservatives were in the opposition now. The Labour Party had long since favoured Indian independence and now took steps to quickly grant it. Sri Aurobindo followed these events with great attention, pleading for avoidance of developments and decisions that might result in a partition of India. But then there was a rift between the Congress and the Muslim League and the latter called for "direct actions". This brought about riots and finally violent attacks, especially against the Hindus in Bengal. When Sri Aurobindo was told about it, he said that they should fight back, which they actually did.[8]

In June 1947 Lord Mountbatten arrived in Delhi to initiate proceedings that would irrevocably bring about independence. When he was asked for a precise date, he said it would be 15 August, so Sri Aurobindo received on his birthday the gift of a free India,

> but complicated by its being presented in two packets as two free Indias: this is a generosity I could have done without, one free India would have been enough for me if offered as an unbroken whole.[9]

When the radio station All India Radio asked him for a message for the occasion of independence, he sent a long statement:

> 15 August 1947 is the birthday of free India. It marks for her the end of an old era, the beginning of a new age. . . . August 15 is my own birthday and it is naturally gratifying to me that it should have assumed this vast significance. I take this coincidence, not as a fortuitous accident, but as the

8 *Twelve Years with Sri Aurobindo*, 250.

9 *Letters on Himself and the Ashram*, 368.

> sanction and seal of the Divine Force that guides my steps on the work . . .[10]

In his text Sri Aurobindo expressed his hope that the partition of the country would one day be overcome because unity would be necessary for India's true future. But his countrymen disappointed him very much. In the subsequent period there followed a terrible carnage of Hindus, Muslims and Sikhs.

However, in his message Sri Aurobindo not only referred to his personal political goals, but also to another dream, ". . . the spiritual gift of India to the world" which he said was already taking place. "India's spirituality is entering Europe and America in an ever increasing measure. That movement will grow."[11]

The Supramental Manifestation

By the middle of the 1940s several journals were started that dealt with the Integral Yoga, such as *Sri Aurobindo Circle, Advent* and *Mother India,* the latter a bi-monthly and later a monthly Ashram journal. In February 1949 the *Bulletin of Physical Education* was added. It was later renamed *Bulletin of Sri Aurobindo International Centre of Education* and appeared every three months in English, French and Hindi. This journal was published in connection with the Ashram School, founded on 2 December 1943 by the Mother and now growing fast. From the beginning she put emphasis on physical education; if the body is well-developed it is helpful in Integral Yoga. Moreover, it was her aim to provide strong self-confidence, to young girls especially, to get them out of the role of the orthodox Hindu wife who is often living a static and one-sided life at home.

These innovations which the Mother introduced over time (which included sportswear such as shorts for the girls) met

---

10 *Autobiographical Notes*, 474, 478.

11 Ibid., 477, 480.

with resistance from some older disciples, but the Mother remained firm and took part herself in sports events, playing table tennis and later, tennis which she had greatly valued since her youth. The Mother's involvement in these activities was so intensive that Sri Aurobindo had to calm some of his disciples by telling them that

> there is no need for anyone to take up sports as indispensable for Yoga or enjoying the Mother's affection and kindness. Yoga is its own object and has its own means and conditions.

He added that "an apotheosis of the Deity of Sport" was not intended.[12]

On a request of the Mother Sri Aurobindo contributed some articles to the *Bulletin* in which he wrote, in general terms, about sports, the true spirit of sports, as well as the perfection of the body, the supermind and the life divine. He also wrote some philosophical and speculative comments on a future divinized body, as a long-term evolutionary perspective.

> The object was to bring in [into the Bulletin] something higher and more interesting than a mere record of gymnasium events but which might appeal to some of the readers and even to wider circles.[13]

The seven articles he wrote were later assembled in the book *The Supramental Manifestation* which can be understood to be a supplement to his work *The Life Divine*. Sri Aurobindo introduces a new term, the Mind of Light, a mind that no longer seeks for knowledge in the ignorance and is "even in its knowledge bound to the Ignorance", but rather "a mind capable of living in the Truth, capable of being truth-conscious

---

12 *Letters on Himself and the Ashram*, 779, 782.

13 Ibid., 138.

and manifesting in its life a direct in place of an indirect knowledge".[14] He continues:

> What we have called specifically the Mind of Light is indeed the last of a series of descending planes of consciousness in which the Supermind veils itself by a self-chosen limitation. . . .[15]

We could say, as an image, that the Mind of Light is a delegate of the supermind on the level of human beings, to reach out to them, supporting and facilitating their ascent from below.

In this important work, consisting of his last written articles, Sri Aurobindo also reflects on the issue of sexuality in a future spiritual life. He states at first that the overcoming of sexual instincts would be required for all those "who would attain to self-mastery and lead the spiritual life". But

> all recognition of the sex principle . . . could not be excluded from a divine life upon earth; it is there in life, plays a large part and has to be dealt with, it cannot be simply ignored, merely suppressed or held down or put away out of sight. In the first place, it is in one of its aspects a cosmic and even a divine principle. It takes the spiritual form of the Ishvara and the Shakti and without it there would be no world-creation . . .[16]

With the male–female principle thus existing on a highest universal plane, it is also reflected on the human level and therefore sex "has its nobler aspects and idealities".[17]

> In all who aspired to [spiritual life] but could not yet take it up in its fullness sex will have to be refined, submit to the

---

14 *Essays in Philosophy and Yoga*: *The Supramental Manifestation*, 585.

15 Ibid., 589.

16 Ibid., 543.

17 Ibid.

> spiritual or psychic impulse and a control by the higher mind and the higher vital. . . . The love of man and woman would also undergo that elevation and consummation; for all that can feel a touch of the ideal and the spiritual must follow the way of ascent till it reaches the divine Reality.[18]

Furthermore, Sri Aurobindo also reflects on the necessity of food and refers to his own experiences with fasting. He had succeeded in receiving cosmic energies without loss of energy, but he could not stop "the wasting of the material tissues of the body, its flesh and substance". However, he thinks it might be possible that one day the necessary means could be found and

> this last invincible obstacle too might be overcome and the body maintained by an interchange of its forces with the forces of material nature.[19]

Even the possibility of a human incarnation without the process of sexual procreation is envisaged by Sri Aurobindo as a long-term evolutionary development. In this context he refers to the concept of a subtle-physical body, well known in Indian Yoga philosophy, and assumes that perhaps this subtler body might be transformed — by whatever unknown process — into a gross material body. In fact, in Indian yogic literature such as Paramahansa Yogananda's *Autobiography of a Yogi* we find several descriptions of specialized *kriyā yogī*s who are temporarily able to manifest a physical body through a comparable process. However, these passages in Sri Aurobindo's work are in the nature of speculation, he writes them as a seer who looks into the future exploring its possibilities, without asserting dogmatically that these developments will exactly take place like that.

---

18 *Essays in Philosophy and Yoga*: *The Supramental Manifestation*, 544.

19 Ibid., 545.

Life with Sri Aurobindo

Nirodbaran has reported with great love and detail on the outer life of Sri Aurobindo during his last twelve years on earth. We are told that the Mother saw him every morning on her way to the balcony *darśan* for a first meeting, starting the day with his blessings, and that later in the day, after his reading the newspapers, she did his hair care and discussed things with him. His dental care was at this stage not done any more through energetic concentration (as at the time of his *yoga* diary) but rather with Neem paste and mouthwash. It was only after 4 p.m. that he took his first and main meal: different vegetarian dishes with sweet desserts and a glass of orange juice, all of it prepared by a *sādhikā* and as a rule served by the Mother on a small table.

In between those times Sri Aurobindo spent much time "doing nothing" as he once called it. Nirodbaran often wondered what might have taken place during these periods, but

> none except the Mother could throw any precise light on it. We were only told that he had a special work to do and must be left alone. . . . All that was visible to our naked eye was that he sat silently in his bed, afterwards in the capacious armchair, with his eyes wide open just as any other person would. Only he passed hours and hours thus, changing his position at times and making himself comfortable. Whether to bring down the Supramental Light, or to dive deep into the nether Hell, to send his force for some world purpose . . . or to solve some difficulties of the Ashram, even of individuals, must have been the nature of his special work.[20]

Around 1945 Sri Aurobindo began to experience problems with his eyes, which resulted in Nirodbaran having still more

---

20 *Twelve Years with Sri Aurobindo*, 49-50.

contact with him, for Sri Aurobindo now dictated texts and had them read out, especially passages from *Savitri* that were constantly revised or rewritten. His last written statement on the state of his *sādhanā* is found in a letter dated 7 July 1947. There he points out that his present effort is not so much to rise to an elevated and distant supramental plane for changing the world from there, "but to bring something of it down here and to stand on that and act by that". At present "the progressive supramentalisation of the Overmind" has first priority and another point is reducing the heavy resistance of the Inconscient. While dealing with world events such as the War, he continues, he has not applied the supramental, but rather the overmental force and this is, in its action in the world, "so inextricably mixed up in the tangle of the lower world forces that its results . . . must necessarily be partial." This would also be the explanation of the "birthday present" in two packets: India and Pakistan.[21]

On 28 June 1950 Sri Aurobindo wrote his last political analysis. His disciple K.D. Sethna, editor of the Ashram journal *Mother India*, sought his guidance regarding a leading article on the invasion in South Korea, after which event President Rhee had asked American president Truman for help. Sri Aurobindo answered Sethna that the matter was perfectly clear, it was the first move

> in the Communist plan of campaign to dominate and take possession first of these northern parts and then of South East Asia as a preliminary to their manoeuvres with regard to the rest of the continent — in passing Tibet as a gate opening to India. If they succeed, there is no reason why domination of the whole world should not follow by steps until they are ready to deal with America. . . . For the moment the situation is as grave as it can be.[22]

---

21 *Letters on Himself and the Ashram,* 368.

22 *Autobiographical Notes,* 507-8.

Truman reacted with great determination since he believed "that firmness would be the only way to deter new actions in other portions of the world . . ."[23] and General MacArthur finally initiated a successful counter-attack. Sri Aurobindo's letter to Sethna was published as a message in August 1950. On 11 November of the same year Sethna noted in an article, when the situation had further aggravated after the invasion of the Chinese into Tibet:

> The basic significance of Mao's Tibetan adventure is to advance China's frontiers right down to India and stand poised there to strike at the right moment and with the right strategy . . .[24]

In 1962 China attacked India via Tibet. A year later the Indian diplomat Sudhir Ghosh showed Sethna's article (based on Sri Aurobindo's analysis) to John F. Kennedy. After Kennedy had read it several times, he remarked,

> Surely there is a typing mistake here. The date must have been 1960, not 1950. You mean to say that a man devoted to meditation and contemplation, sitting in one corner of India, said this about the intentions of Communist China as early as 1950?

And then he added,

> One great Indian, Nehru, showed you the path of non-alignment between China and America, and another great Indian, Aurobindo, showed you another way of survival.[25]

In April 1950 the world-famous photographer Henry Cartier-Bresson visited the Ashram. He was travelling through India

---

23 *Memoirs* by Harry S. Truman, vol. 2 (ed. Signet), 386, quoted in Iyengar, *Sri Aurobindo*, 696.

24 Quoted in Iyengar, *Sri Aurobindo*, 696.

25 S. Ghosh, *Gandhi's Emissary*, 314-15, quoted in *The Lives of Sri Aurobindo*, 402.

and had documented the last days in the life of Ramaṇa Maharṣi in Tiruvannamalai as well as the funeral ceremony. He was admitted to the *darśan* on 24 April to shoot photos but, perhaps due to the powerful energy in the atmosphere, his hands were trembling so that the pictures were spoilt, or had only a reduced quality. However, the next day he was allowed to come to Sri Aurobindo's room where he took a number of photos successfully — the first and the last after 1926.[26]

Sri Aurobindo's Departure

By the middle of 1949 Sri Aurobindo had developed kidney problems which could be reduced, though not completely cured, by changing his diet, giving less starchy food. Nirodbaran assumed it might be a minor prostatic enlargement; this diagnosis was confirmed by P. Sanyal, a reputed Indian physician visiting the Ashram. But some time later Sri Aurobindo said during Sanyal's second visit to the Ashram he had cured the problem.[27]

Meanwhile he continued his work, especially on *Savitri* by dictating verses to Nirodbaran and completing book by book, whereupon the texts were published in booklets. But by the middle of 1950 the symptoms of prostatic enlargement returned and became worse. At the same time Śri Aurobindo's attendants also noted a change in his mood. The talks took place less frequently now and it was hardly possible "to draw him out from his impregnable sanctum of silence . . ." or there were only monosyllabic answers. Finally, Satyendra asked Sri Aurobindo why he was so serious, and the latter answered, "The time is very serious".[28]

---

[26] See M.P. Pandit (ed.), *Champaklal Speaks*, Sri Aurobindo Ashram, 2002, p. 202-3. See also the photos in the picture gallery dated 1950.

[27] *Twelve Years with Sri Aurobindo*, 267.

[28] Ibid., 229.

One day when it was to be decided which work they should do next, Sri Aurobindo told Nirodbaran, "Take up *Savitri*. I want to finish it soon". Nirodbaran was astonished at this response because "in these twelve years this was the first time I had heard him reckoning with the time factor".[29] He reports further:

> When the last revision was made and the Cantos were wound up, I said, "It is finished now." An impersonal smile of satisfaction greeted me, and he said, "Ah, it is finished?" How well I remember that flicker of a smile which all of us craved for so long! "What is left now?" was his next query. "The Book of Death and The Epilogue." "Oh, that? We shall see about that later on." That "later on" never came and was not meant to come. Having taken the decision to leave the body, he must have been waiting for the right moment to go, and for reasons known to himself he left the two last-mentioned Books almost as they were. Thus on *Savitri* was put the seal of incomplete completion about two weeks before the Darshan of 24th November. Other literary works too came to an end.[30]

The last Book Sri Aurobindo had revised was the *Book of Fate* which has some significant lines addressed by Nārada, the messenger of the gods, to Sāvitrī's mother. But we can assume that they also refer prophetically to the role of Mirra, the Ashram-Mother:

> *A day may come when she must stand unhelped*
> *On a dangerous brink of the world's doom and hers,*
> *Carrying the world's future on her lonely breast,*
> *Carrying the human hope in a heart left sole*
> *To conquer or fail on a last desperate verge.*[31]

---

29 *Twelve Years with Sri Aurobindo*, 272.

30 Ibid., 272-73.

31 *Savitri*, 461.

With the beginning of winter, mid-November, Sri Aurobindo's kidney problems had worsened and Nirodbaran consulted Satyabrata Sen, a prominent doctor who had come for *darśan*. It became obvious now that an operation would be the sole means for curing Sri Aurobindo's problems, but it was also evident that Sri Aurobindo and the Mother would not agree to it.

Finally, on 24 November the *darśan* took place despite of the difficulties.

> Not knowing that it was the last Darshan some people seemed to have been drawn in by an unknown force and thought themselves specially blessed. There were others who missed it and nourished a life-long regret . . . Everything went off well, the atmosphere was charged with a solemn silence. The Mother and Sri Aurobindo were love and compassion incarnate.

After about two hours a whisper went round that Sri Aurobindo would like the *darśan* to finish as soon as possible.

> Then in quick steps the long queue passed and everyone received the last memorable look of blessings from him.[32]

The next few days Sri Aurobindo's situation became more serious again; it was decided to contact Sanyal by telegram. The doctor could at first diagnose only a mild kidney infection. Meanwhile Sri Aurobindo himself was not concerned about his condition, he said that there was no trouble ". . . and suffering — one can be above it."[33]

On 1 and 2 December there were the School Anniversary functions which kept the Mother fully occupied. Sri Aurobindo's physical problems were not made known to the public, people had no idea what was going on in his room.

---

32 *Twelve Years with Sri Aurobindo*, 276-77.

33 Ibid., 278.

When Sanyal recommended a detailed blood test to be made, Sri Aurobindo declined and retorted with a smile,

> You doctors can think only in terms of disease and medicine, but always there is much more effectual knowledge beyond and above it. I don't need anything.

So the Mother refused to accept the doctor's proposal to give some strong medication. "He will work out whatever is necessary. Give some simple medicines", was her instruction.[34]

Sri Aurobindo's attendants had so far hoped that he would use, as usually in such cases, his yogic force for curing disease, but when they asked him during a short period of improvement whether he was using it, he answered "No!" giving no explanation, but also added that anyhow they wouldn't understand. However, the Mother knew what was going on and remarked, "He is losing interest in himself". Some time later she said, "Each time I entered his room, I saw him pulling down the Supramental Light."[35]

Finally, on 4 December his blood was examined and the result indicated imminent kidney failure. In the late afternoon Sri Aurobindo lay down with great breathing difficulties and frequently went into trance. Everytime he came out of it, he leaned forward and embraced Champaklal, his faithful attendant who was closest to him, who had served him for decades round the clock with great dedication. Never before had Sri Aurobindo shown this kind of personal touch. Nirodbaran too had received a little earlier some special, affectionate attention from Sri Aurobindo, but only understood its significance later. Some other *sādhaka*s who had a close contact with Sri Aurobindo also reported similar experiences.

The Mother entered Sri Aurobindo's room that night and

---

34 *Twelve Years with Sri Aurobindo*, 279.

35 Ibid., 280-81.

helped him take a drink at 11 p.m. When she came again around midnight, the two looked at each other in a steady gaze and then she withdrew. Some ten minutes before his departure he called Nirodbaran asking him for a drink.

> After this utterance, followed the final plunge and at 1.26 a.m., leaving his physical sheath, "the Colonist from Immortality" departed from the earthly habitation, in the presence of the Mother who stood near his feet with an intense penetrating gaze, an incarnation of divine strength, poise and calm.[36]

The news spread very fast. Ashram photographers were allowed inside to take pictures of Sri Aurobindo's *mahā-samādhi*, the final great inner immersion. Then the other members of the Ashram came into his room for the last *darśana* of their Master. Later the doors were opened to all followers and about 60,000 people passed by in an endless procession. For many observers Sri Aurobindo gave more the impression of a man in sleep rather than one in death.

Meanwhile, Nirodbaran noticed that Sri Aurobindo's body was suffused with a golden crimson light and this experience was so intensive that his gloom seemed to be gone. The Mother confirmed his vision, stating it was the Supramental Light which would prevent the body's decomposition as long as it remained, and it was also seen by other *sādhaka*s.

But in the morning of the fifth day it withdrew and therefore on the evening of 9 December Sri Aurobindo's body was laid in a vault in the Ashram courtyard, which has become known as Samadhi since then. A little earlier a French doctor had been called in accordance with local laws and he certified that the body did not show any signs of decomposition, otherwise a quick burial would have been compulsory.

---

36 *Twelve Years with Sri Aurobindo*, 287.

On 6 December all the big Indian newspapers announced Sri Aurobindo's physical death on the title page. President Rajendra Prasad and Prime Minister Jawaharlal Nehru were among the numberless prominent personalities expressing their respect in various statements in appreciation of Sri Aurobindo's manifold actions for India and for the world. Some newspapers in Europe and America too carried the news. In the British *Manchester Guardian* an author called him "the most massive philosophical thinker that modern India has produced".[37]

In India, Sri Aurobindo is counted today beyond dispute as one of the most important personalities of the twentieth century, which also becomes evident through the numberless visits to the Sri Aurobindo Ashram of highest representatives of the country. However, for many of them his role as an Indian freedom fighter is more easily accessible than his spiritual philosophy or his Integral Yoga. He was a man of powerful dynamism, he had set things in motion visibly and in invisible ways. And according to the Mother's vision and personal experience, he is continuing his action even beyond physical death from worlds hidden to our eyes.

Thus in a message of 7 December she said to her disciples that Sri Aurobindo had assured her in the morning (by way of an inner communication) that he would stay with her until his work is completed "not only as a consciousness which guides and illumines but also as a dynamic presence in action". He had promised, she added, that he would not leave the earth atmosphere "until earth is transformed".[38]

On 6 December the Mother had said to Sanyal:

---

37 *Manchester Guardian*, 6 December, 1950, quoted in *The Lives of Sri Aurobindo*, 411-12.

38 *CWM*, vol. 13, *Words of the Mother I*, 6-7. (See also Nirodbaran, *Twelve Years with Sri Aurobindo*, 298-99.)

> People do not know what a tremendous sacrifice Sri Aurobindo has made for the world. About a year ago, while I was discussing things, I remarked that I felt like leaving this body of mine. He spoke out in a very firm tone, "No, this can never be. If necessary for this transformation, I might go, you will have to fulfil our Yoga of supramental descent and transformation".[39]

Two days later the Mother declared in a message that Sri Aurobindo had renounced personal realization in his body in order to hasten the collective realization.

> When I asked him to resuscitate he clearly answered: "I have left this body purposely. I will not take it back. I shall manifest again in the first supramental body built in the supramental way."[40]

---

39 CWM, vol. 13, *Words of the Mother I*, 8.

40 Ibid., 9.

15

Savitri

WHILE staying in Baroda, Sri Aurobindo had intensively studied the *Mahābhārata*, the great Indian epic of ancient times which has over 80,000 verses. His studies enabled him to conclude that the epic, though not the most valuable work of classical Indian literature, was the most important, and he considered it ". . . the pivot on which the history of Sanskrit literature . . . must perforce turn."[1]

The Sanskrit scholar Sampadananda Mishra summarizes the influence of the epic on Sri Aurobindo's literary works as follows:

> Many of his poems are based on legends from the Mahabharata. The legends of Nala, Citrangada, Urvasie and Uloupy have found expression in his poems in English written in blank verse. "Mandavya" and "Marcundeya", two short poems of Sri Aurobindo, are also from the Mahabharata. He took up the tale of Ruru and Pramadvara of the *adiparva* (cantos 8 and 9) and composed a narrative poem "Love and Death" of 1000 lines in fourteen days of continuous writing. The story of Savitri in the Mahabharata is the basis of his supreme poetic and yogic testament, *Savitri.*[2]

In the epic Sāvitrī is the daughter of King Aśvapati[3] who greatly

---

1 *Early Cultural Writings,* 337.

2 *Sri Aurobindo and Sanskrit,* Pondicherry: Sri Aurobindo Society 2000, 33-34.

3 Sri Aurobindo's original spelling is "Aswapathy".

suffered because he had no offspring. But after having undergone ascetic practices for eighteen years in the forest, the Goddess Gāyatrī appeared to him, granting him the boon that Sāvitrī would be born as his daugther.[4] As she grows up, she develops such a strong and radiant aura that no suitor dares to ask for her hand. Therefore, her father advises her to choose her own bridegroom, which was in accordance with tradition at that time.

After a two-year search she makes her decision in favour of Satyavān, a prince in exile, son of King Dyumatsena who was expelled from his kingdom by an internal opponent. But when Sāvitrī announces her decision in the royal court, the divine Sage Nārada, who happens to be present, declares that she should not choose him as it was his fate to die in twelve months' time.

However, Sāvitrī clings to her decision and on the fateful day she courageously confronts Yama (the God of Death) who has come to take Satyavān into his kingdom. By force of her spiritual penances, which she had performed earlier, and through the power of her fearlessness Sāvitrī succeeds, after a long dialogue, in moving Yama to release her husband and also to bring about the reinstatement of Dyumatsena as a king.

Sri Aurobindo explained the deeper meaning of the story as follows:

> The tale of Satyavan and Savitri is recited in the *Mahabharata* as a story of conjugal love conquering death. But this legend is, as shown by many features of the human tale, one of the many symbolic myths of the Vedic cycle. Satyavan is the soul carrying the divine truth of being with itself but descended into the grip of death and ignorance; Savitri is the Divine Word, daughter of the Sun, goddess of the supreme Truth who comes down and is born to save;

---

[4] Sāvitrī is another name of Gāyatrī. The latter also denotes a Vedic metre and *mantra*.

> Aswapati, the Lord of the Horse, her human father, is the Lord of Tapasya, the concentrated energy of spiritual endeavour that helps us to rise from the mortal to the immortal planes. . . . Still this is not a mere allegory, the characters are not personified qualities, but incarnations or emanations of living and conscious Forces with whom we can enter into concrete touch.[5]

Sri Aurobindo uses this legend of the *Mahābhārata* as a basic motive in his epic which deals, in poetic form, with his goal of transformation of earthly life, with the forces of Ignorance and Death being changed into forces of Light. In the process he describes in detail his own inner experiences on the path of his Integral Yoga, as well as expounding on traditional paths of *yoga*, religion, philosophy and mythology. In numberless letters to some of his disciples he made it clear that his object in *Savitri* was primarily a spiritual message; the poetic appeal was only of secondary importance:

> I have not anywhere in *Savitri* written anything for the sake of mere picturesqueness or merely to produce a rhetorical effect; what I am trying to do everywhere in the poem is to express exactly something seen, something felt or experienced; if, for instance, I indulge in the wealth-burdened line or passage, it is not merely for the pleasure of the indulgence, but because there is that burden, or at least what I conceive to be that, in the vision or the experience. When the expression has been found, I have to judge, not by the intellect or by any set poetical rule, but by an intuitive feeling, whether it is entirely the right expression and, if it is not, I have to change and go on changing until I have received the absolutely right inspiration and the right transcription of it.[6]

---

5 SABCL, vol. 26, *On Himself*, 265.

6 Sri Aurobindo, *Savitri*, Sri Aurobindo Ashram Trust, 1993, 800.

Nirodbaran, who transcribed some major portions of Sri Aurobindo's work for him, has reported in his title *Twelve Years with Sri Aurobindo* how much time the poet-*yogī* was spending revising a text again and again, so that every single line would be written from the highest possible plane of inspiration. It was clearly the most important literary work for him (probably started in 1916) and the Mother too later called it repeatedly his most important creation, "the supreme revelation of Sri Aurobindo's vision".[7]

The epic comprises some 24,000 lines in blank verse (a verse without rhyme), but with a certain mantric rhythm which becomes perceptible particularly when the text is read aloud. The following sample renders the scene in which Sāvitrī announces before her father, King Aśvapati, and her mother and Narada, her irrevocable decision to marry Satyavān:

Once my heart chose and chooses not again,
The word I have spoken can never be erased
It is written in the record book of God.
The truth once uttered, from the earth's air effaced,
By mind forgotten, sounds immortally
For ever in the memory of Time.
Once the dice fall thrown by the hand of Fate
In an eternal moment of the gods.
My heart has sealed its troth to Satyavan:
Its signature adverse Fate cannot efface,
Its seal not Fate nor Death nor Time dissolve.
Those who shall part who have grown one being within?
Death's grip can break our bodies, not our souls;
If death take him, I too know how to die.
Let Fate do with me what she will or can;
I am stronger than death and greater than my fate;
My love shall outlast the world, doom falls from me

[7] *Twelve Years with Sri Aurobindo*, 170.

Helpless against my immortality.
Fate's law may change, but not my spirit's will.[8]

The first book edition of the epic appeared in 1950-51 in two parts, later on the text was several times improved by the editors by way of a thorough checking of the original manuscripts. This is especially true for the edition of 1993 in which every single line was carefully examined once more and several printing errors, as well as errors of transcription from the handwritten manuscripts were removed. In the final version the epic has 23,837 lines, in the *Complete Works* it has been published as volumes 33-34.

Savitri and Faust

Sri Aurobindo had kept his work on *Savitri* more or less secret for a long period of time. It was only his disciple K.D. Sethna — himself a poet and critic — who received some samples of the text as early as 1936. Sethna quickly understood the special meaning of these lines and later contributed several essays to help with understanding the epic. In his book *The Poetic Genius of Sri Aurobindo* which Sri Aurobindo had read out to himself before its publication in 1947 and which he appreciated very much, Sethna draws an interesting comparison with Goethe's *Faust:*

> When we speak of *Savitri* we speak of a unique adventure in poetic creation. From a certain standpoint the only parallel to its development is the second part of Goethe's Faust. Goethe kept it with him for several decades, adding to it, revising it, making it run along with the growth of his own mind, and the last touch was given just a few days before his death. Here the parallel ends. Sri Aurobindo's *Savitri* is not merely a work drawn out over a great number of years: it is a work re-written more than half a dozen times and each time re-written not simply because of poetic defects.

[8] *Savitri*, 432.

> Each version might be poetically satisfying: the difference was of the plane of consciousness from which the writing took place.[9]

The author and professor of philosophy S.K. Maitra has referred to the same subject. In his introduction to a comparative study of *Faust* and *Savitri* he notes that one may consider *Savitri* as a kind of cosmic *Faust*:

> Just as "Faust" represents the varying experiences of the individual soul not satisfied with the kind of knowledge it gets from books and seeking in magic and the wider experiences of life that which it cannot get in traditional learning, so "Savitri" represents the wonderful experiences of the collective human soul moving from world to world in search of that which will remove for ever inconscience and ignorance and their product, death, from Earth. What the one seeks in various earthly experiences, the other seeks in cosmic and supracosmic experiences. Both meet with success in the end. Faust is saved after being tossed heavily on the shore of life, King Ashvapati succeeds in getting from the Divine Mother the boon of a New Birth which will save Earth for ever from the incubus of inconscience and ignorance, symbolized by death.[10]

The Language of Savitri

Sri Aurobindo's vocabulary in *Savitri* is very rich and only fully accessible with comprehensive dictionaries. In this case the difficulty is not — as is mostly the case in other writings — the Sanskrit words, but rather a vocabulary with terms especially of Greek and Latin origin. The American Rand Hicks

---

9 K.D. Sethna (Amal Kiran), *The Poetic Genius of Sri Aurobindo*, 98-99.

10 S.K. Maitra, *the Meeting of the East and the West in Sri Aurobindo's Philosophy*, 242.

has brought out *A Savitri Dictionary*[11] which gives good insight into the exquisite word pool of the epic where we find terms such as ananke, argosy, bacchanal, centaur, centurion, chiaroscuro or kakemono.[12]

But there are also many passages in which Sri Aurobindo uses words of our modern world. Thus we come across "a magic television's glass", the "atomic parcellings of the Infinite", "necessity's logarithmic tables" or "the unprovisioned cheques" which religion signs on the Beyond.[13]

As a contrast to these more technical expressions we close our brief presentation of *Savitri* with a passage taking us into idyllic nature, amply illustrating the whole beauty of Sri Aurobindo's poetry:

I caught for some eternal eye the sudden
King-fisher flashing to a darkling pool;
A slow swan silvering the azure lake,
A shape of magic whiteness, sailed through dream;
Leaves trembling with the passion of the wind,
Pranked butterflies, the conscious flowers of air,
And wandering wings in blue infinity
Lived on the tablets of my inner sight;
Mountains and trees stood there like thoughts from God.[14]

---

11 Dipti Publications, Sri Aurobindo Ashram, 2000.

12 Greek goddess of Necessity; merchant ship; exuberant festival honouring Bacchus; mythical creature representing a state between animal and human; commander of a hundred soldiers; the interplay of light and shadow; Japanese silk painting.

13 *Savitri*, 119, 167, 251, 269.

14 Ibid., 405.

16

The Mother and the Ashram
(1951-73)

THE story of the Mother's life has already been told in another book.[1] Therefore, in this present chapter we will only briefly summarize how she continued the joint project of a supramental manifestation in the Ashram.

After Sri Aurobindo had departed, the Mother tried to counteract the general depression in the atmosphere and declared repeatedly that Sri Aurobindo had not left them, but that he was present to support the work.[2] After a break of twelve days all activities were resumed. She especially spent much time with the children in the Ashram, personally giving them lessons.

Since 1951, talks with the young students took place regularly on Wednesdays with all kinds of questions on spiritual life discussed. After some time the talks (which were conducted in French) were recorded on tape and later published as books.[3] The number of students steadily increased now and so the Mother established an Ashram institution in 1951 under the name of *Sri Aurobindo International University Centre,* which was renamed in 1959 as *Sri Aurobindo International Centre of Education.* It was the Mother's objective to try new

1 *The Mother : A Short Biography* (see Literature).

2 *CWM,* vol. 13, *Words of the Mother I,* 7.

3 *Entretiens,* 1950-58. English edition *Questions and Answers,* 1950-1958.

methods in tune with the principles of Integral Yoga, with great emphasis on free development — without concentration on marks and diplomas — and, on physical education. The instruction is given up to the BA level and students who wish to continue their studies elsewhere in India or in foreign countries are able to do so.

The Supramental Descent

In 1953 the Mother gave some hints on the state of her own *sādhanā* and said that the (already mentioned) "mind of light" had been realized within her, as Sri Aurobindo was withdrawing from the body. The supermind, she said, had descended long ago into the mind and vital and was also active in the physical being, though only indirectly through these intermediaries.

> The question now was about the direct action of the Supermind in the physical. Sri Aurobindo said it could be possible only if the physical mind received the supramental light. . . . This physical mind receiving the supramental light Sri Aurobindo called the Mind of Light.[4]

Already in 1931 the Mother had said that the supramental descent

> will be the successful consummation of our work, a descent of which the full glory has not yet been or else the whole face of life would have been different. By slow degrees the Supramental is exerting its influence; now one part of the being and now another feels the embrace or the touch of its divinity; but when it comes down in all its self-existent power, a supreme radical change will seize the whole nature.[5]

In the evening of 29 February 1956 the Mother had a very

---

4 *CWM*, vol. 13, *Words of the Mother I*, 62-63.

5 *CWM*, vol. 3, *Questions and Answers 1929-1931*, 180.

significant experience during a meditation in the playground (a sports field) near the Ashram main building. She saw herself facing a big golden door that separated the world from the Divine, and when she looked at it, she felt "that the time has come . . ." and she shattered the door to pieces with a golden hammer. "Then the supramental Light and Force and Consciousness rushed down upon earth in an uninterrupted flow."[6]

In a message dated 24 April she declared:

> The Manifestation of the Supramental upon earth is no more a promise but a living fact, a reality. It is at work here, and a day will come when the most blind, the most unconscious, even the most unwilling shall be obliged to recognise it.[7]

But the Mother later cautioned her disciples against too much euphoria, because the resistances of the earth were tremendous and

> all the Force that was coming down was swallowed up and it is again from inside the Inconscient that it has to work itself through. That is why things take so much time here.[8]

On 3 February 1958 the Mother saw in a vision a boat, on which humans were prepared for the supramental life. She was able to identify all persons on board as members of the Ashram or seekers outside. They were first inspected by some extremely tall beings and then accepted for disembarking or sent back to the boat for further training. The people on the boat did not wear clothes, but a kind of consciousness-tissue which could assume various forms.

> Life created its own forms: There was *one single* substance

6 *CWM*, vol. 15, *Words of the Mother III*, 94.

7 Ibid., 96.

8 The Mother in *About Savitri*, quoted in Iyengar, *On the Mother*, 795.

in everything; it changed the quality of its vibration according to need and use.[9]

The Yoga of Physical Transformation

In the final phase of her life the Mother dedicated herself to the *yoga* of physical transformation, that is working on the cells of the body, their purification and liberation from accumulated negative impressions. Ultimately, the objective was to bring about a new functioning of the cells, opening them to the divine Light. This was an endeavour that went beyond the aims of the Indian spiritual tradition, excepting the path of the Vedic *ṛṣis* who, according to Sri Aurobindo's conviction, had made a similar attempt.

We are well informed of this new body-*yoga* of the Mother, because she had weekly talks about it with her French disciple Satprem who was particularly interested in this subject. He recorded the talks on tape after some time. Since 1964 extracts were published quarterly in the *Bulletin of Sri Aurobindo International Centre of Education* under the title *Notes on the Way*. Here, at times, the Mother gave very detailed information on her current progress or difficulties and obstacles. Also she discussed a great number of spiritual questions.

The Mother was experiencing great suffering and pain during this period, due to the manifold resistances against the intrusion of Light into so far not illumined layers, but she also had experiences of bliss, as for instance on 1 January 1969 when an intermediary power between man and the future supramental being descended:

> During these few hours (three or four), I understood absolutely what it was to have the divine consciousness in the body. . . . But that state, which lasted for several hours,

---

[9] *CWM*, vol. 9, *Questions and Answers 1957-58*, 79.

> nothing similar to that happiness has this body ever felt during the ninety-one years it has been here upon earth: freedom, absolute power and no limits. . . .[10]

In March 1972 the Mother saw for the first time in an inner experience her supramental body, or a transitional body preceding it. The body was sexless, very slim, made for an uncomplicated digestion of simple food, and

> . . . what will change very much, which had become very important, was breathing. It is upon this that this being greatly depended.[11]

The Mother's Departure

In her talks the Mother had repeatedly reported problems: the massive resistance in earth nature and in humans, which occasionally resulted in serious physical difficulties such as paralysed legs. After the celebrations in connection with Sri Aurobindo's centenary in August 1972 her health became increasingly weaker and from the beginning of April 1973 access to her was very much restricted. On 15 August she gave her last *darśan*, under great difficulties, to 8,000 *sādhaka*s and visitors from the terrace on the eastern side of the Ashram. Thereafter she withdrew more and more and spent most of her time in trance. When an attendant asked her why she was always keeping her eyes closed, she replied: "Because I can see everything with my eyes closed."[12]

Since the middle of November the Mother's crisis became still more serious, her heart weakened and she was hardly able to eat anymore. On 17 November 1973 at 7:25 p.m. she

---

10 *CWM*, vol. 11, *Notes on the Way*, 158-59.

11 Ibid., 303-04.

12 *Souvenir*, Annual Conference 1973, 38, quoted in Iyengar, *On the Mother*, 800.

left her body in the presence of some disciples and Sanyal (who had been called to her room). On the following morning her body was laid in state on a bed in the Meditation Room where tens of thousands of followers passed by her for a last *darśan*. In the morning of November 20 her body was laid in a second, upper chamber of the Samadhi, which she had asked to be prepared in 1950 during its construction.

The next day Nolini Kanta Gupta, Secretary of the Ashram, issued the following message:

> Mother once told me — "If ever I leave my body, my consciousness will remain with you". Mother is present amongst us and Her work continues . . .[13]

Her followers are convinced that the Mother remains active on the subtle-physical planes to further advance the transformation of humans, and the earth, and to work towards the goal of a new creation. In this endeavour, Auroville plays an important role.

---

[13] *Mother India*, December 1973, p. 1.

17

Auroville

Sri Aurobindo's evolutionary philosophy includes an aspect of individual as well as collective development, both of them closely connected. Interaction within the community opens opportunities for a greater inner growth of the individual, but the community can only develop truly if the members are advancing on their individual path.

The Sri Aurobindo Ashram as it had been taking shape since the 1920s under the Mother's guidance was a first attempt to infuse the energies released by Sri Aurobindo into a greater community, and to envisage its transformation according to his vision. But although life in the Ashram was developing on very broad lines as compared to traditional Indian *āśrama*s, it was none the less an experiment within a limited framework, and during the 1960s the Mother felt increasingly the need to start a project on a larger basis.

On 28 February 1968 she therefore founded Auroville, "the City of Dawn", situated some 7 miles north-west of Pondicherry.[1] The Indian president and many other prominent personalities were present when representatives from 124 nations, in a symbolic act, put earth from their home countries into an urn which was then sealed. Auroville has been conceived as a universal town and belongs to "nobody in particular" but

1 The name Auroville is derived from French *l'aurore* (dawn) but most people rather associate the name with "Aurobindo".

rather "to humanity as a whole". Furthermore, it says in the Mother's text,

> Auroville will be a site of material and spiritual researches for a living embodiment of an actual Human Unity.[2]

The rules of life were different now from those in the Ashram: a personal inner turning to Sri Aurobindo and his Integral Yoga was not a necessary pre-condition for joining Auroville (although certainly helpful). It was sufficient to have a sincere aspiration to live progressively, to be ready to be guided by a higher consciousness in trying new forms of life and basically to accept the ideal of collective living in a community in unity and harmony.

Furthermore, families could be founded now — with or without marriage certificates — and there would be children.[3] Some members of the Ashram moved to Auroville eventually, when they found the living conditions there more suitable to their natures. According to some reports, about two-thirds of the Aurovilians live in a temporary or long-term partnership and children form 22 per cent of the population.[4] A number of schools take care of their education, with some schools especially receiving Tamil children from the surrounding villages.

The spiritual centre of Auroville is the Matrimandir, "temple of the Mother", designed as a large spherical globe and built on a scaffolding of four pillars. Inside there is a spacious hall for inner concentration and silent meditation, with a huge crystal globe placed in the centre. If there is a blue sky, sun rays are constantly projected into this hall and directed to the globe with the help of some technical device. All of this has been

---

[2] *Auroville : A Dream Takes Shape*, 1.

[3] In the Ashram, married couples with children were admitted in some cases, though only at a later stage and with restrictions.

[4] According to a census dated November 2009.

constructed according to visions of the Mother: for her, Matrimandir was "the soul of Auroville" and of great importance:

> Sri Aurobindo taught that it is in matter that the Divine must be manifested, and has insisted on the understanding of this notion of the creatrix Mother.
>
> Matrimandir is to teach people that it is not by retiring from this world nor by ignoring it that they will realise the Divine during their lifetime.
>
> I do not want it to become a religious place; there must be absolutely no dogmas, nor rules, nor rituals.
>
> Indians, for the great majority, do not need any explanation; they understand it because of their culture. But only one Westerner out of a million will understand that such a building is necessary.[5]

Today some 2,000 people from more than forty nations reside in Auroville. The large majority of them are Indians, followed by the French and Germans.[6] There is a great intercultural multiplicity in Auroville and during the regular plenary meetings there is a vivid exchange of opinions by the inhabitants who basically have equal rights: "The former university professor from New York, the erstwhile resident of the noble 18th arrondissement in Paris, the emigrated Siberian engineer, the German eco-freak and the Indian peasant who hails from the neighbouring village — all of them have equal rights", that is how Wolfgang Schmidt-Reinecke has described it in an essay.[7] However, decision-making is a rather complicated process because there is also a governing board

---

5 *Auroville : A Dream Takes Shape*, 10.

6 According to a census dated November 2009.

7 *Evolution statt Erosion. Ein Rückblick auf 40 Jahre Zukunft in Auroville*, Kurskontakte, Ausg. 157 (2008), p. 38. English translation by W.H. The author was a member of the Board of Auroville International Germany for a long period of time.

constituted by the Indian government, which has a voice since 1988 when Auroville obtained the legal structure of a non-profit foundation, with a kind of extra-territorial status.

Among the greatest achievements of Auroville are the amazing accomplishments in the afforestation of an area that was completely desiccated and has been transformed into a green oasis with 1.5 million trees and shrubs, with many houses, gardens, sportgrounds, enterprises and schools. Schmidt-Reinecke describes the state of affairs in 2008 as follows:

> For many years Auroville had been busy almost exclusively with its own, really difficult initial development. But meanwhile it gives increasingly impulses to other parts of the world in the fields of city ecology, reforestation and alternative techniques of construction. There is another core task of society — to form a city model of supranational unity — which Auroville pursues in its daily practical life in manifold ways and with at times remarkable results. However, a point has not yet been reached where the Aurovilians would be able to reflect, document or communicate these approaches and solutions on a larger scale. This remains one of the future tasks which is also more and more recognized as such.[8]

Among the highlights in the life of Aurovilians are visits as that of the Dalai Lama, who came for instance in 2009 for the inauguration of the Tibetan Pavilion, or that of the Unesco General Director Irina Bokova who visited the community just a few months after her appointment. Actually, Unesco has supported Auroville since its foundation, through various resolutions. In 2009 a statue of Sri Aurobindo was placed in

---

[8] *Evolution statt Erosion. Ein Rückblick auf 40 Jahre Zukunft in Auroville,* Kurskontakte, Ausg. 157 (2008), p. 38. English translation by W.H. The author was a member of the Board of Auroville International Germany for a long period of time.

the Paris headquarters of the organization. It was the Mother's wish that in the long run many pavilions should be built in the "international zone" of Auroville in order to symbolize and realize the essence and soul of the respective countries in manifold forms, thus to lay a solid foundation for the goal of a world unity in multiplicity.

Experience has shown that some visions of the Mother regarding Auroville can only be realized after long periods of time and manifold processes of development — as was also the case with Matrimandir, which has been completed after a construction time of four decades. The processes are different from those known to us in the familiar world of economy and technology and they follow their own laws. Learning to understand them is part of the game. Roger Anger, who had been for a long time the chief architect of Auroville, said in an interview in 1972:

> It is important that Auroville is constructed on the level of individual experience. You could say that Auroville is at the opposite end of the tradition of contemporary urbanization where you create a city on paper . . . and then ask people to live there. Here the way ahead is just in the opposite direction. People are living the experience, and out of this experience they will create their personal circumstances, their surroundings, their ways of life.[9]

---

[9] *Rundbrief Auroville International Deutschland e.V.*, Sommer 2010, 13 (text retranslated into English by W.H.).

Picture Gallery

PART 1
Historical Photos

Design: Gaby Mahler

The photos of the first part are printed with the kind permission of Sri Aurobindo Ashram Trust.

1. Sri Aurobindo, 1950

Childhood and Youth

2. Loreto Convent School

3. Sri Aurobindo with his parents, his sister and brothers, 1879

4. Sri Aurobindo in England, *c.* 1886

Baroda, Surat and Calcutta

5. Sri Aurobindo with his wife Mrinalini Bose, 1901

6. The bungalow of the Maharaja of Baroda in Nainital in the westerm Himalayas, where Sri Aurobindo stayed as a guest with Mrinalini in 1901

7. Sayajirao, the Maharaja of Baroda

8. Sri Aurobindo with his students of French in Baroda, 1906

Bande Mataram

Weekly Edition.

PUBLISHED EVERY SUNDAY.

Vol. I.	CALCUTTA, SUNDAY, SEPTEMBER 29, 1907.	No. 18.

OUR PICTURE GALLERY.

SJT. AUROBINDO GHOSE.

9. Sri Aurobindo as editor of the newspaper *Bande Mataram*, September 1907

10. Sri Aurobindo presiding over a meeting of the Nationalists in Surat, December 1907. Standing on his left Bal Gangadhar Tilak

11. S. Majumdar's house in Baroda, where with Lele's guidance Sri Aurobindo first experienced the silent mind, in 1908.

12. Vishnu Bhaskar Lele

13. Sri Aurobindo in Baroda after the Congress in Surat, 1908

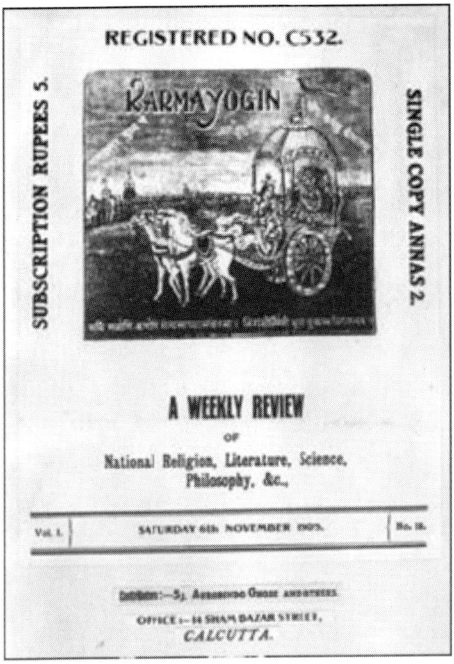

REGISTERED NO. C532.

SUBSCRIPTION RUPEES 5.

SINGLE COPY ANNAS 2.

KARMAYOGIN

A WEEKLY REVIEW

OF

National Religion, Literature, Science, Philosophy, &c.,

Vol. I.

OFFICE:—14 SHAM BAZAR STREET,

CALCUTTA.

14. Facsimile of the cover page of the journal *Karmayogin*

15. The landing site in Chandernagore from where Sri Aurobindo started his journey to Pondicherry via Calcutta

16. Historical view of the coast of Pondicherry

17. The house of Sankara Chettiar

18. Sri Aurobindo writing articles for the journal *Arya* 1914-21

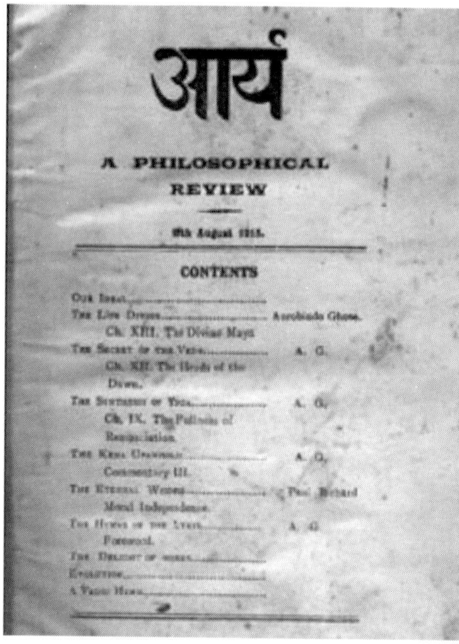

19. Facsimile of the first page of the *Arya*

20. Sri Aurobindo with some disciples, 1918-20

21. Sri Aurobindo's Symbol

22. Sri Aurobindo and the Mother giving Darshan, 24 April 1950

23. Sri Aurobindo in his room, 1950

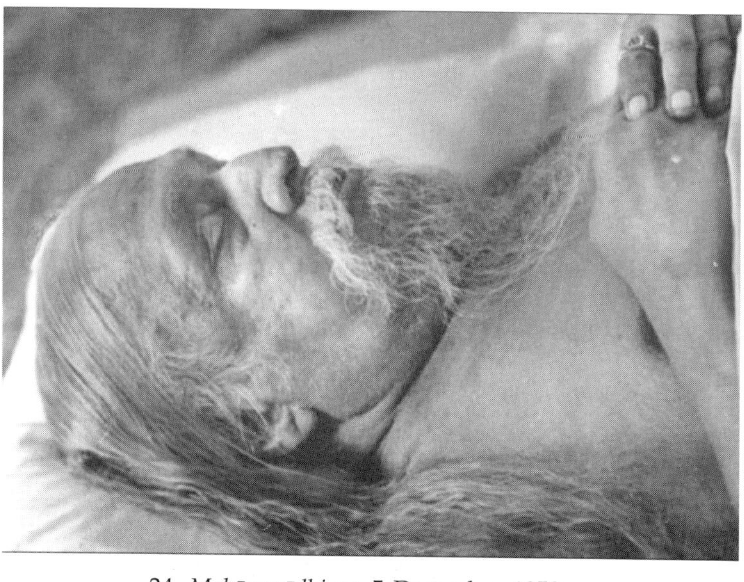

24. *Mahāsamādhi* on 5 December 1950 —
Sri Aurobindo after leaving his body

25. The Mother in France, 1897

26. The Mother in Japan, 1916

27. Balcony Darshan of the Mother, April 1956

28. A scene from the epic poem "Ilion", Sri Aurobindo Ashram, 1960

29. The Mother in the Ashram, 1954

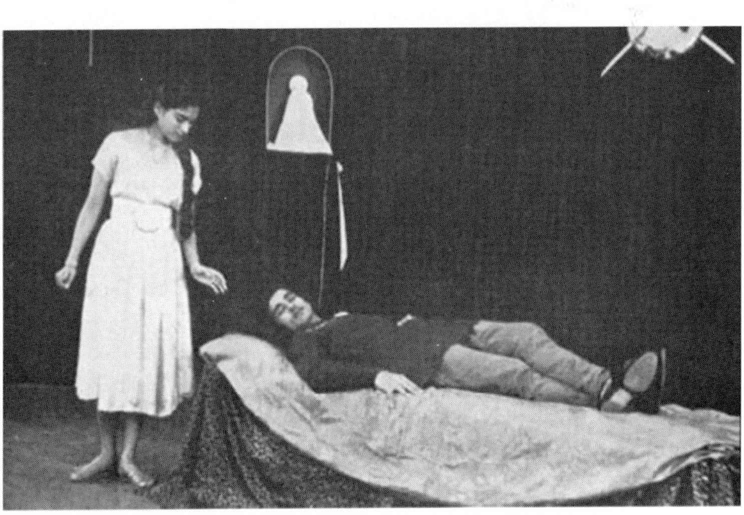

30. A scene from the play "Eric", Sri Aurobindo Ashram, 1963

31. Meditation around Sri Aurobindo's Samadhi on 9 December 1972

PART 2

Recent Photos

Photos: Kathrin Dannebauer [K.D.]
Gaby Mahler [G.M.]
Sri Aurobindo Ashram [S.A.A.]

The photo of the Samadhi is printed with the kind permission of the Sri Aurobindo Ashram Trust.

Sri Aurobindo Ashram and surroundings

32. The gate of the Sri Aurobindo Ashram (G.M.)

33. The Mother's room in the main building of the Ashram (K.D.)

34. The Ashram's book distribution, SABDA (K.D.)

35. Site of the Mother's balcony Darshan on the northern side of the Ashram (G.M.)

36. Gandhi statue in Pondicherry (G.M.)

37. Park Guest House (G.M.)

38. A view of the garden at Park Guest House (K.D.)

39. A view of the Matrimandir (G.M.)

40. Sri Aurobindo's Samadhi in the Ashram courtyard (S.A.A.)

41. The Mother's symbol as a glass mosaic (G.M.)

Appendices

Sri Aurobindo on India

India's Mission and Culture

MOTHER India is not a piece of earth; she is a Power, a Godhead, for all nations have such a Devi supporting their separate existence and keeping it in being.[1]

Each nation is a Shakti (power) of the evolving spirit in humanity and lives by the principle which it embodies. India is the Bharata Shakti, the living energy of a great spiritual conception, and fidelity to it is the very principle of her existence. For by its virtue alone she has been one of the immortal nations; this alone has been the secret of her amazing persistence and perpetual force of survival and revival.[2]

India recognised the authority of spiritual experience and knowledge, but she recognised still more the need of variety of spiritual experience and knowledge. Even in the days of decline when the claim of authority became in too many directions rigorous and excessive, she still kept the saving perception that there could not be one but must be many authorities.[3]

. . . But it is perfectly true that Indian culture has always set the highest value on that in man which rises beyond the terrestrial preoccupation; it has held up the goal of a supreme

---

1 SABCL, vol. 22, *Letters on Yoga*, 424.

2 *The Renaissance in India*, 57.

3 Ibid., 187.

and arduous self-exceeding as the summit of human endeavour. The spiritual life was to its view a nobler thing than the life of external power and enjoyment, the thinker greater than the man of action, the spiritual man greater than the thinker.[4]

India's Greatness

The Rishi in ancient India was the outstanding figure with the hero just behind, while in later times the most striking feature is the long uninterrupted chain from Buddha and Mahavira to Ramanuja, Chaitanya, Nanak, Ramdas and Tukaram, and beyond them to Ramakrishna and Vivekananda and Dayananda. But there have been also the remarkable achievements of statesmen and rulers, from the first dawn of ascertainable history which comes in with the striking figures of Chandragupta, Chanakya, Ashoka, the Gupta emperors and goes down through the multitude of famous Hindu and Mahomedan figures of the middle age to quite modern times.[5]

When we look at the past of India, what strikes us next is her stupendous vitality, her inexhaustible power of life and joy of life, her almost unimaginably prolific creativeness.[6]

Spiritual Foundation

The tendency of the normal Western mind is to live from below upward and from out inward. A strong foundation is taken in the vital and material nature and higher powers are invoked and admitted only to modify and partially uplift the natural terrestrial life. The inner existence is formed and governed by the external powers. India's constant aim has been, on the contrary, to find a basis of living in the higher spiritual truth and to live from the inner spirit outwards, to exceed the present

---

4 *The Renaissance in India*, 125f.

5 Ibid., 246.

6 Ibid., 7.

way of mind, life and body, to command and dictate to external Nature. As the old Vedic seers put:

> Their divine foundation was above even while they stood below; let its rays be settled deep within us.[7]

[7] *The Renaissance in India,* 74.

Quotations on Sri Aurobindo and His Action

THE MOTHER

Sri Aurobindo does not belong to the past nor to history. Sri Aurobindo is the Future advancing towards its realisation.[1]

What Sri Aurobindo represents in the world's history is not a teaching, nor even a revelation; it is a decisive action direct from the Supreme.[2]

India

RABINDRANATH TAGORE

. . . The French steamer on which I was travelling touched Pondicherry and I came to meet Aurobindo. At the very first sight I could realise that he had been seeking for the soul and had gained it, and through this long process of realisation has accumulated within him a silent power of inspiration. His face was radiant with an inner light. . . . I said to him, "You have the Word and we are waiting to accept it from you. India will speak through your voice to the world, 'Hearken to me'."[3]

SWAMI SIVANANDA

The crest jewel of renascent India, the bravest among the

---

1 *CWM*, vol. 13, *Words of the Mother*, 5.

2 Ibid., 4.

3 *The Modern Review*, July 1928, quoted in *Mother India*, August 2009, 699-700.

patriots, the sharpest among the intellectuals, and the subtlest among the seers, Sri Aurobindo fulfilled the glorious purpose of demonstrating to the world that real India, the India of the Vedic seers, could survive and absorb into herself all alien cultures, and that at the hands of one who knew the proper synthesis, Eastern and Western cultures could find their happy blend, without necessarily having to antagonize one another. Sri Aurobindo's *Life Divine*, the divine life that he lived and preached — will live for ever, inspiring mankind. Posterity will hail him as a member of the galaxy of Vedic seers. May his Light ever shine.[4]

Europe

ROMAIN ROLLAND

He is today the greatest interpreter of India who has realized the most perfect synthesis that the genius of the West and the East may be able to reach. Seeking to harmonize the spiritual impulses of India with the activities of the Occident, he directed all the powers of his mind to an ascending movement.[5]

TIMES LITERARY SUPPLEMENT

Of all modern Indian writers Aurobindo . . . is the most significant and perhaps the most interesting. . . . In fact, he is a new type of thinker, one who combines in his vision the alacrity of the West with the illumination of the East. To study his writings is to enlarge the boundaries of one's knowledge.[6]

MAURICE SCHUMANN

After all these years, what do you still recollect of your meeting with Sri Aurobindo? An inner impression. . . .

---

4 dlshq.org/saints/aurobindo.htm (14 August 2010).

5 Quoted in Otto Wolff, *Sri Aurobindo*, Rowohlt Verlag 1995, p. 149, English tr. W.H.

6 *Times Literary Supplement*, London, 8 July 1944.

The extraordinary radiance of the divine life, the Life Divine. The radiance that was there on his face. I always thought that faith manifested as a breath. One feels, in certain circumstances, the Breath of God, Spiritus — it means "breath" . . . and I felt it as soon as I saw him. One had the impression — there was no artificial light falling on him — one had the impression that he was himself a radiant centre.[7]

ALEXANDRA DAVID-NÉEL

In the evening I had a conversation with a Hindu [Sri Aurobindo]. . . . I spent two wonderful hours reviewing the ancient philosophical ideas of India with a man of rare intelligence. He belongs to that uncommon category that I so much admire, the reasonable mystics. I am truly grateful to the friends who advised me to visit this man. He thinks with such clarity, there is such lucidness in his reasoning, such lustre in his eyes, that he leaves one with the impression of having contemplated the genius of India such as one dreams it to be after reading the noblest pages of Hindu philosophy.[8]

America and South America

GABRIELA MISTRAL

While Tagore awakened the latent music in me, another Indian Sri Aurobindo, brought me to religion. He opened the way to my religious consecration. Indeed my debt to India is very great and is due in part to Tagore and in part to Sri Aurobindo.[9]

---

7 Quoted in *Mother India*, August 2009, 704. Maurice Schumann was a confidant of Charles de Gaulle in the Second World War and later foreign secretary of France. He was in charge of the negotiations regarding the liquidation of the French colonies in India and met Sri Aurobindo twice. Pournaprema, the Mother's granddaughter, had a long interview with him.

8 Quoted in *Mother India*, August 2009, 625.

9 sriaurobindosociety.org.in/sriauro/theysaw.htm.

KEN WILBER

Sri Aurobindo, India's great modern sage, has written extensively on just this viewpoint — Brahman getting lost in involution and then evolving back — from matter to prana to mind to over-mind to supermind and Atman, and he sees it occurring cosmologically as well as psychologically.[10]

RAYMOND PIPER

Sri Aurobindo's epic "Savitri" has already inaugurated the New Age of Illumination and is probably the greatest epic in the English language. . . . The most comprehensive, integrated, beautiful and perfect cosmic poem ever composed. It is perhaps the most powerful artistic work in the world for expanding man's mind towards the Absolute.[11]

---

10 Ken Wilber, *Up from Eden,* Boston: New Science Library, 1983, 313.

11 sriaurobindosociety.org.in/sriauro/theysaw.htm. Raymond Piper was a Professor of Philosophy at Syracuse University, NY, USA.

The Meaning of the Symbols of Sri Aurobindo and the Mother

Sri Aurobindo's Symbol

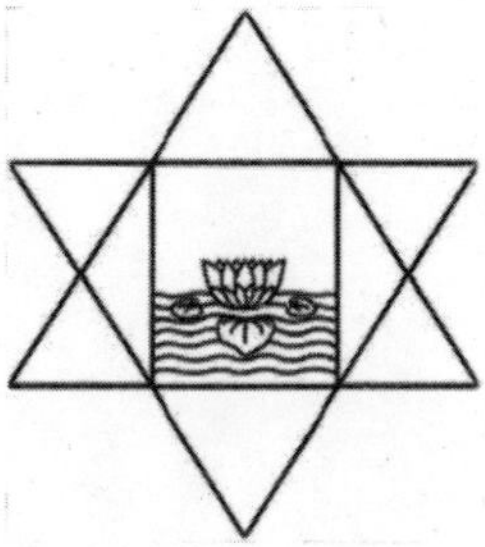

- The descending triangle represents *Sat-Chit-Ananda*.[1]
- The ascending triangle represents the aspiring answer from matter under the form of life, light and love.
- The junction of both — the central square — is the perfect manifestation having at its centre the Avatar of the Supreme — the lotus.
- The water — inside the square — represents the multiplicity, the creation.

The Mother's Symbol

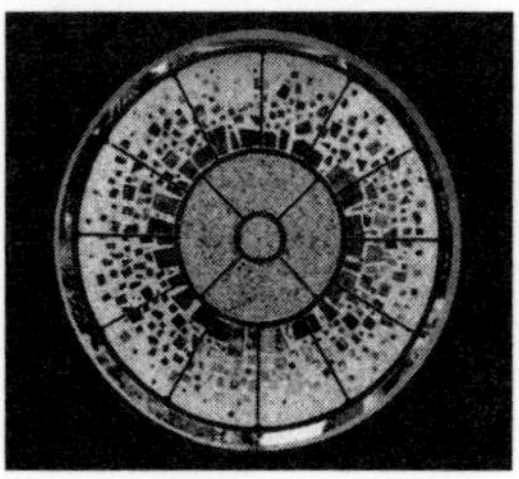

- The central circle represents the Divine Consciousness.
- The four petals represent the four powers of the Mother.[2]
- The twelve petals represent the twelve powers of the Mother mani-fested for Her work.[3] — The Mother[4]

References

[1] Existence, Consciousness, Bliss.

[2] See p. 207 of this present title.

[3] Gratitude, humility, peace, equality, sincerity, aspiration, courage, progress, receptivity, perseverance, goodness and generosity.

[4] Quoted from *Sri Aurobindo and His Ashram*, Sri Aurobindo Ashram, 2006, 43-44.

Chronology of Events

Childhood and Youth

1872	Born on 15 August in Calcutta as the son of Krishna Dhan Ghose and Swarnalata Ghose. Childhood in Rangpur, East Bengal.
1877-79	Attends the Loreto Convent School in Darjeeling.
1879-84	Stays in Manchester, England with Mr and Mrs Drewett who give him private lessons in Latin, French, mathematics and other subjects.
1884-89	Moves to London to Drewett's mother. Admits to St. Paul's School. In 1887 new independent lodgings. In 1889 Matriculation from St. Paul's with very good results, especially in Greek and Latin.
1890-92 —	Starts studies for a career in the Indian Civil Service (ICS) and secured a scholarship at King's College in Cambridge. On successful completion of the studies in October 1892, returns to London. Member of a secret society for the national liberation of India. Failure to take the horse-riding examination for the ICS, therefore disqualifies for this career. During this period writes some literary texts.

1892	In November meets the Maharaja of Baroda who gives Sri Aurobindo employment in the State Service.

Baroda and Calcutta

1893	Returns to India and joins the Baroda State Service. Publication of a series of articles titled "New Lamps for Old" in the *Indu Prakash*.
1895–1900	Publication of his *Songs to Myrtylla,* a collection of poems. Works as a lecturer in French at Baroda College, later as a Professor of English. First contacts with national leaders.
1901	Marries Mrinalini Bose.
1902-03	Contacts with a revolutionary secret society in west India.
1903	Accompanies the Gaekwad of Baroda on his tour of Kashmir, at the latter place experiences of the vacant infinite.
1904	Begins his own practice of *yoga.*
1905	Sri Aurobindo becomes Vice-Principal of Baroda College, a little later acting Principal. The Partition of Bengal, accompanied by unrest in the population. Sri Aurobindo writes the nationalistic pamphlet *Bhavani Mandir.*
1906	Moves to Calcutta and writes some articles for the journal *Jugantar.*
1907	Helps to start the newspaper *Bande Mataram,* in August charged with sedition, acquittal in September.

1908	In January meeting with Vishnu Bhaskar Lele, experience of the complete silence of mind. On 2 May arrested in connection with the violent activities of his brother Barin. In Alipore prison experience of Krishna as the omnipresent divinity.
1909	On 6 May acquitted. In June publication of the journal *Karmayogin* in English. In August publication of the Bengali weekly *Dharma*.

Pondicherry

1910	In February Sri Aurobindo leaves Calcutta and travels to Chandernagore. At the end of March returns to Calcutta and from there the voyage to Pondicherry. Arrival on 4 April, staying in Sankara Chettiar's house. In November writes a letter to *The Hindu*, stating his place of stay and announcing his withdrawal from politics.
1911-13	Several times changes residence, however without leaving Pondicherry.
1914	On 29 March first meeting with Mirra Richard; with Mirra and Paul Richard joint editing of the journal *Arya*. The first edition on 15 August, many later main works are serially published in the journal.
1915-16	On 22 February Mirra's departure to France, in 1916 journey to Japan.
1920	Long letter to Barin with a survey of the state of his *sadhana* and other subjects. On 24 April final return of Mirra to Pondicherry.

1921	On 15 January last edition of the *Arya.*
1922	Mirra takes charge of Sri Aurobindo's household. Evening talks with Sri Aurobindo and meditations.
1926	On 24 November descent of Krishna, the godhead of the overmind, into the physical. Sri Aurobindo withdraws to develop his *sadhana* with intensive concentration. Henceforth, contact with the disciples through Mirra, "the Mother".
1930-38	Sri Aurobindo writes thousands of letters on *yoga* and other subjects to his disciples.
1938	Sri Aurobindo breaks his right leg in an accident on 24 November. A small group of attendants has regular access to him, among them Nirodbaran who records many talks with him in the years to come.
1939	In November the first part of *The Life Divine* is published.
1940	In July publication of the second part. In September Sri Aurobindo and the Mother publicly declare their support to the Allies in the Second World War.
1943	Foundation of the Ashram School.
1947	India's Independence on 15 August.
1949	On 21 February publication of the first edition of the *Bulletin of Physical Education,* later renamed *Bulletin of Sri Aurobindo International Centre of Education.* On the same day publication of the Ashram journal *Mother India.*

1950		Part 1 of *Savitri* is published as a book. On 5 December Sri Aurobindo leaves his body which on 9 December is laid in a vault in the Ashram courtyard, henceforth called the Samadhi.
1951	—	Publication of parts 2 and 3 of *Savitri*. The Sri Aurobindo University Centre is founded, later renamed Sri Aurobindo International Centre of Education.
1968	—	On 28 February foundation of Auroville.
1973	—	On 17 November the Mother leaves her body, which is laid in the upper chamber of the Samadhi.

Glossary

In the glossary below some important Sanskrit terms as well as English words newly-introduced by Sri Aurobindo are explained. For more comprehensive explanations, see the *Glossary of Terms in Sri Aurobindo's Writings*.[1]

āśrama	– spiritual centre in which disciples gather around a *guru*
ānanda	– joy, bliss
asura	– a hostile being, opposed to the Divine
avatāra	– incarnation of the Divine on earth
bande mātaram	– Indian national hymn "I bow before the Mother"
Bhagavad-Gītā	– sacred writing of India in which Kṛṣṇa teaches the threefold *yoga* of works, love and knowledge
bhakti	– devotion, adoration
Brahman	– the supreme Absolute, the all-encompassing divine Being
darśan	– lit. seeing, from Sanskrit *darśana; darśan* is the Hindi version. The seeing of a *guru* or saint and the blessings connected with that seeing. On *darśana* days Sri Aurobindo and the Mother used to show themselves to their followers (21 February, 24 April, 15 August, 24 November)
dharma	– law, true law of being, the rule of true social and moral action; also duty, religion

[1] Pondicherry, Sri Aurobindo Ashram, 1978.

Gītā – see *Bhagavad-Gītā*

karma – work, the fruit of works; result of past actions; the law of retributive justice for all actions and works

karma-yoga – *yoga* of selfless works, dedicated to the Divine

Kṛṣṇa – well-known God and *avatāra*

mokṣa – spiritual liberation

mukti – spiritual liberation

Nārāyaṇa – name of Kṛṣṇa

Overmind – an "overhead" plane, the highest level below *supermind*. A subordinate level of the supreme Light which supports the current human evolution from the Ignorance and forms a bridge to Knowledge. The overmind receives the Light of supermind, but divides it into separate aspects and forces; it is the world of the Gods

prāṇāyāma – control of breath, control of the energy currents in the body through particular breathing techniques

psychic being – the soul in evolution through which the contact with the Divine is established. While the *ātman* is the unchanging immortal Self beyond death and birth, the psychic being enters into the transitory world of becoming, like a delegate of the ātman and develops from life to life. It exerts an increasing influence on the thinking, feeling and action of humans until everything is ready for a union with the Divine.

Referring to the psychic being in the Indian tradition, Sri Aurobindo said: ". . . What [the Upanishads] say about the Atman is that it is in all and all is in it, it is everywhere and all this universe is the Atman. What they speak of as situated in the deeper inner heart is the *purusha* in the heart or Antaratman. This is in fact what

		we call the psychic being, *chaitya purusha.*" — *Letters on Himself and the Ashram,* 171
ṛṣi	–	a seer who has the vision of spiritual truths
sādhaka	–	someone who practises *sādhanā.* The term is often used to refer to the members of the Ashram. The feminine form is *sādhikā.*
Sādhanā	–	*yoga* practice, spiritual practice
samādhi	–	ecstasy, inner immersion, also refers to the tomb of Sri Aurobindo and the Mother in the Ashram courtyard
śakti	–	energy, force; the effective force of the Divine in Nature; Śiva's spouse or female partner of a spiritual personality
Śāstra	–	any systematized teaching. The term mostly refers to the sacred writings of India in the Vedic tradition
siddhi	–	success; the perfection of a yogic path; extrasensory powers such as telepathy
Supermind	–	the dynamic Truth-consciousness, the infinite wisdom and will of the Creator. That plane through which the supreme Absolute, *sat-cit-ānanda,* organizes Creation; an intermediary power between the two spheres of the Infinite and the Finite, which extends to both of them
swarāj	–	self-rule, independence
swadeshi	–	lit. belonging to one's own country; goods produced in one's home country
Vedānta	–	the "end (or culmination) of the Veda". A system of philosophy and spiritual discipline based on the Upaniṣads, teaching the culminating knowledge of the Absolute

Literature

English Complete Editions

Sri Aurobindo Birth Centenary Library (SABCL), Pondicherry: Sri Aurobindo Ashram 1972. Complete edition in 30 volumes, not available any more.

Complete Works of Sri Aurobindo (CWSA), Pondicherry: Sri Aurobindo Ashram, from 1995. Complete edition in 36 volumes. Some volumes have currently not yet been published. Info: sabda.in/ Collected Works:

1. *Early Cultural Writings;* 2. *Collected Poems;* 3-4. *Collected Plays and Stories;* 5. *Translations;* 6-7. *Bande Mataram;* 8. *Karmayogin;* 9. *Writings in Bengali and Sanskrit;* 10-11. *Record of Yoga;* 12. *Essays Divine and Human;* 13. *Essays in Philosophy and Yoga;* 14. *Vedic and Philological Studies;* 15. *The Secret of the Veda;* 16. *Hymns to the Mystic Fire;* 17. *Isha Upanishad;* 18. *Kena and Other Upanishads;* 19. *Essays on the Gita;* 20. *The Renaissance of India with a Defence of Indian Culture;* 21-22. *The Life Divine;* 23-24. *The Synthesis of Yoga;* 25. *The Human Cycle: The Ideal of Human Unity – War and Self-Determination;* 26. *The Future Poetry;* 27. *Letters on Poetry and Art;* 28-31. *Letters on Yoga;* 32. *The Mother with Letters on the Mother;* 33-34. *Savitri: A Legend and a Symbol;* 35. *Letters on Himself and the Ashram;* 36. *Autobiographical Notes and Other Writings of Historical Interest;* 37. Reference Volume

Collected Works of the Mother (CWM), Pondicherry: Sri Aurobindo Ashram. Complete edition in 17 volumes:

1. *Prayers and Meditations;* 2. *Words of Long Ago;* 3. *Questions and Answers 1929-1931;* 4. *Questions and Answers 1950-51;* 5. *Questions and Answers 1953;* 6. *Questions and Answers 1954;* 7. *Questions and Answers 1955;* 8. *Questions and Answers 1956;* 9. *Questions and Answers 1957-58;* 10. *On Thoughts and Aphorisms.* 11. *Notes on the Way;* 12. *On Education;* 13-15. *Words of the Mother*

I-III; 16. *Some Answers from the Mother*; 17. *More Answers from the Mother*.

Talks and Correspondence

Nirodbaran, *Correspondence with Sri Aurobindo*, Pondicherry: Sri Aurobindo Ashram, 1983.

———, *Talks with Sri Aurobindo*, Pondicherry: Sri Aurobindo Ashram, 2001.

Purani, A.B., *Evening Talks with Sri Aurobindo*, Pondicherry: Sri Aurobindo Ashram, 2007.

Secondary Literature

Banerji, Debashish, *Seven Quartets of Becoming: A Transformative Yoga Psychology Based on the Diaries of Sri Aurobindo*, Los Angeles: Nalanda International; New Delhi: D.K. Printworld 2012.[1]

Gupta, Nolini Kanta, *Reminiscences*, Pondicherry: Sri Aurobindo Ashram, 1969.

Heehs, Peter, *The Lives of Sri Aurobindo*, New York: Columbia University Press, 2008.[2]

Iyengar, K.R. Srinivasa, *Sri Aurobindo: A Biography and A History*, Pondicherry: Sri Aurobindo Ashram, 1972.[3]

———, *On the Mother*, Pondicherry: Sri Aurobindo Ashram, 1978.

Nirodbaran, *Twelve Years with Sri Aurobindo*, Pondicherry: Sri Aurobindo Ashram, 1973.

Maitra, S.K., *The Meeting of the East and the West in Sri Aurobindo's Philosophy*, Pondicherry: Sri Aurobindo Ashram, 2000.

Purani, A.B., *The Life of Sri Aurobindo*, Pondicherry: Sri Aurobindo Ashram, 1978.

Roy, Dilip Kumar, *Sri Aurobindo Came to Me*, Pondicherry: Sri Aurobindo Ashram, 1952.

---

[1] A high-level study of *Record of Yoga* which also examines Integral Yoga in the context of other Indian *yoga*s and in relation to various Western philosophies.

[2] A critical biography, conceived and written for the modern Western mind. The author evaluates many new sources and documents.

[3] A very voluminous standard work, the author also presents in great detail several literary works of Sri Aurobindo.

Satprem, *Sri Aurobindo or the Adventure of Consciousness*, Mysore: Mira Aditi, 2000.[4]

———, *Mother's Agenda*, Paris: Institut de Recherches òvolutives, 1982.

Sethna, K.D., *The Poetic Genius of Sri Aurobindo*, Puducherry: Clear Ray Trust, 2008.

Vrekhem, Georges van, *Beyond Man: The Life and Work of Sri Aurobindo and the Mother*, New Delhi: Rupa & Co., 1997.[5]

Wilfried, *The Mother: A Short Biography*, Pondicherry: Sri Aurobindo Society, 1990.

Glossaries and Dictionaries

Glossary of Terms in Sri Aurobindo's Writings. Pondicherry: Sri Aurobindo Ashram 1978.

Hicks, Rand, *A Savitri Dictionary*, Pondicherry: Dipti Publications, 2000.

Pandit, M.P., *Dictionary of Sri Aurobindo's Yoga*, Pondicherry: Dipti Publications, 1973.

Journals

Mother India: Monthly Review of Culture, Pondicherry: Sri Aurobindo Ashram.

The Bulletin of Sri Aurobindo International Centre of Education. Pondicherry: Sri Aurobindo Ashram.

All India Magazine, Pondicherry: Sri Aurobindo Society.

Auroville

Auroville: A Dream Takes Shape, Auroville, 2010.

The Auroville Handbook, Pondicherry: All India Press, 2007.

Auroville References in Mother's Agenda, Auroville: Auroville Press, n.d.

---

[4] A valuable introduction to Sri Aurobindo's life and Integral Yoga.

[5] The author mainly focuses on the inner biographies and discusses with great insight the processes of spiritual transformation and other subjects.

The Auroville Experience: Selections from 202 Issues of Auroville Today, November 1988 to November 2005, Auroville: Auroville Today, 2006.

Internet Addresses

sriaurobindoashram.org

The website of the Sri Aurobindo Ashram. The Complete Works of Sri Aurobindo as PDF files are found under the keys Sri Aurobindo/ His Writings; the Glossary for *Record of Yoga* under Research/ Archival Research/Glossary. The key "Music" on the Start page takes you to the organ music of the Mother and Sunil's New Year music as well as his Savitri compositions.

sriaurobindoashram.com

Full-text search for the works of Sri Aurobindo and the Mother.

auroville.org

Auroville.

auroville.org/research/academics.html

A list of more than 120 articles and dissertations on Auroville, Integral Yoga and Sri Aurobindo.

Index